Human Predicaments

Human Predicaments

AND WHAT TO DO ABOUT THEM

John Kekes

The University of Chicago Press

Chicago and London

John Kekes is the author of many books, most recently *The Human Condition* and *How Should We Live?*, the latter also published by the University of Chicago Press.

The University of Chicago Press, Chicago 60637
The University of Chicago Press, Ltd., London
© 2016 by The University of Chicago
All rights reserved. Published 2016.
Printed in the United States of America

25 24 23 22 21 20 19 18 17 16   1 2 3 4 5

ISBN-13: 978-0-226-35945-8 (cloth)
ISBN-13: 978-0-226-35959-5 (e-book)
DOI: 10.7208/chicago/9780226359595.001.0001

Library of Congress Cataloging-in-Publication Data
Names: Kekes, John, author.
Title: Human predicaments and what to do about them / John Kekes.
Description: Chicago : The University of Chicago Press, 2016. | Includes
    bibliographical references and index.
Identifiers: LCCN 2015041741 | ISBN 9780226359458 (cloth : alk. paper) |
    ISBN 9780226359595 (e-book)
Subjects: LCSH: Philosophical anthropology. | Ontology.
Classification: LCC BD450 .K366 2016 | DDC 128—dc23 LC record available
    at http://lccn.loc.gov/2015041741

♾ This paper meets the requirements of ANSI/NISO Z39.48-1992
(Permanence of Paper).

For J. Y. K.

Contents

A Note to the Reader

The human predicaments I discuss in this book are connected, in one way or another, with how we have reason to live now in our present conditions. The resulting problems are deep because they arise out of our nature and conditions. We can understand the problems, but that leads to the realization that again and again we have to make difficult choices between conflicting possibilities of life we reasonably value. And we have to keep making them for ourselves, since no one else can do it for us. But not even the deepest understanding can solve the resulting problems once and for all, no matter how hard and reasonably we try. That is why I call them human predicaments. This book is intended as a contribution toward a deeper understanding of them.

This is not an academic exercise, but a matter of interest to all of us who do not just try to live as well as we can in the circumstances in which we find ourselves, but also stand back from time to time and reflect on the hurly-burly of life, on the conflicts we face, and on the difficult choices we have to make. The aim of such reflection is a deeper understanding.

This kind of reflection is, in the broadest sense of the word, philosophical. But most philosophers now are specialists who write about technical problems using a technical vocabulary that is largely inaccessible to non-specialists. They perhaps begin with a general human predicament, but very soon break it down into many small problems, which are further broken down into even smaller problems that are discussed in specialist journals in articles that draw ever finer distinctions in order to accommodate ever more far-fetched fictional examples of the what-would-you-do-if sort. The result is that the initial predicament is ignored and it is mentioned only when specialists have to explain and justify to administrators what they are doing.

My discussion of human predicaments proceeds differently. It focuses on familiar problems of everyday life and compares our customary responses to them with quite different possibilities of life derived from anthropology, history, and literature. It ranges far beyond the usual philosophical confines and abstractions. But as philosophers have always done, I am centrally concerned with giving reasons for the claims I make. I do my best to write plainly, avoid technicalities, and address the human predicaments and the problems to which they lead directly. I write for reflective non-specialists, including students, who used to look to philosophers, and I hope still do, for a deeper understanding of the predicaments, problems, conflicts, and choices that concern all of us. I say this now to avoid disappointing readers who expect something else.

Acknowledgments

Paul Hollander, Anthony O'Hear, Krisanna Scheiter, and George Sher read and commented on papers that have eventually become chapters of this book. I gratefully acknowledge their help and thank them for it.

I am particularly grateful to one of the readers commissioned by the press. He or she offered exceptionally helpful criticisms and suggestions about my discussion of boredom. I very much appreciate the sympathy and deep understanding of my aims shown by this reader's report. I wish I could acknowledge by name the help he or she gave me. Alas, the anonymity of the reviewing process prevents me from doing so.

This is the second book of mine that has been seen through from submission to publication by my editor, Elizabeth Branch Dyson. There may be an editor somewhere more helpful and receptive to the sort of work I do than she is, but I doubt it. It gives me great pleasure to thank her for all that she has done toward transforming the typescript into a book.

I dedicate the book to my wife with gratitude and love for all her help and for our long marriage.

Ithaka
Charlton
New York

1 Human Predicaments and Problems

The Question

Suppose you ask yourself during a sleepless night: do you regret any of the major decisions you have made? Are you content with your personal relationships, the work you do, your health, the state of your finances, where and how you live, your sex life, the respect and appreciation you get from others? Do you have lasting feelings of shame, guilt, anxiety, boredom, envy, regret, or resentment about how your life is unfolding? Do you think you have missed valuable opportunities or failed in ways that matter? Would you say that all in all your life is going as you want, that you want it to continue without significant changes, and that you feel good about it? Are you just willing to put up with your life as it is or do you actively like it? I doubt that many of us could honestly say that our life is not just good enough, but really good. Most of us want it to be better than it is, but we are uncertain about how to make it better. And that is the source of human predicaments and the particular problems involved in them.

The aim of this book is to arrive at a deeper understanding of these predicaments and to consider what we could do about them. The "we" in question are adults living in affluent, democratic societies in North America and Europe, roughly from the 1950s on. This is a narrow context that excludes many people, societies, and historical periods in which people face or have faced similar predicaments, just as we do in ours. Although I focus on our context, I will stress again and again that comparisons with other contexts are centrally important for understanding our predicaments and how we might reasonably respond to them. Still, our predicaments arise in our context and it is in it that we have to understand and cope with the resulting problems.

Our context, however, is different from the others with which I will compare it. In the others, poverty is more widespread; political regimes are more repressive; and the burdens of the past restrict present possibilities more than they restrict ours. We enjoy better living standards, medical care, education, political stability, and democratic governance than what was possible for most people, apart from a few privileged ones, ever before in human history. Nevertheless, we are troubled by problems in the midst of our better conditions. Why?

We emerge from childhood with an upbringing that has taught us timeless truths, prudential proverbs and catchphrases, silly mistakes, pernicious prejudices, important information, basic skills, and rules drummed into us. Out of such material we form a vague, unstable, and inarticulate view of how we think we should live. It is usually a mixture of unexamined beliefs, emotions, desires, values, experiences, preferences, and aspirations. I will refer to them jointly as our personal attitude to life. It motivates us to live and act in ways that—unsurprisingly—often conflict and change in response to changes in the conditions of our context and in our attitude. One source of our predicaments and problems is this ill-formed and uncritically held personal attitude that initially guides how we think we should live. We need something more reliable, better tested, less labile to guide how we should live than the largely unchosen and often shifting personal attitude of our early years. This something is the evaluative framework of our society.[1]

It is a system of widely shared aesthetic, economic, educational, legal, literary, medical, moral, political, religious, scientific, and other modes of evaluation. The evaluations derived from them often conflict, their relative importance is frequently controversial, and the conditions to which they guide possible responses continually change. The evaluative framework is not a rigid structure but a flexible social construct always in a state of flux. Some of its parts are temporarily stable, others are being questioned, enlarged, abandoned, or reformed in the light of criticisms and changing conditions. Think of what has been happening to our evaluations, for instance, of beauty, chastity, culture, faith, honor, modesty, privacy, or thrift.

If we proceed from our point of view as participants, we can say that the context of our evaluative framework is usually the society in which we live, although it may cut across several societies. We share our commitment to it with others, even though we do not know many of them. Yet we are bound together by a tacit agreement that we should be guided by many of the same evaluations. We are unlikely to agree about all of them, but we do share at least some of the important ones, draw some of the same distinctions, favor or condemn many of the same possibilities of life, and pursue many of the same aims. We largely agree about what evaluative considerations are relevant, even if we act contrary to them and disagree about their relative importance. It may be said, metaphorically, that what we share is an evaluative vocabulary, although we may use it to make very different evaluations.

Ideological and religious differences, waves of immigration, multiculturalism, and secularization have transformed our society and made it much less homogeneous than it used to be. Now, several evaluative frameworks coexist in greater or lesser harmony. If we share an evaluative framework, we have a bond, but it is not a bondage. Some of its evaluations are controversial, others are changing, priorities shift. Yet its hold on us is very strong because it provides the evaluations that enable us to distinguish between good and bad, better and worse, important and unimportant possibilities in our lives. The evaluative framework is an essential part of the context in which we can try to live as we think we should.

In fortunate circumstances when the evaluative framework is good enough, we need not pay attention to it in the routine conduct of our affairs. We know what we can and cannot, should and should not do, and how to do what we want or must. We keep appointments, pay bills, enjoy what we can, raise our children, and do our job. There are difficult situations, of course, and then we have to stop and think. But when all goes well that does not happen often.

If our routine transactions become fraught with conflicts, if we are frequently uncertain about how to evaluate the possibilities we might pursue, then our life becomes uncertain. The bond we used to share with others is fraying. If our conflicts spread from occasional difficult situations to the routines of everyday life, then they cast doubt on our entire evaluative framework. We lose confidence in how we think we should live, in what we owe to others and they to us, and in our ability to cope with our increasingly frequent conflicts. But even in fortunate circumstances we have to contend with our conflicting evaluations and difficult choices about marriage, love affairs, raising children, political matters, and the relative importance we attribute to beauty, death, friendship, honor, justice, loyalty, money, privacy, recognition, sex, and so forth. The difficult choices these conflicting evaluations force us to make are not irrevocable, but they do change us. We may also find that our conflicting evaluations are changing as we change partly as a result of past choices we have made or failed to make. Our evaluative framework provides the means of evaluating the possibilities between which, if all goes well, we can choose. And we choose reasonably if we find an acceptable fit between the evaluations we have derived from the modes of evaluation of our evaluative framework and from our own often inarticulate, fallible, and changing personal attitude that guides how we think we should live.

Participation in an evaluative framework is the key to a life in which we can cope with our conflicting evaluations and difficult choices. If the evaluative framework is threatened, the conditions of life as we know them are threatened. The threat is that we will become unable to make reasonable choices between good and bad possibilities of life. We come to doubt that the evaluative framework on which we rely is actually reliable. And we come to doubt also our personal attitude because we realize that it may be based on wishful thinking, or it is misled by fear or lack of imagination, or that it involves false beliefs, misdirected emotions, and contrary desires.

Our doubts make it very difficult for us to choose between the conflicting evaluations that follow from our evaluative framework and personal attitude. We become uncertain about how we should live. And that leads to the predicaments of life this book is about. I will discuss the problems involved in them in the chapters that follow. They are deep conflicts, difficult choices, vulnerability to fate and to the contingencies of life, our divided self, the complexities of evaluations, inescapable hypocrisies, the miasma of boredom, the prevalence of evil, and the danger of innocence. These problems occur in different, often very different, forms in different contexts. Still, chapters 2–6 are about problems that are easily recognizable in different contexts, while chapters 7–11 are about problems that are particularly acute in our present context; they are perhaps even characteristic of our lives here and now. All these problems are exceptionally hard because our efforts to cope with them are affected by the problems with which we are trying to cope. Such self-referential problems are part of the human condition, but the forms in which they occur and have to be faced vary with contexts. I will discuss them as they are in our context.

The Aim

Each chapter has a constructive and a critical aim. The constructive one is to show that we can understand and respond to a particular problem of life reasonably, but only by considering the context-dependent conflicts, choices, and possibilities that give rise to that problem. The critical aim is to show that we cannot arrive at a reasonable understanding and response by a theory that abstracts from individual differences and appeals to an ideal that reason requires everyone in all contexts to follow.

These constructive and critical aims are contrary to the widely shared assumption that pervades contemporary thought that there could be an ideal theory.[2] The ideal has been variously identified as *eudaimonia*, the love of God, natural law, the categorical imperative, the common good, rationality, autonomy, justice, happiness, and so on. Whatever the ideal is supposed to be, a theory of it claims that reason requires everyone to follow it. I do not think that such a theory could be found. This needs to be shown, of course, not just said. And I will show it again and again in the following chapters, in which I consider how we might cope with particular problems and why no ideal theory could help us do that.

If we reject ideal theories, we must face the question of how we should cope with the problems of life. We find, then, that we have to rely on our evaluative framework and personal attitude regardless of our doubts about them, because we have no other way of evaluating the available possibilities of life. We can sometimes make a considerable effort and transfer our allegiance to another evaluative framework or form another personal attitude, but it will have its own problems. In our life as it now is, we depend on the prevailing aesthetic, economic, educational, legal, literary, medical, moral, political, religious, scientific, and other modes of evaluation, and on our personal attitude. They are as much part of us as our native language, gender, sexual preferences, manual dexterity, and limbs.

We do not have to accept all the evaluations that follow from them. We may reject an entire mode of evaluation or change our personal attitude. Nevertheless, it is impossible not to be strongly influenced by many of the evaluations that follow from them, even if we are critical of some of them. But if we are critical, it is because they conflict with other evaluations we also derive from our evaluative framework or personal attitude. These conflicts make us conflicted, force us to make difficult choices between our own evaluations, and lead to the problems of life we have to face and cope with in our context.

These problems indicate that something is wrong with the prevailing evaluative framework, its modes of evaluation, or with our personal attitude. They may be faulty, but the problems would occur even if they were faultless. For the possibilities of life we value may conflict and we may be conflicted about the choice between them. We may be divided between ambitious striving and peace of mind, present enjoyments or hoped-for future ones, prudence and truthfulness, compassion and justice, duty and happiness, and so on. These and many other problems are familiar experiences in most of our lives, and force us to make difficult choices.

Part of what makes problems of life very hard is that we have strong reasons for valuing both of the conflicting possibilities of life between which we have to choose. These reasons follow from how we think we should live. We value the conflicting possibilities from that point of view. Yet we must choose between them because we cannot have both. Whichever we choose, we must give up a possibility we genuinely and reasonably value. We give it up in order to pursue another possibility we value even more, but that does not make the loss of the possibility we value easier to bear, nor the choice easier to make. We will find the problems of life hard even if we are as reasonable as possible.

Many different evaluative frameworks, modes of evaluation, and personal attitudes that guide how we should live render our problems even more onerous. We value their diversity because they enrich the possibilities of life. But we pay for it by having to cope with the resulting problems, conflicts, and choices. Doing that depends on distinguishing between reasonable and unreasonable evaluative frameworks, modes of evaluation, and personal attitudes. Each of the following chapters draws that distinction, as we try to find the best way of coping with a particular problem of life in a particular context.

What that way is depends on what the particular problems are, what context they occur in, and what alternative possibilities are available. Their unavoidable particularity rules out the sort of universal answer that ideal theorists seek. But that still leaves reasonable particular answers, as I will show. However, there are some minimum conditions that must be met by all reasonable evaluative frameworks, modes of evaluation, and personal attitudes that might guide our efforts to find reasonable ways of coping. They must make it possible to satisfy basic needs we all have; provide some way in which we can evaluate and choose between conflicting possibilities; have sufficient flexibility to respond to changing condition; and have modes of evaluations in terms of which we can live a meaningful and worthwhile life.

We cannot reasonably accept any evaluative framework, mode of evaluation, or personal attitude if it fails to meet these minimum conditions. There is a great diversity of ways in which these conditions can be met. And those that meet them may still be more or less reasonable, depending on the extent to which they fulfill these conditions. Diversity, therefore, does not lead to the relativistic denial that it is possible to provide reasons for and against our acceptance of evaluative frameworks, modes of evaluation, and personal attitudes. There are reasons beyond these minimal ones, but I postpone discussion of them.

My overall aim is to arrive at a deeper understanding of human predicaments and of how we might reasonably cope with them. Each chapter is centrally concerned with comparing our ways of understanding and coping with the particular problems to which general human predicaments lead with other ways recognized in anthropological, historical, and literary contexts that are often very different from ours. We can then consider whether our ways are more or less reasonable than these others. This may allow us to improve our ways, if we find other ways better. These comparisons deepen our understanding of the possibilities of life by giving us imaginative entry into possibilities recognized in other contexts. This enriches us, makes us less parochial, and provides points of view external to our own from which we can evaluate how we think we should live. The aim of this approach is not to justify or criticize how others live in other contexts, but to learn from their good or bad examples and thereby evaluate more reasonably how we live in our context.

I write as a philosopher, but my approach is not in the mainstream of English-speaking philosophy, as it is currently understood and practiced. I approach philosophy as a humanistic discipline[3] that is concerned with how we should live from our unavoidably changing, context-dependent, and fallible human point of view. This approach and point of view are part of an old but continuing tradition that regards philosophy as a way of understanding and coping with human predicaments.[4] This is of concern to thoughtful people, not an academic specialty. I do my best to write accessibly to nonspecialists and avoid unnecessary jargon and technicalities. There are, of course, other approaches and points of view, but they are not my own.

My approach is evaluative and practical. It aims to understand, evaluate, and respond to the relevant facts from the point of view of living as we think we should now in our context. It is not an amateur venture into social science that aims to explain the economic, historical, political, psychological, or sociological conditions that give rise to human predicaments. Whatever the best social scientific explanation turns out to be, there is no reason why the approach I favor could not be consistent with it. The human predicaments I am concerned with have been familiar long before they were studied by social scientists. The particular problems to which they lead vary with contexts, but in one form or another they are recurrent features of human life. We know what our problems are. What we do not know is how we should understand, evaluate, and cope with them.

No one can have the last word on these difficult subjects. The particular forms in which the problems I will discuss now occur are part of how life now is for us. They are here to stay as long as our life and context are what they are. The best we can do is to understand, evaluate, and cope with them here and now as reasonably as we can. I offer a modest contribution to that.

2   Deep Conflicts

The Standard View

According to the standard view, we all have a more or less inarticulate view that guides how we think we should live. It is the joint product of the evaluative framework of our society, the modes of evaluation, and of our personal attitude. They form the background of our evaluations of the possibilities of life. The possibilities and our evaluations of them often conflict, and their conflicts reflect wider conflicts between the components of our personal attitude and the modes of evaluation of our evaluative framework. The result is that how we think we should live becomes a problem. It adds to the problem that both our evaluations and personal attitude are changing in response to new experiences and changing circumstances and preferences. The standard view is that deep conflicts are the source of the problem and self-knowledge is the solution. I think that the standard view is mistaken.

The aim of self-knowledge is to surmount this problem by examining the conflicting components of our personal attitude, evaluating their relative importance, learning from our past experiences, successes, and failures, and planning for a future that would be an improvement over the past. The ideal of self-knowledge is to live an examined life. Conflicts are seen by defenders of the standard view as obstacles to it and self-knowledge is supposed by them to be a means of overcoming them. The more conflicts we have, the less likely it is that we can live as we think we should. According to the standard view, the cultivation of self-knowledge is the key to overcoming such conflicts.

The standard view has had influential defenders ever since Plato had Socrates articulate it. The ideal is for each human being to be his own ruler . . . well regulated, and has internal concord . . . once he has bound all the factors together and made himself a perfect unity instead of a plurality, self-disciplined and internally attuned. . . . It is conduct which preserves and promotes this inner condition of his that . . . he describes as fine, and it is the knowledge which oversees this conduct that he regards as wisdom.[1]

The following quote from Stuart Hampshire is representative of the contemporary version of the standard view:

It is through the various degrees of self-consciousness in action, through more and more explicit knowledge of what I am doing, that in the first place I become comparatively free, free in the sense that my achievements either directly correspond to my intentions, or are attributable to my incompetence or powerlessness in execution, which may or may not be venial. . . . A man becomes more and more a free and responsible agent the more he at all times knows what he is doing, in every sense of this phrase, and the more he acts with a definite and formed intention. He is in this sense less free the less his actual achievements, that which he directly brings into existence and changes by his activity, correspond to any clearly formed intention of his own.[2]

The ideal was inscribed on the portal of the temple at Delphi as (in translation) "Know Thyself." The Socratic dictum—the unexamined life is not worth living—has been so often repeated as to have become virtually a cliché. Its central importance has been insisted on by Plato in many works,[3] as well as by Aristotle, Augustine, Montaigne, Kant, and their numerous followers. It is an essential part of autonomy that is central to liberal political and moral theory. It has a pivotal place in the genres of autobiography, bildungsroman, and stream of consciousness works.[4] There has also been a vast amount of psychological work done—under the name of cognitive dissonance theory—on the frustration caused by conflicts and the importance of coping with them by cultivating self-knowledge.[5] And, of course, the cultivation of self-knowledge is a central aim of psychoanalysis and various other forms of psychotherapy.[6]

Self-knowledge does not require constant examination of the beliefs, emotions, desires, experiences, and preferences that form our personal attitude. We need to rely on it only when we have to cope with our conflicts, or want to explain or justify to ourselves or others what we are about. Ordinarily, however, for most of us self-knowledge can remain a silent presence. Only when we face conflicts or have to make difficult choices do we need to activate whatever self-knowledge we have managed to arrive at.

There are countless influences that have shaped how we live. We may recall many of them, or be ignorant of or have forgotten many others. Some are trivial, others important. Self-knowledge selects, interprets, and evaluates them from the point of view of how we think we should live. It is likely to be strengthened or weakened by prevailing economic, legal, moral, political, religious, and the other modes of evaluations and by our relationships with others. It is unlikely therefore that self-knowledge will be entirely self-centered.

Self-knowledge is not only of our beliefs, but also of our emotions and desires. It would be pathological to know how we should live, but have no hopes, fears, regrets, satisfactions, or dissatisfactions about how our life is going. It demands explanation if self-knowledge does not include knowledge of our emotions and desires. How much of them it includes varies with persons, contexts, and the relative importance of what is known. We are so constituted, however, as to have not only beliefs, but also emotions about what we have or lack in our life, how much we value or miss them, the ways we should like to change, and how important to us are our achievements and failures. Such beliefs, emotions, and desires motivate us to act in various ways or not to act at all. But we are prone to make mistakes about them because self-deception, wishful thinking, inattention, lethargy, or disappointment may mislead us.

One indication of whether our self-knowledge is genuine is that it actually guides how we live and act by making us conscious of the reasons that guide us. If we are reluctant, ambivalent, or doubtful about wanting the consequences of possible actions, or are tempted by other actions, or are uncertain about what we want to do, then we have reason to distrust what we take to be our self-knowledge. According to the standard view, whether we live and act as we think we should partly depends on whether our actions are guided by self-knowledge. It is in our interest to be guided by it because it is in our interest to live and act as we think we should.

I mention now and discuss later some reasons for doubting the standard view. If the complexities of conflicts and self-knowledge are recognized, it becomes apparent that not all conflicts are avoidable or indeed obstacles to living as we think we should. Furthermore, we are often as wrong about what we take to be self-knowledge as we are about what we take to be our beliefs, emotions, and desires. And even when self-knowledge is genuine, it might be better to live with some conflicts than with some truths that self-knowledge might reveal. We often have strong reasons both for and against living with our conflicts and cultivating self-knowledge.

The difficulty of evaluating these reasons cannot be met by acquiring more self-knowledge. For, even if we evaluate our conflicting reasons as best as we can, we do so in a particular context. But contexts change and we have to keep making difficult choices throughout our life because the reasons vary with the changing contexts and the changing beliefs, emotions, and desires involved in our conflicts.

Furthermore, given the great importance defenders of the standard view attribute to self-knowledge, they must think that those who lack it are prevented by their conflicts from living as they themselves think they should. Their lack of self-knowledge, therefore, must make them dissatisfied with their lives. The fact is, however, that most human beings have always lived and continue to live without cultivating self-knowledge. They follow the conventional practices of their society, earn a living, raise children, mature and grow old, get sick and with luck recover, have friends and enemies, allies and rivals, enjoy what they can, try to avoid falling afoul of the law, hope for something better, fear what may be worse, and live as well as they can in the circumstances in which they find themselves. No doubt they have conflicts, but they deal with them by following the time-honored conventions of their religion, morality, ethnicity, tribe, occupation, or family, not by relying on self-knowledge. It is unreasonable to suppose that the multitudes who had lived throughout history or are now living without cultivating self-knowledge must be doomed to lifelong dissatisfactions by their lack of self-knowledge.

I think that the cultivation of self-knowledge is how affluent, well educated, reflective people committed to our evaluative framework have come to value living, not a way that all human beings should live. In order to make this concrete, I turn to the place of conflicts and self-knowledge in the context of what used to be the traditional evaluative framework of Shilluk society for hundreds of years until the first half of the twentieth century. This will show that the standard view is a socially conditioned preference of some people for a particular way of life, not a requirement that all human beings have reason to follow. There are strong reasons, however, why that preference is unreasonable even in our own evaluative framework.

The Shilluk[7]

In the evaluative framework of the Shilluk conflicts have a central and constructive place and the cultivation of self-knowledge would endanger their entire evaluative framework. In fact, self-knowledge has hardly any role in their lives. For centuries, they have gotten along quite well without it. This surely counts against the standard view according to which conflicts are the problem and self-knowledge is the solution. For the Shilluk, the opposite is true.

The Shilluk numbered over 100,000. They lived on the bank of the Nile in Sudan in several hamlets. Their economy was based on cattle. Each hamlet had a leader who was head of the lineage and a prince. There were about a hundred such Shilluk lineages. Above all these lineages and princes stood the king, who claimed mystical descent through close to forty generations from God. Not only the king but also the princes were thought to be linked to God in this way. This was why the king ruled over the Shilluk and the princes ruled over their lineages. Kings and princes died, but the lineage and the mystical union with God endured.

> The kingship stands at the center of Shilluk moral values. . . . Everything they value most in their national and private life has its origin in him [i.e. in the King]. . . . When a king dies the Shilluk say . . . the centre of the Shilluk world has fallen out. It is restored by the investiture of a new king. . . . Because of the mystical values associated with the kingship and centred in the person of the king he must keep himself in a state of ritual purity . . . and in physical perfection. . . . The Shilluk believe that should the king become physically weak the whole people might suffer, and, further, that if the king becomes sick or senile he should be killed to avoid some grave national misfortune, such as defeat in war, epidemic, or famine. [The sign of the king's failing is] if he fails to satisfy his wives or shows signs of illness or senility (201–2).

Apart from the physical appearance of rude good health and the gratifying public testimony of satisfied wives, a further evidence of the king's robustness was to prevail in conflicts. Any prince could "at any time challenge the king to mortal combat, in which the king may not call for help" (202). The combat was not always interpreted by the Shilluk literally as a physical fight between the king and the challenging prince. Sometimes a prince may have led a political rebellion against the king. Still, the result was the same as that of physical combat: the death of the challenged or of the challenger. But

> Shilluk rebellions have not been made against the kingship. On the contrary, they were made to preserve the values embodied in the kingship which were being weakened . . . by the individual who held office (208–9). . . . It is the kingship and not the king who is divine. . . . The kingship . . . is changeless and acknowledged as a supreme value by all the Shilluk. In that permanence and in that acknowledgement the unity of the nation is manifested (210–11).

There was, of course, much more to the evaluative framework of the Shilluk society than what I have just sketched. But this much is enough to show that conflicts occupied a central place in Shilluk life. Lineages competed with other lineages for the available resources. There were constant strifes within each lineage as others high up in a lineage prepared to challenge physically or politically the ruling prince. And the different princes and different lineages were forever strengthening themselves and trying to weaken the others in order to maneuver themselves into a position where they might successfully challenge the king.

As the Shilluk saw it, these conflicts were not obstacles to living as they should, but the very means by which they assured their well-being and the continuity of the evaluative framework of their society. They knew that they faced adversities, that they were vulnerable to defeat in war, and threatened by epidemics and starvation, and they knew that they had to protect themselves by relying on the king, and to a lesser extent on their prince, to make the right decisions on which the continuity of their lineage, and the Shilluk life and society depended. "Everything they most value in their national and private life has its origin in him [the king] (201)." And the competitions, strifes, and conflicts that permeated their lives were the means of assuring that the king and the princes are fit to make the right decisions on which what they most valued in life depended.

Defenders of the standard view may say that the value the Shilluk attributed to conflicts made their life worse than it might have been. It is important, they might say, to have competent leaders who make the right decisions, but there are better ways of testing their competence than relying on the testimony of their sexual prowess by their wives and prevailing in physical or political mortal combat. This is no doubt true, but it does not affect the point that conflicts need not be seen as obstacles that have to be surmounted. They might be seen instead as means to making life better by testing the relative strength of alternative possibilities before accepting one of them, and thereby leading to the improvement of life.

Furthermore, it would be a mistake to dismiss the value the Shilluk attributed to conflicts as a rare anomaly in the natural history of humanity. There are numerous aspects of our own evaluative framework in which conflicts have a reasonably valued place. Consider, for instance, competition in free market economies, in funding for alternative research programs, and in sports; the adversarial process in criminal trials; the constitutional requirement of checks and balances in the separation of powers; the contests of political parties in democratic elections; the ever-present tension between traditionalists and reformers in the arts, law, morality, politics, and religion; in historical reconstructions of the causes of wars, revolutions, and international tensions; and so on and on in many other areas of life now and in the history of our society. If we start looking at our past and present, conflicts will be seen as ubiquitous and many of them as beneficial.

It should not be thought that all these conflicts, both in Shilluk and in our own society, are merely social. It is true that they are social, but they are also personal, between the beliefs, emotions, and desires that guide how we live. The conflicts occur because the Shilluk and we identify with the values that we can pursue in different but conflicting ways, and we think and feel that it is important to test which way is better than the others. Conflicts are such tests. These values and conflicts are part of our personal attitude that guides how we think we should live. That is why the conflicts are not just social but also personal. The Shilluk's conflicts aimed at determining who should be the king or the prince who will make the best decisions in matters that affect their well-being. And our conflicts aim at strengthening the values we attribute to the prosperity to which economic competition leads, to the growth of scientific knowledge, to the adversarial system as a means to justice, to checks and balances as a way of guarding against the abuse of power, and electoral contests as making democracy function as we think it should.

We ourselves value the conflicts that lead to prosperity, scientific progress, justice, liberty, the accountability of politicians, and so on. The conflicts are both social and personal because we are conflicted about the reasons both for and against constant economic, scientific, judicial, political, and democratic tensions in our society. The reasons for them are the benefits they yield, and the reasons against them are the burdens of living on a society in which conflicts are ubiquitous and change constant. These conflicts are means of protecting what we and others in our evaluative framework value.

This does not mean that conflicts always strengthen the contested value. Conflicts are often cynically corrupted by paying lip service to the value that is being betrayed by pursuing aims contrary to it. But that does not alter the fact that when we struggle with conflicts about the best way of trying to realize something we value, we do so because we are committed to the value. The conflicts are personally felt, because they are about finding the best way of pursuing what we value. Conflicts need not be obstacles to living as we think we should, but means of doing so. And we often have to make difficult choices between the reasons for and against coping with them in one way or another.

There are also other conflicts even more intimately connected with how we think we should live. Most of us have to grapple with conflicts between long- and short-term satisfactions, truthfulness and prudence, integrity and ambition, private life and political involvement, familiar comforts and hoped-for improvements, present enjoyments and saving for the future, self-interest and moral obligations, sexual experimentation and close family life, responsibilities to our parents and to our children, keeping and sharing, caution and exploration, and so on. Such conflicts are among the problems with which we have to find some way of coping. And we often find out how we think we should live by facing the conflicts and deciding how we should cope with them. These conflicts are not obstacles to living as we should, but familiar struggles in our life that enable us to grow, enlarge our possibilities, and form our mature personal attitude to how we should live.

I am not suggesting that all conflicts are like this. Some are symptoms of confusion about how we should live; of doubts about the values of our society or of our own; of ambivalence about our beliefs, emotions, or desires; of fear of failure; and so on. There are many different kinds of conflicts and they have many different sources. That is why the standard view that sees conflicts as obstacles to living as we should is half true. Half-truths come with half-untruths. The half-truth of the standard view is that some conflicts are obstacles. The half-untruth of it is that some other conflicts are not obstacles but means to living as we think we should.

Part of life is to decide whether the particular conflicts we face are obstacles or means. Making the choice is often difficult because we have reasons for and against both alternatives. One of the available possibilities is usually more reasonable than the others, but which one that is depends on the context, on the value we aim at, on the possibilities of the evaluative framework of our society, and on our often imperfectly formed and changing personal attitude that guides how we live. There is no theory, blueprint, or universally applicable prescription of how to make that choice, because it is context-dependent and individually variable.

The standard view proposes just such a theory. According to it, the cultivation of self-knowledge is a requirement that all human beings either follow or render themselves helpless in the face of their conflicts. This is a mistake even in the context of our own evaluative framework. It rests on three mistaken assumptions, which I call exclusivist, parochial, and optimistic.

The Exclusivist Mistake

One of these assumptions is that the connection between conflicts and self-knowledge is exclusive: we either cope with conflicts by cultivating self-knowledge or we cannot cope with them at all. As the example of Shilluk shows, conflicts need not be problems that must be solved by cultivating self-knowledge and self-knowledge may be destructive rather than constructive.

It may be said in favor of the standard view that even if its evaluation of conflicts is only half true, self-knowledge is still necessary for responding reasonably to many conflicts. This is also only half true.

Thinking further about the Shilluk will make this clear. If the Shilluk evaluative framework is interpreted literally, it rests on false factual assumptions. There is no reason to believe that there was a mystical union between each of the kings and princes throughout forty generations and whatever God was supposed by the Shilluk to be. Given intermarriage between Shilluk lineages and with neighboring Arabs and other Africans, given also adultery, polygamy, and the absence of written records, there is no reason to believe that the genealogical descent of kings and princes could be accurately traced through forty generations. Nor is there reason to believe that sexual potency and physical or political combat are effective ways of choosing leaders capable of making the best practical decisions.

Suppose that the Shilluk cultivated sufficient self-knowledge and it forced them to realize that the factual basis of their evaluative framework was mistaken. They would have concluded that the conflicts that were central features of their life could not make their lives better, and the strife and bloodshed that the conflicts involved made their lives worse. This would have undermined the foundation of their evaluative framework and deprived them of their conventional and successful ways of coping with the adversities of war, hostilities between lineages, and epidemics that threatened them or their cattle on which their livelihood depended. They were incomparably better off without self-knowledge that would have led to such disastrous consequences. And they would also have had very strong reasons to silence imprudent advocates of self-knowledge, had there been any, just as the Athenians may have had—dare I say it—for silencing Socrates.

Defenders of the Shilluk evaluative framework, who may have been thoughtful Shilluk, may acknowledge that the literal interpretation of the factual basis of their evaluative framework is untrue. But they may deny that this matters. They may say that what matters is the metaphorical interpretation of their genealogical descent from divinity. The Shilluk have endured through many generations in the face of great adversities because they relied on their evaluative framework and valued conflicts as a means of selecting good leaders. That is surely reason enough, they may say, for believing that their evaluative framework is divinely inspired. They had no other explanation of their survival under adverse conditions. Their connection with God will be interpreted literally by common people and metaphorically by thoughtful ones.

These thoughtful ones may be supposed to have discovered for themselves the doctrine of double truth: metaphorical one for the learned, literal one for others. The doctrine has been attributed to Averroes, who may only have discussed it without actually accepting it. But numerous Christians, including Boethius, at least toyed with it, until it was condemned as heresy. But neither thoughtful Shilluk, nor defenders of the standard view, need be disconcerted by the checkered history of the doctrine. The defense of the standard view may be that it does not matter whether an evaluative framework has a divine origin. What matters is that people in a society are by and large guided by it, turn to it when they face adversities, appeal to its values to resolve their conflicts, interpret the world and their experiences in terms they derive from it, and thus maintain the cohesion of their society on which they think their well-being depends.

Defenders of the standard view may say that the untruth of the literal interpretation of the Shilluk—or of any other—evaluative framework does not affect its importance and guiding force. Those who are led by self-knowledge to conclude that the factual assumptions on which their evaluative framework rests are untrue can reasonably adopt a metaphorical interpretation of it. It avoids the catastrophic consequences the untruth of the literal interpretation would have, if they had no alternative to it. But the metaphorical interpretation is an alternative, and there are good reasons for accepting it. Defenders of the standard view, therefore, may claim that self-knowledge need not have unacceptable consequences for those who are steeped in their evaluative framework.

Whatever we may think of this cavalier attitude to the truth, there is a strong reason why the acceptance of the metaphorical interpretation would doom the standard view. The reason is that it is inconsistent with the importance defenders of the standard view attribute to self-knowledge. They suppose that self-knowledge is the means whereby we resolve conflicts between our beliefs, emotions, desires, and actions. But the metaphorical interpretation makes self-knowledge irrelevant to resolving conflicts. What matters to conflict-resolution then is the conventional and successful approach to conflict-resolution—which was sexual potency and physical or political combat for the Shilluk—not the weighing of reasons for and against the components of our personal attitude that guides how we think we should live. The reason for following conventional approaches is to maintain the evaluative framework of our society that enables us to live as we think we should. This is what the thoughtful Shilluk may accept, what the heretics of double truth advocate, and what the Church had condemned.

The metaphorical interpretation justifies an evaluative framework if it endures. But that does not show the pivotal importance of self-knowledge. It shows instead that it does not matter whether our supposed knowledge of our the personal attitude that guides how we live is genuine. What matters is to live as we think we should, not whether we have genuine self-knowledge. If an evaluative framework is interpreted literally by its participants, then the cultivation of self-knowledge may have disastrous consequences for those who are guided by it. If it is interpreted metaphorically, then self-knowledge is irrelevant to its justification. My interim conclusion is that the standard view rests on the exclusivist mistake about the importance of self-knowledge and about the interpretation of social and personal conflicts as obstacles to living as we think we should. Conflicts are often not obstacles but means to living as we think we should.

It may be said in defense of the standard view that these criticisms of the importance of self-knowledge are based on cases in which self-knowledge fails. Self-knowledge is important, its defenders would say, provided it is genuine, not when it is mistaken. If so, it becomes crucial for the defense of the standard view to distinguish between genuine and mistaken cases of self-knowledge. I will now argue that it is a parochial mistake to attribute great importance even to genuine self-knowledge.

The Parochial Mistake

Some years ago I had a memorable conversation with a strikingly intelligent Muslim economist. We were at a research establishment, he was negotiating a commercial agreement on behalf of his country that was to be worth a great deal of money, and I was trying to finish a book. We had both worked hard during the day, and wanted to get away from it for a few hours. By chance we sat side by side during dinner, which was excellent, the wine was plentiful, and we both helped ourselves to it rather freely. He said to me with a smile about the wine he obviously enjoyed that he is not as good a Muslim as he should be. And I replied that fortunately I feel free to drink what I like. He asked, perhaps with a touch of envy, what my permissive religion was, and I said that I am not religious at all. This amazed him. He asked how a respected scholar, as he took me to be, could be without religion. I explained that I thought there were serious questions about the assumptions of all religions known to me and instead of relying on them I prefer to make up my mind about how I should live. I asked him in turn how he deals with questions about the assumptions on which his faith rests. He said that he knows that there are such questions, but he does not think about them much, and when he does and has no answers, he asks his mullah, his religious authority, who gives him the answers. He then asked me how I handle no less complicated questions about economics. I had to say that I do not think much about them and that I leave it to experts to worry about them. He thought that this was perfectly reasonable. But I did not think that his answer to my question was perfectly reasonable. I thought that he should cultivate self-knowledge of the reasons he has for his religion rather than rely on the authority of his mullah.

This difference between us stuck in my mind. I thought about it a great deal and concluded that he was right and I was wrong. He did not and I did make the parochial mistake. The difference between us was that I thought that cultivating self-knowledge is more reasonable than relying on authority and he did not. But he did not go on to think that relying on authority was more reasonable than cultivating self-knowledge. He thought that he is reasonable in following the way of his religion and I am reasonable in following my own judgment. He does it his way, I do it my way, and that is that. What he does about religion is his affair, and what I do is my affair. I was reminded by his view to Gibbon's gem:

> The various modes of worship which prevailed in the Roman world were all considered by the people as equally true; by the philosophers as equally false; and by the magistrates as equally useful. And this toleration produced not only mutual indulgence, but even religious concord.[8]

I eventually saw that my attitude was what Gibbon rightly calls philosophical, my dinner companion's personal attitude was what Gibbon attributes to the people, but his reflective judgment was that of the magistrate. I was thinking about religion from a theoretical and he from a practical point of view. I thought that religious beliefs are either true or false and it is important to have self-knowledge of our reasons for deciding which they are. He thought about religious beliefs as a way of life. What is important is to follow the one we have, and it does not much matter which one, provided it is kept within reasonable limits. He could leave problems about his way of life to religious authorities, but I could not because I thought that reliance on authority would not be a reasonable substitute for the cultivation of self-knowledge. Self-knowledge is important from the theoretical point of view, authority is important from the practical one. My theoretical view was parochial because I mistakenly supposed that only my view is reasonable. His practical view was not parochial because he recognized that reasons for the relative importance of the cultivation of self-knowledge and reliance on authority depend on the point of view from which they are being considered.

I realized later that I do not even think that the cultivation of self-knowledge is always more important than relying on authority. I confidently rely on the authority of scientists and historians when I have questions about the assumptions of science or history, just as my dinner companion relies on the authority of his mullah for answers to questions about religious assumptions. I realized that the difference between us is not simply that I thought that the cultivation of self-knowledge is more reasonable than relying on authority, but that self-knowledge is more reasonable than authority when the questions are religious, but not when they are scientific or historical. And this brought me to the embarrassing further realization that I was evaluating my dinner companion's evaluative framework from the point of view of my own. And that is the parochial mistake. It is the cardinal sin of historians to evaluate what was done in the past from the point of view of present values; of anthropologists to evaluate a culture by the standards of another culture; and for philosophers to evaluate a metaphysical theory from the point of view of another metaphysical theory. By making the parochial mistake, I convicted myself of this kind of cardinal sin.

My acknowledgment of this did not make me doubt my evaluative framework and accept my dinner companion's. I continued to think that the assumptions on which religion rests are doubtful, while the assumptions on which science and history rest are not. But I could no longer think that cultivating self-knowledge is always more reasonable than relying on authority.

Defenders of the standard view, however, think just that. They think that the cultivation of self-knowledge is necessary for living as we think we should. And in this they are as mistaken as I was. Countless people live by and large as they think they should, try to follow the conventions of their religion, morality, tribe, ethnicity, or family, rely on their authorities when they need to, and neither cultivate self-knowledge, nor suffer from its lack. Perhaps the most that can be reasonably claimed by champions of self-knowledge is that given our evaluative framework, self-knowledge is more reasonable for us in several areas of life than authority. But I do not think that even that attenuated claim is defensible for reasons I will now give.

The Optimistic Mistake

The mistake is to suppose that self-knowledge makes our life better, its lack makes it worse, and the more self-knowledge we have, the more likely it is that we will live as we think we should. This view makes the cultivation of self-knowledge a moral imperative. Hampshire's succinct expression of it is as follows:

> He explains himself to himself by his history, but by the history as accompanied by unrealised possibilities on both sides of the track of actual events. His individual nature, and the quality of his life, do not depend only on the bare log-book of events and actions. His character and the quality of his experience emerge in the possibilities that were real possibilities for him, which he considered and rejected for some reason or other. From the moral point of view, it is even a significant fact about him as a person that a certain possibility, which might have occurred to him as a possibility, never did occur to him. In self-examination one may press these inquiries into possibilities very far, and this pressure upon possibilities belongs to the essence of moral reflection.[9]

There are many questions that cry out to be asked about this self-examination, as Hampshire calls the cultivation of self-knowledge. One of them is about how far it should be pressed? Say that I have rejected certain possibilities in the past. I said to myself: I will not distrust my friend; I will not forgive the injustice done to me; I will not apologize for telling the truth; and so on. If I am committed to the cultivation of self-knowledge, I will not stop here. I will ask, What has led me to reject these possibilities? Why did I choose the possibilities I have accepted instead of others? Suppose the answer I give to myself is that I have trusted my friend because he was always true to me; I have not forgiven the injustice because it was motivated by ill will toward me and caused me serious unnecessary injury; and I have told the truth because I was asked to tell it, and have nothing to apologize for.

If I am serious about cultivating self-knowledge, I will not think that these answers are the end of the matter. I will go on to ask myself whether my need for friends may not have blinded me to the occasions when my supposed friend was false? Whether what was done to me was really unjust rather than injury to my pride? And whether I might have told the truth tactlessly because I was insensitive? If I answer these questions to my satisfaction, it will be still far from the end of the matter, because I will ask myself whether I might not be judging myself too self-indulgently? Whether my recollection of the facts is accurate? Whether my moral judgments are not too rigid or too permissive? And this cultivation of self-knowledge can be pressed very far indeed. How far is too far? When is it right to stop it?

The point of these questions is not deny the importance of self-knowledge, but to deny that its cultivation is always good and that the more self-knowledge we have, the more likely it is that we will live as we think we should. Excessive cultivation of self-knowledge may well be a bad substitute for an active life. We may get lost in the unending questioning of our motives. Just as skeptical questioning can go on ad infinitum, so the cultivation of self-knowledge can be an endless process of aiming at the authentication of the latest revelation of self-knowledge.

Suppose, however, that we have enough self-knowledge to know when we do not need more of it. Why should we think that self-knowledge will make our life better? Why might it not make us ashamed, guilty, regretful, or chagrined about how we have lived and acted, and make us despise ourselves? The answer defenders of the standard view might give is that realizing this about ourselves is the first step toward becoming better. But why should the self-knowledge we have gained make us want to change? Why might we not say instead that this is the way we are, we accept it, reject the values that make us feel badly about ourselves, and we will make the most of life, given what we are? Or we might say, cynically, that we are despicable, but so is everyone else. The difference is that we admit it, at least to ourselves, but others are ignorant of it or hypocritical about it.

The cultivation of self-knowledge can go wrong in these ways, but it need not. Its defenders may optimistically claim that since it is in our interest to cultivate genuine self-knowledge in order to correct those parts of ourselves that are obstacles to living as we think we should, we will do all we can to prevent our self-knowledge from going wrong. Most of the time, therefore, we can reasonably rely on the self-knowledge we have managed to acquire. Let us suppose, contrary to the facts, that this is true. We have enough self-knowledge to be realistic about our beliefs, emotions, and desires. We do not deceive ourselves, are not led astray by wishful thinking, we avoid self-indulgent evaluations of ourselves, and we do not get lost in the futile process of trying to authenticate our authentications. If these very favorable conditions were met, would self-knowledge enable us to live as we think we should?

It may or it may not, depending on whether the components of our personal attitude of which we have genuine self-knowledge are in some way mistaken. It is an optimistic fallacy to suppose that the beliefs, emotions, and desires of which we have successfully cultivated self-knowledge are ones we should have. What if we are motivated by our beliefs and emotions to seek power over others, impose our will on them, subjugate foreign lands, manipulate the stock market, try to communicate with the dead, collect pine cones, avenge insults to honor, or protect racial purity? Just because we know what beliefs, emotions, and desires guide how we live does not make them valuable, nor should being true to them always guide how we live. They may be deplorable or absurd, even if our self-knowledge of them is not. And we should not be motivated in these ways even if they are endorsed by the evaluative framework of our society, because that too could be deplorable or absurd, as were those of many fortunately extinct societies.

Finally, it is yet another mistake to suppose that what self-knowledge reveals actually guides how we live. It may reveal that we are confused about how we do or should live, or that our beliefs, emotions, and desires conflict and lead us to act in incompatible ways, or that they keep changing depending on our momentary successes or failures. The optimistic mistake is to suppose that genuine self-knowledge will reveal our deepest concerns, what may be called our moral center, when, in fact, it might reveal that our concerns are shifting, that we have no moral center, and that the self we get to know is riddled with ambivalence. We might then be better off following the conventional ways of our society's evaluative framework, getting on with life as well as we can, and forgetting about the conflicts at the core of our being. We certainly have reasons for cultivating self-knowledge, but we also have reasons against it. And the weight of these reasons shifts as we age, our circumstances change, and new experiences influence our personal attitude that guides of how we live.

Facing Conflicts

I have been arguing that conflicts are not always bad and self-knowledge is not always good. Conflicts need not be obstacles to living as we should but the means to it. They may lead us to realize that our personal attitude needs to be revised and made more coherent. And the cultivation of self-knowledge need not be the best way of coping with our conflicts. It may be preferable to live with conflicts than to face the despicable truths we may come to know about what we really believe, feel, or desire to do. Self-knowledge may be misled by the various tempting ways of seeing ourselves in a favorable light. It may make us question the entire evaluative framework of our life, and thus threaten to destroy the conditions on which we depend for living as we think we should. And in cultivating it, we have to rely on some of the same beliefs, emotions, and desires whose conflicts have led us to seek self-knowledge in the first place, thus casting doubt on the reliability of whatever results self-knowledge yields.

The conclusion is not that conflicts could not be bad and self-knowledge could not be good. Of course they could be. The conclusion is that they need not be, and when we try to decide whether they are bad or good, whether they are obstacles or means to living as we think we should, then we often have strong reasons both for and against regarding them as bad obstacles or as good means. This is what makes our choices between them difficult.

Most of us have to make difficult choices, but how we make them depends on the evaluative framework of our society and on our personal attitude that guides how we live. It may be that we are committed to a primarily theoretical approach, and then our main concern will be seeking the truth by cultivating self-knowledge, or it may be primarily practical aiming at an acceptable way of life, in which self-knowledge will seem much less important. It may be one in which a social point of view is dominant, and then self-knowledge may not be all that important, or it may be primarily a personal point of view to which self-knowledge may be essential. But that point of view will only be personal, not one that everyone should either adopt or be doomed to a life of frustration.

If the point of view is derived from a hierarchical evaluative framework at whose peak there is a highest value or an overriding principle, then conflicts will be seen as having relatively easy casuistical resolutions by applying to them whatever the value or principle is, and then the need for self-knowledge will not be keenly felt. Or the point of view may be personal, both conflicts and self-knowledge may have great importance in it, or it may be conventional and then reliance on conventions obviates the need to worry much about either conflicts or self-knowledge, since the conventional authorities will do the worrying for us. How we make difficult choices depends on the evaluative framework and how we think we should live.

There will be reasonable and unreasonable ways of making difficult choices in evaluative frameworks that enable us to make sense of our life, have the means of evaluating the available possibilities, and provide sufficient freedom to act on our evaluations. There are many evaluative frameworks that meet these conditions. The importance we attribute to conflicts and self-knowledge depends on the evaluative framework and our personal attitude.

In the light of these considerations, it becomes apparent that we cannot make difficult choices reasonably if we suppose that we can make them once and for all. Our conflicts—for instance between having and not having children, getting a divorce and staying with an imperfect marriage, or accepting and rejecting a lucrative but possibly corrupting job—need not be obstacles to living as we think we should but crucial junctures at which we have to make difficult choices about how we should live. And part of the difficulty of making such choices is to decide whether the self-knowledge we seem to have—for instance of our merits or demerits, confidence or its lack, talents or weaknesses, successes or failures—is genuine or the result of self-deception, or of being misled by the possibly mistaken evaluative framework of our society, or of the narrowness or permissiveness of our upbringing. If what seems like self-knowledge is not genuine, it will exacerbate our conflicts, rather than help to overcome them.

The difficult choices we have to make when we face such conflicts and have to make up our mind about the reliability of what may or may not be genuine self-knowledge unavoidably depend on what the possibilities of life are in our context, on the objects of our supposed knowledge, on our experiences in making similar choices, on the particular beliefs, emotions, and desires involved, and on the changing possibilities of the society in which we live. The choices are difficult because there are reasons both for and against the conflicting possibilities and because even if we make a reasonable choice at particular time, in a particular context, the times, alternatives, and contexts change, and make the new choice as difficult as the previous one was. This need not be our fault, although, of course, it often is. Having to make difficult choices will remain human predicaments, even if we are as reasonable as possible.

The preceding critical remarks should not be taken as expressing doubts about self-knowledge. They express doubts about the exaggerated claim made by defenders of the standard view that the pursuit of self-knowledge is a necessary condition of living as we think we should. In some fine lives, the pursuit of self-knowledge does have an important and rightly valued place. But in many other no less fine lives, it has much less importance. The widely accepted standard view does not recognize this rather obvious fact.

3   Difficult Choices

Commitments

At critical junctures of our lives, we have to make choices between conflicting commitments. We have to decide how deeply we are willing to compromise our self-respect in order to keep a job we love and need. Or whether to help a beloved, needy, but undeserving family member. Or whether to tell the truth to a friend who asked for it but would be deeply hurt by it. Or to strive for excellence or for peace of mind. Such choices are not easy, but we can make them by evaluating the relative strength of reasons for and against the alternative possibilities from the point of how we think we should live. We ask ourselves whether we should be the kind of person who values love over justice, self-respect over security, truthfulness over hurting a friend, or excellence over peace of mind, and then choose the one that the person we think we should be would choose. We may regret that we cannot honor both commitments, but we can readily explain and justify to ourselves or to others why we have made that particular choice. The choice may still turn out to be mistaken, but it is not arbitrary because we have what we take to be strong reasons for acting on one commitment rather than the conflicting one.

A choice we need to make becomes difficult when we have strong reasons both for and against the conflicting commitments and after weighing the reasons we cannot decide which are stronger. If we value both of the conflicting commitments as important to living as we think we should, then the choice becomes difficult indeed, and we have to look further for a reasonable way of making it. The problem is to find out what that way might be.

We all have countless different commitments ranging along a continuum from trivial to important. I will refer to the most important ones as primary. If our primary commitments conflict, then whichever we opt for will prevent us from living as we think we should. Damaging as this is, it is exacerbated by other consequences. If we dishonor a primary commitment, as we must if a difficult choice requires it, then we unavoidably see ourselves as dishonorable. We condemn ourselves in the supreme court of our own judgment. But that is still not all. Added to the self-condemnation is the loss of something we deeply value, like love or justice, self-respect or security, truthfulness or friendship, the pursuit of excellence or peace of mind. By making a difficult choice either way, we knowingly have to act contrary to being the kind of person we think we should be. It is the joint force of these considerations that makes the choice we have to make between conflicting primary commitments difficult.

Given the conflicts and difficult choices to which primary commitments lead, perhaps it would be best then to avoid making primary commitments. Then we would not have to make difficult choices between them. We can do this either by making only one primary commitment, or by making none. Neither expedient will enable us to live as we think we should.

Take the first possibility. Our primary commitment will be to something we value more than anything else. If it conflicts with anything else, we resolve the conflict in its favor. We could have only one such commitment because there could be only one thing we value more than anything else. Such a primary commitment is unconditional. It may be to creativity, family, happiness, honor, justice, love, pleasure, a political or religious ideal, and so on. If it conflicts with anything else, we resolve the conflict in favor of our unconditional commitment. That choice will not be the difficult, but it will be no less problematic than a difficult choice would be.

There are some people who live by following an unconditional commitment. They subordinate all else to living according to it. Typically, it is a religious or a political ideal, or a life of pleasure or creativity. For its sake they are willing, if necessary, to sacrifice friends, livelihood, happiness, beauty, goodness, truth, or indeed themselves. Such people are fanatical. They incapacitate themselves from living a human life in which they could recognize the importance of a variety of economic, legal, medical, moral, personal, political, religious, and other modes of evaluation. Most of us are not fanatics, and we struggle with our conflicting commitments. Fanatics do not have to struggle. Their unconditional commitment overrides all else that interferes with living according to it, and they are true to it.

Looking at the lives of such people from the outside, we wonder how they could be so confident that they have made the right commitment. Are they not as fallible as we are? How could they know that they are not misled by self-deception, wishful thinking, dogmatism, prejudice, ignorance of the importance of other valuable possibilities of life, or by fear of uncertainty or of serious conflicts? We think that there are no convincing answers to such questions. We distrust fanatics because they are dangerous. They do not recognize normal restraints. We think that they should question their certainties and recognize that there are legal, moral, political, religious, and other limits. If they do not, there is something wrong with them. even if we do not know exactly what that is. If they were more reasonable, they would realize it and then they would not be fanatical.

We have these doubts because we recognize that we are fallible. The best we can do is face our conflicts, and then reflect on them. We know that we may be misled by false beliefs, misdirected emotions, or misguided desires. We struggle to understand, evaluate, and correct these mistakes, and find some way of coping with our conflicts. We do what we can for a loving family life, friendship, interesting work, varied enjoyments, good health, financial security, some beauty, respect from others, deeper understanding, or a life without debilitating fear, guilt, shame, regret, boredom, and dissatisfaction. And we rightly think that a fanatical life, governed by an unconditional commitment, is incompatible with seeking these or other good things in life.

Our problem is that if we do not make an unconditional commitment, we are left with various conditional and conflicting primary commitments to possibilities we regard as important to living as we think we should. And then we have to make difficult choices between them. If we are to make them reasonably, we need to have some reasons for making them one way rather than another. These reasons cannot be evaluations that follow from any of the modes of evaluation of our evaluative framework, because they also conflict. In fact, our conditional primary commitments often conflict precisely because we have derived them from conflicting modes of evaluations. It seems then that we do not know how to make difficult choices between them. Perhaps a deeper understanding of the kind of difficulty they involve might point to possible ways of making them less difficult.

Difficult Choices

Difficult choices between conflicting primary commitments are like tragic ones in some ways, but unlike them in others. Antigone faced a tragic choice between her political and religious obligation; Captain Vere between following naval law in time of war and hanging Billy Budd who was morally, if not legally, innocent; and the Grand Inquisitor in Dostoevsky's fable between defending Christianity and ordering the killing of Jesus. Tragic choices are between exclusive alternatives. Those facing them must choose between life and death, keeping or not keeping a promise, telling or not telling the truth, speaking or remaining silent, and so forth. Confronted with such a choice, making no choice is in fact to choose by default one of the conflicting primary commitments.

If we face a difficult but non-tragic choice, we have an alternative that is unavailable in tragic choices. We can abandon both of the conflicting primary commitments. The very difficulty of the choice may persuade us to make only conditional commitments. Then we will not regard any of our commitments as crucial to living as we should. If they conflict, we sometimes act on one at the expense of the other, and sometimes do the opposite without thereby going against how we think we should live. If how we think we should live is flexible enough, we will not have to make difficult choices.

We will, however, have to pay the heavy price for it that we will be uncertain about how we should live. We will have many commitments, choose to act sometimes on one, sometimes on another, but all our choices will be episodic and opportunistic. We will be living day to day and our life will lack lasting interests, intimate relationships, or long-term goals whose pursuit could give meaning and purpose to what we do. The foreseeable result is that the choice between making and not making primary commitments will be as difficult as the choice is between conflicting primary commitments. Most of us can certainly be more flexible than we are, but flexibility will come to an end if we really care about something, like love, our children, self-respect, justice, and so on. But then our commitments to those things are all too likely to conflict on occasions, and then the choice between them will be difficult.

Another way in which might try to make choices between primary commitments less difficult is to become more critical of them. Commitments are not arbitrary acts of will of the kind Sartre and other existentialists thought we have to make if we are honest enough not to live in bad faith. They are acts of will, but they unavoidably involve a personal attitude formed of various beliefs, emotions, and desires we have about ourselves, the conditions of our society, the available possibilities, and the modes of evaluation of our evaluative framework. These beliefs may be false, emotions misdirected, and desires misguided, and, it may be thought, that is what makes some choices difficult. If one of our conflicting commitments is in one of these ways mistaken, while the other is not, or if one is more likely to be mistaken than the other, then the choice between them will not be difficult. Perhaps we find the choice difficult only because we have not been sufficiently critical of the commitments we have made. And then we can make the choice less difficult by becoming more critical of our commitments.

A strong reason for cultivating such a critical personal attitude is that we often make commitments because we are intimidated by some authority, unquestioningly follow prevailing conventions, are too lazy or timid to think for ourselves, or are misled by self-deception and fantasies, or mistaken about what possibilities are actually available in our context. The cultivation of a critical personal attitude toward our commitments is not easy. We are reluctant to question them if they are to people, causes, or interests we value. But there is a strong impetus to question them if we are forced to make a difficult choice between them and if we find that our conflicts and the difficulty of our choices make us uncertain about how to live as we think we should. It is possible that we are to be blamed for having conflicts and having to make difficult choices because we have not been critical enough of our commitments.

The fact remains, however, that eliminating this possibility is exceptionally difficult. If we have a critical personal attitude toward our commitments, then we must have some standard with reference to which we can criticize or justify them. Applying to them whatever that standard is, however, must involve one or more of our beliefs, emotions, and desires, since we have no other way of justifying or criticizing anything. But when we try to justify or criticize our commitments, then the beliefs, emotions, and desires involved are among the ones that we are trying to criticize or justify. If those beliefs, emotions, and desires are questionable, so will be the criticisms and justifications based on them. And then the reliability of what our critical personal attitude yields will be as questionable as the beliefs, emotions, and desires are on which our commitments are based. Our choices, therefore, will remain difficult no matter how critical we are of them.

There is yet another reason why choices between commitments are difficult. We often find it hard to do what we recognize as our onerous obligation because it is contrary to our inclination; or to choose between two of our duties when it is impossible to fulfill both; or not to allow embarrassment, fatigue, weakness, or inattention to divert us from doing what we know is right. It is often difficult to do what we think we should. But in such cases we know what is right and wrong. Difficult choices are different precisely because we do not know what is right or wrong to do. Who could be certain of what the reasonable limits are of truthfulness, loyalty, compassion, or prudence? Or when it is permissible to take a human life? Or, what could justify doing what is normally wrong? Or when should a legal, moral, political, or religious obligation override a conflicting obligation that follows from another mode of evaluation?

These questions lead to what has been called the problem of dirty hands.[1] Much has been written about it, but the problem of difficult choices should not be assimilated to it. The problem of dirty hands is the conflict between political and moral obligations. Political office holders are sometimes obligated to do what is morally wrong. If they fail, they fail in the discharge of the responsibilities of their office. If they act as political necessity dictates—lie to those who trusted and elected them, compromise their principles, torture terrorists—then they must dirty their hands and act immorally. It is usually hard to evaluate how far politicians can reasonably go in dirtying their hands. But that is not the problem of making difficult choices.

The conflict between politics and morality can be generalized to other modes of evaluations. Economic, legal, medical, moral, prudential, religious, and other evaluations may also conflict, and in resolving their conflicts we will have to dirty our hands as much as politicians may have to do. Making difficult choices calls for decisions. What is a difficult choice for one person, however, may not be difficult for another. What makes choices difficult are the commitments we have made. Different people often have different commitments. And we can change, revise, abandon, or demote the importance of our commitments. We cannot do that with legal, moral, political, or religious evaluations. They are not up to us, although of course we may accept or reject them. But we accept or reject them on the basis of our commitments. What makes choices difficult is that we do not know how to resolve conflicts between our commitments. If we knew it, we would know whether to accept or reject the evaluations that follow from conflicting modes of evaluation. In doing this, of course, we may be wrong, and then it is proper to hold us legally, morally, politically, or otherwise responsible. We must begin, however, with making a decision about what commitments we should make.

Decisions

Reasonable decisions involve finding a fit between the evaluations that follow from the modes of evaluations in our context and our personal attitude that guides how we think we should live. Whether we live that way depends on how successful we are in finding a good enough fit. This involves understanding and evaluating the available possibilities and our personal attitude toward them. We are prone to make mistakes about both. Reasonable decisions depend on avoiding such mistakes and trying to achieve as much control as we can over how we live. This is a lifelong process because both our possibilities and personal attitude change. Making a commitment to living in this way is one of the most basic ideals of our contemporary evaluative framework. And many of the problems of life in our context are attributed to our failure to follow it.

The possibilities we are trying understand and evaluate exist independently of us. Our control over them is minimal. The prevailing economic, legal, medical, moral, political, religious, and other possibilities are what they are and the best we can do is to make the most of them. What we can decide, at least to some extent, are our evaluations and personal attitude toward them. That is supposed to be the key to living as we think we should. The ideal is to make as reasonable decisions as we can. If we are committed to it, we must do it for ourselves. No one can decide for us what the best fit is between our evaluations, personal attitude, and the possibilities available in our context. Others may know better than we what the possibilities and perhaps even what our beliefs, emotions, and desires really are. But our personal attitude to how we should live goes beyond that. It involves our evaluations of the relative importance we attribute to our possibilities and to the components of our personal attitude. And that we can only do for ourselves. Others may tell us what our evaluations should be, but whether we accept or reject what they tell us is still a decision that only we can make.

As Montaigne put it,

> Things in themselves may have their own weights and measures and qualities; but once inside, within us, she allots them their qualities as she sees fit. . . . Health, conscience, authority, knowledge, riches, beauty, and their opposites — are all stripped on entry and receive from the soul new clothing, and the coloring she chooses — and which each individual chooses; for they have not agreed together on their styles, rules, and forms; each one is queen in her realm. Wherefore let us no longer make the external qualities of things our excuse; it is up to us to reckon them as we will. Our good and our ill depend on ourselves alone. Let us offer our offerings and vows to ourselves, not to Fortune; she has no power over our character.[2]

It is not contrary to making decisions to be guided by a mode of evaluation, or the advice or example of a teacher, a friend, or an admired person. If our decisions to follow such guidance are based on adequate understanding and evaluation of what they involve, then they are genuinely ours, even if we have been helped by others to make them. Of course, our decisions may go wrong. The test is whether they aid or hinder us in living as we think we should. But, according to the ideal, that is also up to us to decide. Others can evaluate whether we are right or wrong in how we think we should live, but no one can decide for us whether we are satisfied or dissatisfied when we live as we think we should. We are the ultimate authority on that.

According to the ideal of decision making, individual responsibility depends on our decisions. We are responsible both for acting and not acting on our decisions. We evaluate actions on the basis of whether their agents had or could have made a decision to act or not to act that way. In an admirable study of the history of this ideal, Schneewind writes that it has emerged by the end of the eighteenth century centered on the belief that all normal individuals are equally able to live together in a morality of self-governance. All of us, on this view, have an equal ability to see for ourselves what morality calls for and are in principle equally able to move ourselves to act accordingly, regardless of threats or rewards from others. These two points have come to be widely accepted. . . . In daily life they give us the working assumption that the people we live with are capable of understanding and acknowledging in practice the reasons for moral constraints we all mutually expect ourselves and others to respect. . . . The conception of morality as self-governance provides a conceptual framework for a social space in which we may each rightly claim to direct our own actions without interference from state, the church, the neighbors, or those claiming to be better or wiser than we.[3]

Decision, then, involves choosing one among some possibilities available in our context, making a commitment to it, distinguishing between our more and less important commitments, and resolving conflicts between them. And they will conflict because our economic, legal, medical, moral, political, religious, and other modes of evaluation of the possibilities to which we are committed often conflict. We have to make such decisions when we have to deal with our conflicting commitments to love and justice, self-respect and security, truthfulness and friendship, pursuit of excellence and peace of mind, and the like. Living as we think we should, then, depends on acting on our commitments, but if two of them conflict, then we cannot live as we think we should. We must go against one of our conflicting commitments even though we have strong reasons for acting on both. Doing so is contrary to our will. Yet we must make a decision about which we choose to act on when we cannot act on both. Whichever we decide to act on will prevent us from living as we think we should. And we must condemn ourselves for being untrue to our own commitments.

The problem of finding a way of making reasonable decisions is therefore unavoidable and basic for those of us who are guided by the evaluative framework of our society in which central importance attributed to the ideal of decision making. The intractability of this problem is a strong reason for considering whether there might not be reasonable alternatives to this ideal.

The alternatives I will now sketch are two very different evaluative frameworks in which decision making is far less important than it is for us. Those who are guided by these frameworks have fewer conflicts and have to make fewer difficult choices than we do. If we compare these alternatives with our own, we realize that the possibilities of life are richer than they appear to be if we are confined to our evaluative framework. It will also provide two different external points of view, which will help us form a better understanding, more informed evaluation, a wider possibility of recognizing and correcting the mistakes of our evaluative framework and personal attitude, and perhaps even suggest a better approach to decision making when we face conflicts and difficult choices.

I derive these two alternatives from anthropological reconstructions of the rapidly disappearing evaluative frameworks of Hindus in India and of Balinese in what is now Indonesia. Each flourished for many centuries, until around the second half of the nineteenth century when they began to undergo accelerating change, so much so that except in a few isolated rural communities they now exist largely as part of the imperfectly remembered past. The anthropological reconstructions I rely on are far richer than my sketch of them. I will focus mainly on the place decision making has in these evaluative frameworks.

I have found both reconstructions wonderful feats of sympathetic imagination firmly anchored in facts. Both have been much discussed, sometimes critically, by anthropologists. I cannot make an informed judgment about their accuracy. But that is not important for present purposes. I take from them the suggestive account of two possible ways of making sense of life and understanding, evaluating, and coping with the vicissitudes of human predicaments. The imagined possibilities are enough to provide two external points of view with which we can compare our own. We do not have to accept or admire them, and I certainly do not, but that is not needed for relying on them for a better understanding of our own.

The Hindu and Balinese Alternatives

The first of these anthropological reconstructions is the work of Louis Dumont, a far from uncritical follower of Durkheim and Mauss.[4] The basic evaluative terms in the Indian Hindu evaluative framework he reconstructs are purity and impurity. Purity is the highest ideal whose approximation is the aim of life. Impurity is what stands in its way. In human lives, as Hindus see them, purity and impurity are unavoidably mixed, but in different lives they are mixed in different proportions. The purer a life is, the higher its social standing; and the greater the proportion of impurity, the lower its social standing of those in whose lives impurity dominates. Impurity is natural and biological. Purity is to be free of it. The purest are the Brahmins. They occupy the peak of the social hierarchy. The most impure are the Untouchables whose social rank is the lowest. Between Brahmins and Untouchables there are various castes whose standing in the hierarchy depends on the degree of purity of their lives.

The origin of impurity is external. It depends on contact with corpses, excrement, human or animal excretions like semen, saliva, menstrual blood, or sweat; sex or other physical contact with other impure human beings; or eating impure food. External impurity becomes internal through contact with it. The Brahmins are the purest because they have the least contact with impure things or people, like the Untouchables or of those in castes lower than the Brahmins'. Each caste has specific services to perform. The Brahmins' are the priestly functions. The Untouchables handle corpses, excrement, and unclean food, and do the cleaning. What the castes do is thought of as performing necessary services for others, not as optional productive labor.

Each person is born into a caste, destined to provide the appropriate services, and thereby be exposed to greater or lesser impurity. There is no upward mobility at all that would enable a person to rise to a higher caste, although it is possible to sink lower. Those who belong to the same caste can marry only others of the same caste. Through conception and physical contact children inherit the caste of their parents. Good intentions, ambition, wealth, talent, education, and effort can at best raise the status of individuals within their caste, but there is no way out from it. People are born into a caste depending on the mixture of purity and impurity they have accumulated in previous existences, and they carry over the mixture from this life into the next.

The caste system is the social representation of the scheme of things that nothing human beings could do will change. The only escape from it is to become totally pure, with no admixture of impurity, and that means pure disembodied existence, which is possible but its achievement is extraordinarily difficult because it depends on leaving behind all impure human things, including the body, and becoming one with the scheme of things.

Insofar as there are conflicts between commitments in this evaluative framework, it is clear that they should be resolved in favor of the commitment that brings one closer to purity, the incomparably highest ideal of this hierarchical evaluative framework. There are choices to be made, but they are not difficult—in the sense of there being strong reasons for both of the conflicting primary commitments—because reasons overwhelmingly favor doing all individuals can to approximate purity. Those who nevertheless opt for impurity do so as a result of stupidity, ignorance, weakness, or succumbing to the temptations of impurity. They are irrational, act against their own interests, and doom themselves to a worse life than the one they already have.

In this evaluative framework the ideal of decision making has a role, but it is very limited compared to the importance it has in our own. Individuals can make some decisions about how they live, but it extends only to preventing them from worsening the lot they unavoidably have. Intention or hard work cannot change the impurity individuals carry over from their previous existences. Ambition is a wasted effort. The pursuit of anything but purity is a delusion. Most people do not understand the inexorability of the scheme of things. If they catch a remote glimpse of it, they can gain from it only an understanding of the futility of their efforts to escape it. Disenchantment, alienation, or rebellion are useless because they cannot change the ineluctable conditions of life.

The second alternative to our evaluative framework is Balinese, as reconstructed by Clifford Geertz.[5] I will draw from his rich account only the elements that I take to be relevant to decision making. I begin with how the Balinese think of persons. Geertz writes that

> some conception of what a human individual is, as opposed to a rock, an animal, a rainstorm, or a god, is, so far as I can see, universal. Yet, at the same time, as these offhand examples suggest, the actual conceptions involved vary from one group to the next, and often quite sharply (59).

Geertz explains the variable element of the Balinese conception of persons thus:

> There is in Bali a persistent and systematic attempt to stylize all aspects of personal expression to the point where anything idiosyncratic, anything characteristic of the individual merely because he is who he is physically,

psychologically, or biographically, is muted in favor of his assigned place in the continuing . . . never-changing pageant that is Balinese life. It is dramatis personae, not actors, that endure. . . . Physically men come and go, mere incidents in a happenstance history, of no genuine importance even to themselves. But the . . . stage they occupy, the parts they play, and, most important, the spectacle they mount remain, and comprise not the facade but the substance of things, not least the self (62).

"Dramatis personae," "stage," "play," and "spectacle" are not metaphors. The Balinese see life in those terms. The ceremonial performance of the roles that go with their social positions is the essence of the Balinese evaluative framework. That is why the subtitle of Geertz's book is *The Theatre State*. Each individual has many such roles. And the identity of individuals consists in enacting the roles of the positions they occupy, such as: "king," "grandmother," "third-born." It is not just others who identify individuals in this way. Individuals identify themselves with their positions and roles "in the never-changing pageant that is Balinese life."

Just as the Indian Hindus are born into a caste, so the Balinese are born into various social positions. And just as caste determines the services Hindus must provide throughout their lives, so the Balinese must perform the ceremonial roles that attach to the social positions into which they are born. What the Balinese fear, as Hindus fear impurity,

is that the public performance to which one's cultural location commits one will be botched and that the . . . individual will break through to dissolve his standardized public identity. . . . It is the fear of the faux pas . . . that keeps social intercourse on its deliberately narrowed rails and protects the dramatical sense of self against the disruptive threat (64).

In the Balinese evaluative framework there are no conflicts between commitments. The Balinese know that they must do what their social positions require. The decisions they can make concern only better or worse ways of doing it. As Geertz puts it, their individuality is "muted." What matters to them is to occupy their "assigned place in the continuing . . . pageant that is Balinese life." The ideal is that the individual should not "break through to dissolve his standardized public identity." As our central concern is "to direct our own actions without interference from state, the church, the neighbors, or those claiming to be better or wiser than we,"[6] so the central concern of the Balinese is with following the unchosen requirements of the roles into which they were born.

Consequences

These comparisons enable us to see that decision making is an ideal only in our evaluative framework. In the Hindu one, personhood is a burden, the source of impurity, and the cause of human misery. The aim of life is to be free of impurity, the unavoidable consequence of being a person. And in the Balinese evaluative framework, decisions endanger the all-important performance of the unchosen roles each person inhabits from birth. The ideal is to live as one's roles require, and for that decisions are as irrelevant as they are for breathing. Decisions are not involved in how life should be lived.

The point of these comparisons is not to say that our evaluative framework is better or worse than the Hindu or the Balinese. It is rather that the basic importance we attribute to decision making is one possible ideal of life, but there are others. If we acknowledge this, we will realize that our commitment to this ideal is not a universal and necessary ideal of how all human beings should live. Yet, in our contemporary evaluative framework, decision making is regarded as a universal and necessary requirement of morality and reason, and deviations from that as immoral and irrational.

By thinking about the comparison between the Hindu and Balinese evaluative frameworks and ours we may realize that the ancient ideal of eudaimonia that all reasonable human beings are supposed to aim at is mistaken. For Hindus aim at purity and the Balinese at faithfully enacting the roles into which they were born, regardless of how it affects their eudaimonia. We can also realize that it is not a universal requirement of reason to be motivated by the categorical imperative to act as we would want everyone to act. The Hindus think that reason requires different people to perform the different services of the caste into which they were born and to carry different burdens of impurity accumulated in their previous lives. And the Balinese think that reason requires everyone to enact the very different roles of the social positions that is his or hers from birth on. And we can then see as well that it is not a universal and necessary requirement of reason to aim at the greatest happiness for the greatest number. For reason requires Hindus to aim at as much purity as possible, regardless of how it affects others, and the Balinese to aim at the performance of their own roles, not at anyone's happiness.

Decision making, therefore, is not a universal ideal, but only one that is central in our evaluative framework. The recognition that our ideal of decision making is a contingent product of contingent historical circumstances is not a reason against it. On the contrary, it may strengthen our commitment to it, provided we realize that we do not need to make an all-or-nothing choice between adhering to or abandoning it, or between being rational by following it or be doomed to an irrational life. We may reasonably deny that the ideal of decision making is a universal and necessary requirement of reason. Instead, we may try to improve it by seeking better reasons for it than mistakenly insisting on its universality and necessity.

One reason for seeking better reasons is that even now in our context, not just in other places and times, there are countless people who live reasonable and morally acceptable lives although decisions do not have a central place in their lives. They, like Hindus and Balinese, are born into a community they have neither chosen nor have made a decision to accept. They simply and unquestioningly follow the legal, moral, political, or religious modes of evaluation they have learned from their parents or teachers. They are surrounded by family, friends, teachers, neighbors, employers, and employees with whom they share many of their inherited evaluations, and they live decent, productive lives. Such communities are now on the wane, at least in our society. I am not celebrating them. I am calling attention to their possibility even in our context. And that is sufficient to show that the ideal of decision making is not a universal and necessary requirement of reason even for us here and now. To deny its universality and necessity is not to deny that decision making is an important ideal for us. It is that, and I myself accept and try to follow it. But it is not an ideal that reason requires everyone to accept and try to follow.

Another reason for revising the central importance we attribute to the ideal of decision making is that it imposes on us the burden of making difficult choices without helping to make them. If we aim to decide how we should live, we must choose some among the possibilities of life provided by our evaluative framework. We will be driven to realize that we value more than one of the possibilities to which we are committed than others, and then we will become committed to those we value more. As I have argued throughout this chapter, these commitments will conflict, we will have strong reasons for both, and we will have to make difficult choices between them. It is a problem for us now in our evaluative framework how to make these difficult choices reasonably, rather than arbitrarily. And that is a burden in our life that accounts for many of our problems. Hindus and Balinese do not have to make difficult choices, and do not have this burden. They can choose by asking which of their conflicting possibilities is more conducive to purity or more in accordance with the performance of their roles.

Our evaluative framework however is unlike the Hindu or the Balinese in not being hierarchical. We do not have a generally recognized highest value—like purity or role playing—so we cannot appeal to it as a standard with reference to which we could make difficult choices between our conflicting commitments. Nor can we appeal to how we think we should live, because living according to both of the our conflicting commitments is an important part of how we think we should live. That is precisely why the choice between them is difficult. And if we accept the hierarchical evaluative framework of a political ideology or a religious faith, we in effect abandon the ideal of decision making by relying on an ideological or religious authority to decide for us how we should make the difficult choice we could not make. This predicament is then another reason for revising the ideal of decision making by accepting that it is contingent, not universal and necessary, and thus revisable. In conclusion, I turn to a suggestion—no more than that— of how we might nevertheless make reasonable decisions about coping with our conflicts, choices, and problems.

Toward Reasonable Decisions

If we remain committed to our evaluative framework and its ideal of decision making, then conflicts and difficult choices are unavoidable. Perhaps some exceptionally fortunate people living in exceptionally fortunate circumstances can live idyllic lives in which they do not have to face such conflicts and choices, but for most of us they are among the facts of life, not exceptional episodes or sudden emergencies, but ordinary routine events. The acceptance of this is the first of three steps toward a reasonable response to our conflicts and difficult choices. It avoids dramatizing them by resisting Promethean melodrama.

The second step is a way of defusing the problem I discussed earlier in this chapter. The problem is that our commitments are either unconditional or conditional. If we hold one of them unconditionally, it will override any other commitment that may conflict with it, so we can have only one unconditional commitment. If that one is based on some reason, then commitment to it is conditional on that reason, and it cannot be unconditional. If it is unconditional but not based on any reason, then it is arbitrary and we cannot rely on it for making reasonable decisions about difficult choices between conflicting conditional commitments.

If none of our commitments is unconditional, then they are all conditional and some of them will conflict. If there is some consideration on which we can rely for a reasonable way of resolving their conflicts, then that consideration overrides conditional commitments, and it must be unconditional. And then we are back with the problem about unconditional commitments. If there is no consideration to which we could appeal to resolve conflicts between our conditional commitments, then the choice between them remains difficult and we do not have a reasonable way of making decisions about it. It seems, then, that regardless whether one of our conflicting commitments is unconditional, or whether they are all conditional, difficult choices will remain and we will need but do not have a reasonable way of making decisions about them.

This problem can be avoided by making only defeasible commitments.[7] I do not mean by this that our commitments may be mistaken. Of course that is always possible. But commitments remain defeasible even if they are not mistaken, because they may yet be defeated by sufficiently strong countervailing reasons. Defeasible commitments, therefore, are not unconditional. Are they then simply conditional?

They are conditional, but not simply. Only one kind of reason can be sufficiently strong to defeat an unmistaken commitment: a more important unmistaken commitment. And a commitment is more important than another if it is more important to living as we think we should than the conflicting commitment. Living as we think we should is more important than any of our particular commitments, because the reason why we have made that particular commitment is that we think that living as we think we should depends on it. But if a commitment is important to living that way, then is it not unconditional?

No, because reasonable decisions about how we should live should be flexible, not rigid. They should be responsive to the concrete and particular circumstances in which we have to make difficult choices. Decisions about the relative importance of our conflicting commitments should be conditional on these concrete and particular circumstances. There is no general formula, universal principle, or highest good on which we could rely to guide us in making the decisions we need to make. We can nevertheless make them reasonably.

Consider the examples of difficult choices and decisions with which I began: whether to continue to help a family member who does not deserve it; compromise our self-respect in order to keep a secure job we love; tell the humiliating truth to a friend who will be deeply hurt by it; strive for excellence or settle for what is good enough. Reasonable ways of making decisions when we face such difficult choices have to be concrete and particular. They depend on how serious is the offense of the undeserving family member; what makes our help undeserved and what the help we might give involves; how robust is our self-respect and how deeply we will have to compromise it; how secure is our job and how much we love and need it; how humiliating is the truth we might tell and how easily is our friend hurt and how difficult it might be for him to get over it; and whether our talents are sufficient for the excellence we might strive for and how much we are motivated by fear or love of comfort; and so on.

The reasonable evaluation of the relative importance of conflicting commitments depends on answering such concrete and particular questions. There are reasonable and unreasonable answers to them, and we can distinguish between them, even if it is often difficult and painful. The truth may hurt, but it is there to be found. And if we find it in case of the particular and concrete decision when we have to make a difficult choice, we will have a reasonable way of making it then and there. But this will not carry over to other difficult choices because the concrete and particular features of different difficult choices will be different. In each case, however, there will be a reasonable decision we can make about which of two conflicting commitments is important enough to living as we think we should to defeat the other.

The second step toward making a reasonable decision about difficult choices is to maintain our commitment to the ideal of decision making but revise it by accepting its contingency and context-dependence and denying—on the basis of comparisons of our evaluative framework with others—that it is a universal and necessary requirement of reason. This has implications which bring us to the third step of reasonable decision making.

One of these implications is that the widely shared optimistic contemporary expectation that if how we think we should live conforms to the requirements of reason, then we will be able to live as we should. The need to make decisions and difficult choices shows that this expectation is illusory. No matter how reasonable and successful our efforts are in making reasonable, concrete, and particular decisions about to the particular difficult choices we have to make, we will not be able to live as we think we should.

The reason for this is that making decisions about difficult choices between conflicting commitments will unavoidably lead to the loss of a possibility on which living as we think we should depends. The lost possibility will be the one to whose pursuit we have made the commitment that we now override by deciding to act on another commitment. But in being commitments, they are both important to living as we think we should. If the overridden commitment were not to an important possibility we value, then we would not have made it. A reasonable decision, therefore, compels those who make it to accept also that, barring exceptional good fortune, life without serious loss is impossible. The optimistic contemporary expectation rests on the illusion that if we are reasonable enough we will not have conflicts, face difficult choices, and make decisions that involve serious risks.

If we give up the illusion, hard as that is, we may be tempted to swing to the opposite pessimistic view that sees even our most reasonable efforts as futile. This is also an illusion. That we cannot have all we really and reasonably want does not mean that we cannot have much of it. Accepting the pessimistic view of the futility of our efforts would guarantee that we will have even less of it.

The reasonable view is an alternative to both optimism and pessimism. I cannot improve on the following description of it:

> The delicate and difficult art of life is to find, in each new turn of experience, the *via media* between two extremes: to be catholic *without* being characterless; to have and apply standards, and yet to be on guard against their desensitizing and stupefying influence, their tendency to blind us

to the diversities of concrete situations and to previously unrecognized values; to know when to tolerate, when to embrace, and when to fight. And in that art, since no fixed and comprehensive rule can be laid down for it, we shall doubtless never acquire perfection.[8]

But this reasonable view has consequences. One of them is that conflicts, difficult choices, and decisions will remain problems for us no matter how reasonable we are in finding the *via media* in particular contexts as we face particular and concrete conflicts, choices, and decisions. Another consequence is that if we bear in mind the possibilities of other evaluative frameworks, like those of the Hindu's and Balinese's, then we should realize that these are problems only for us, not for all human beings. We have to face them because we accept our evaluative framework and the ideal of decision making, even if it is revised in the way I have suggested. And this will give us, whether or not we are willing to face it, strong reasons against our evaluative framework. But if we do face it, we will also realize that we have strong reasons for it. We genuinely think that how we should live should be based on our decisions, we value the freedom and responsibility that come with making them, and we value also the social arrangements that enable us to live in this way.

These reasons for and against our evaluative framework conflict. Most of us will resolve the conflict in favor of the reasons for it, even as we chafe under the undeniable faults of our evaluative framework. We will not think that our evaluative framework is perfect. But we will think that it is less imperfect than the alternatives to it. That, however, has the cost of having to live with problems, deep conflicts, and difficult choices. That is now one of our predicaments. We can make it less imperfect, but we cannot change it as long as we remain committed to our evaluative framework.

4 The Force of Fate

What Is Fate?

According to the *Random House Dictionary* "fate" is a noun that denotes "something that unavoidably befalls a person; fortune; lot." The corresponding adjective is "fateful." It connotes, among other things, that what befalls a person has "momentous significance or consequences"; and it is "decisively important; portentous," "controlled or determined by destiny; inexorable," and "ominous." This leaves much vague. The features I am concerned with are that fate is *necessary*, not accidental; *personal*, individually variable; *significant*, not commonplace; and involves something *serious that unavoidably befalls* a person, not a minor mishap. Each requires further explanation.

A classic example of fate is what happened to Oedipus. His fate was to murder his father and commit incest with his mother. Both were deeply abhorrent to him and to his society. What kind of necessity was it that made these actions unavoidable? It was certainly not logical. Oedipus would not have made a logical mistake if he had not killed his father or committed incest with his mother. Nor was the necessity dictated by the laws of nature. It would not have been contrary to them if Oedipus had refrained from actions he found abhorrent. The necessity was psychological: it followed from the kind of person Oedipus was. Another person might have acted differently, but the character of Oedipus dictated his actions. When Luther, martyrs, heroes, soldiers, and dissenters, led by conscience, honor, or integrity, say, "Here I stand, I can do no other," they express the psychological necessity that compels them to act in a certain way. Someone else in their situation might not be compelled. It is the character of those on whom fate befalls that makes their fate not just necessary, but also personal.

There is, however, more to fate than this. Most actions follow from the character of the agent. Honesty prompts honest actions, cowardice cowardly ones, stupidity stupid ones, and so on. Such actions are banal, not fateful. Fate enters when the characteristic action is significant because it threatens to have ominous, rather than trivial, consequences for the agent and for others, as did the parricide and incest of Oedipus. "Ominous" is the right word here because the fate that befalls a person is very bad, has decisive importance, and cannot be evaded. Such were the consequences of Antigone's response to Creon's edict, Hamlet's to his father's ghost, and Othello's to Iago's insinuations. In the memorable words of a philosopher whose pessimistic voice has been drowned out by Enlightenment optimism, fate concerns

> the terrible side of life. The unspeakable pain . . . wretchedness and misery, the triumph of wickedness, the scornful mastery of chance, and the irretrievable fall of the just and the innocent . . . the suffering of mankind which is produced partly by chance and error . . . personified as fate.[1]

A fateful action is not just an episode, but a significant one that follows from the character of the agent and the context of the action. The same action may be fateful for one person and not for another. Their brothers' deaths was an episode in both Antigone's and Ismene's lives, but it had elicited very different actions from them. Antigone's actions were intransigent, Ismene's prudent. Given her character, Antigone's fate was to respond as she did, but it was not Ismene's fate. Someone other than Hamlet might have treated the appearance of his father's ghost as a paranoid delusion. And a person more perceptive than Othello might have seen through Iago. But they could not because their character compelled them to act as they did.

In addition to character, fate depends also on the context that makes the episode significant. The context of the death of Antigone's brother and her response to it was the awful history of the House of Atreus; of Hamlet's response to the ghost was his fraught relationship with his mother, the murder of his father, and the usurpation of the throne; and of Othello's jealousy it was yearning for a safe haven after the dangers of war and his uneasy position as a black Moor in white Venice. What happened to them, then, was fateful because of the nature of the episode, its context, and their character.

It might be said that if these conditions are met, then their fate had to happen. We should be careful, however, not to take this as a commitment to fatalism. According to fatalists, whatever happens necessarily has to happen, regardless of what we do or do not do.[2] "Que sera, sera" may have been a popular song, but the idea it expressed is mistaken. What happens may be dictated by ineluctable necessity, but the conditions in which the necessity holds can sometimes be changed. We can prevent all kinds of things from happening to us, for instance by abandoning all contact with others, becoming a hermit, and giving no hostage to fortune. What happened to Antigone, Hamlet, and Othello would not have happened if their characters and contexts had been different. And they could have prevented the calamitous events that transpired by killing themselves at the beginning rather than dying at the end of the fateful train of disasters. Fatalism is mistaken. But it is no less mistaken to conclude that the justified dismissal of fatalism warrants the dismissal of fate.

If fate befalls a person given a particular episode, character, and context, might we say that the fate is determined? Yes, provided we do not suppose that this implies determinism. Determinism is an impersonal and universal theory about everything that happens, including human actions, as the effect of inexorable laws—natural or divine—antecedent causes, and specifiable conditions. If determinism is true, it is true also of fate, but it does not follow that if fate is determined, then determinism is true. Some things may be determined even if not everything is. Fate involves some adversity that befalls a particular person in a particular context. The nature of the adversity and the response to it vary with those who are subject to it. The adversity faced by a person (a death, a parting, a quarrel, a defeat, an experience) may be ominous for one person but not for another.

Fate depends not only on what happens but also on how it affects those to whom it happens. And that, in turn, depends on individual differences in personal relationships, past experiences, and the possession or lack of inner resources, such as strength of character, intelligence, sensitivity, preparedness, vulnerability, and so on. We cannot undo the adversity that befalls us, but we can respond to it in better and worse ways. The seriousness of the adversity does not depend only on whether it is by some impersonal measure greater or smaller, but also on the personal attitude of those who are subject to it. Between the causes and effects of fate are differences in character, context, and attitude. If determinism is true, it is true universally and impersonally of all that happens, including adversities and responses to them. What is fateful, however, depends not only on the causes of an adversity, but also on its nature, how it affects those on whom it befalls, and how they respond to it.

What Is Autonomy?

In our evaluative framework little or no importance is attributed to fate. Luck, especially what has been called moral luck, is much discussed, but luck can be good or bad, and, unlike fate, it need not involve unavoidable, portentous, ominous adversity. We marginalize fate. In this respect, our evaluative framework differs from numerous others in which central importance is attributed to fate: as it is to ancient Greek *moira* and *daimon*, Roman *fatum*, Vedic *rta*, Egyptian *maat*, Hindu and Buddhist *karma*, Arab *kismet*, Renaissance *fortuna*, and by various West African religions under a variety of different names.[3]

One reason why fate has become marginalized for us is that it conflicts with the ideal of autonomy that is as central to our evaluative framework as decision making is. One clear expression of this ideal is that

> to be autonomous is to be one's own person, to be directed by considerations, desires, conditions, and characteristics that are not simply imposed externally upon one, but are part of what can somehow be considered one's authentic self. Autonomy in this sense seems an irrefutable value, especially since its opposite—being guided by forces external to the self and which one cannot authentically embrace—seems to mark the height of oppression.[4]

Another expression of it is

> I wish to be the instrument of my own . . . acts of will. I wish to be a subject, not an object; to be moved by reasons, by conscious purposes, which are my own, not by causes which affect me, as it were from the outside. I wish to be a doer—deciding, not being decided for, self-directed and not acted upon by external nature. . . . I wish, above all, to be conscious of myself as a thinking, willing, active being, bearing responsibility for

my choices and able to explain them by references to my own ideas and purposes.[5]

It is not a mere accident in the history of ideas that fate has a central importance in some other evaluative frameworks, but not in ours. Marginalizing fate is a consequence of the basic evaluative attitude we have toward our lives and their vicissitudes, not one that participants in all reasonable evaluative frameworks must share. The difference between our evaluative framework and these others is not that they do and we do not recognize that fate may derail our lives. We do recognize it. The difference is that we attribute to it far less importance than it is done in some other evaluative frameworks. We marginalize its importance because we stress the importance of autonomy. Our evaluations of individuals and actions fundamentally depend on whether they are wholly, partly, or not at all autonomous. We assume that the extent to which we can control how we live and act depends on our autonomy, and we see fate as contrary to it. We want to be autonomous because we want to reduce our vulnerability to fate.

This favorable evaluation of autonomy is central to our evaluative framework, but it is open to question. Part of the significance of ancient tragedies, especially those of Sophocles, is that they question it. *Oedipus the King* shows that autonomy may—not will!—have disastrous consequences for ourselves and others. Why should we think, tragedies may prompt us to ask, that autonomy may not lead to adversities as great as does fate? Why should we not question our evaluation that it is good to be autonomous? It is not absurd to suppose that fate and autonomy may both have bad consequences. Oedipus was as autonomous as it was possible for him to be, and that was just the problem. Reflection on tragedies may lead us to understand that Oedipus blinded himself because he realized that his autonomous actions were essential links in the causal chain that led to the misfortune that befell both him and others who depended on him. And it is not only tragedies—which are, after all, literary inventions—but also the hard facts attested to by history and the news that great atrocities are perpetrated by autonomous ideological or religious fanatics who are convinced that their cause is righteous.

These questions do not show that our favorable evaluation of autonomy is mistaken. But they do show that it is questionable. It is pervaded by the optimistic confidence that autonomy will make our lives and actions better. What is the reason for this confidence? Why are our efforts to cultivate autonomy not as vulnerable to fate as anything else we might try to do? Why could not autonomy be instrumental to bringing about the very adversity that we are trying to control by being autonomous? What is the reason for preferring the optimistic view that permeates our evaluative framework to the pessimistic tragic view of life as unavoidably vulnerable to fate? These questions can be answered only by providing the needed reasons. But the questions are rarely asked and the reasons are not given. The importance of autonomy and the unimportance of fate are taken for granted by participants in our evaluative framework.

Perhaps we can learn from tragedies and from evaluative frameworks in which fate is not neglected. This possibility has not been much explored in our context, although there are exceptions. But the neglect of fate is not a good enough reason for persevering with it now. Perhaps our evaluative framework rests on a Pollyannaish view of the human condition? It has been well said by the author of one of the exceptions that

> there are areas of philosophy which might be supposed to have a special commitment to not forgetting or lying about the horrors, among them moral philosophy. No one with sense asks it to think about them all the time, but, in addressing what it claims to be our most serious concerns, it would do better if it did not make them disappear. Yet this is what almost all modern forms of moral philosophy effectively does. This is above all because it tries to withdraw our ethical interest from both chance and necessity. . . . The very plain fact [is] that everything that an agent most cares about typically comes from, and can be ruined by, uncontrollable necessity and chance.[6]

The upshot of the preceding discussion is that the optimism that permeates our evaluative framework is called into question by the pessimism prompted by the tragic view of life. I do not think that one of these views is more reasonable than the other. But they do conflict. The greater is the importance attributed to autonomy, the less importance is fate supposed to have, and vice versa. I turn now to three familiar and historically influential metaphors that suggest different ways of understanding these views and the conflict between them.

Three Metaphors

The first is a Stoic one about a dog who is leashed to a cart drawn by a horse. If the cart moves, the dog can move with it willingly or be dragged unwillingly. If the cart is at rest, so can be the dog. It can move a little, but not much because the leash is not very long. It is certainly not long enough to allow the dog to get at the horse. The dog can bark but that will not ease its lot. Stoics ask: if the dog could have an attitude, what attitude would be reasonable for it to have? And their answer is: accept the conditions of its life it cannot change and do as well as possible within the unavoidably narrow limits. It is a waste of energy to inveigh against the prevailing conditions. This is the lesson Oedipus at Colonus[7] — that precocious Stoic — tells us he has learned after many years of wandering as a blind beggar: "Acceptance — that is the great lesson suffering teaches (6) . . . no more fighting with necessity (210), . . . there is no escape, ever (303) . . . [and comes to understand] the final things in life" (656).

The attitude this Stoic metaphor suggests is not fatalism but the recognition that we are vulnerable to fate regardless of our efforts. The best policy is to accept it and make the most of the few possibilities we have within the many limits we cannot overcome. The limits restrict the extent to which we can change the conditions of our life and cultivate autonomy. The idea that we can make ourselves less vulnerable to fate by becoming more autonomous is an illusion sustained by wishful thinking and the refusal to face the facts of life. Optimistic efforts to enlarge our possibilities beyond their unavoidable limits by cultivating autonomy are as futile as the dog straining against its leash.

We are capable of some autonomy, but it is severely limited by what our leash happens to be. The one respect, according to Stoics, in which we are not limited is our capacity to reflect on and try to come terms with our conditions. Such reflection cannot change them, but it can enable us to live within them with as much equanimity as we can muster. We can come to a better understanding of "the final things in life." In the Stoic attitude to life fate is pervasive, autonomy is limited, and if we are reasonable, we understand and accept these facts of life.

The second metaphor is of a sculptor who is creating a work of art out of the rough material that happens to be his medium. He has an imaginative ideal of the potential shape he wants to realize and his creative effort is an interplay between the envisioned ideal, the available tools, and the possibilities of the medium. He works and works, and tinkers and tinkers, and ends up with a sculpture that may or may not satisfy him. He may be influenced by what other sculptors have done, but his creativity and creation are his own, bear the marks of his individuality, imaginative ideal, and what talents and skills he can bring to shaping his material.

What the sculptor does with the medium with which he starts is what we each, consciously or otherwise, have done or are now doing to make ourselves the person we think we should be. Like the sculptor, we may or may not be satisfied with the end product, but a sure sign of failure is imitation. For the ideal we want to realize is a unique mixture of the innate and acquired predispositions with which we start, the conditions in which we live, our capacities and incapacities, the possibilities of our context, what we have learned from the examples of others, and the influences that have formed our ideal. This unique mixture makes each of us a unique individual. The emerging individual may be good or bad, better or worse, approximate the ideal more or less closely, and even if it comes as close to it as possible, it may still fail because the ideal may be flawed.

> The source of this metaphor is romanticism. The romantic ideal presents itself in the form of a categorical imperative: serve inner light within you because it burns within you, for that reason alone. Do what you think right, make what you think beautiful, shape your life in accordance with those ends which are your ultimate purposes, to which everything in your life is a means, to which all must be subordinated (187–88). . . . That is the romantic ideal in its fullest . . . form (192).[8]

In the resulting attitude to life, autonomy dominates fate. Fate affects only the personal and social conditions we start out with in life. The all-important task of autonomy is to make ourselves come ever closer to our ideal. Life is a struggle to impose our autonomous will on the recalcitrant aspects of our personal conditions and make the most we can of our social conditions. Fate may be an obstacle to complete success, but it leaves us with many possible ways of pursuing the ideal we want at least to approximate. This is one source of the optimism that pervades our evaluative framework.

Defenders of the pessimistic Stoic and the optimistic romantic attitudes charge each other with unreasonably over- or underestimating the extent to which human lives are vulnerable to fate. Pessimists adduce in support of their attitude the awful events of human history and the imperfectibility of human nature. Optimists point at human perfectibility as evidenced by progress throughout history toward more inclusive and compassionate morality, less repressive regimes, and the spread of objectivity and rationality. It is characteristic of the apparent conflict between these attitudes that their historically informed defenders may agree about all the relevant facts and yet go on to disagree about how they should be evaluated. Additional facts will not resolve this disagreement because they will disagree also about their evaluation. Are we to conclude then that we have run out of reasons and reached a basic impasse that reflects conflicting temperaments?

I think the answer is no because both attitudes are inconsistent in allowing the possibility of autonomy; they differ only about how much autonomy they inconsistently allow. It is, however, a consequence of both attitudes that autonomy actually presupposes fate. If our fate is to die in infancy, become insane, fall into a coma, suffer brain damage, live with a debilitating disease, or be enslaved, addicted, or tormented, then it would be impossible for us to be autonomous. It is question begging to deny this by claiming that we could be autonomous if we were not handicapped adults or live in a barbaric society. How autonomous we could be and whether we are unhandicapped adults and live in a civilized society are not controllable by autonomy. It follows from both attitudes that whether we have any autonomy at all cannot depend on autonomy. This is just what determinists claim. The inconsistency of both attitudes is that they presuppose determinism, insofar as they accept fate; and they reject determinism, insofar as they accept autonomy. The resolution of the impasse they have reached is to reject both metaphors and the attitudes that go with them. We can rely instead on a third metaphor that combines salvageable portions of the other two.

The third metaphor is Plato's myth of Er at the end of the *Republic*.[9] The Fates to which human lives are subject are the daughters of Necessity. One controls birth, the other life, the third death, and jointly they control the thread of life which stretches from birth to death. As yet unborn souls appear before the Fates and choose a life that will then become irrevocably theirs.

> Every single life was included among the samples . . . there were dictatorships . . . lives of fame for one's physique, good looks . . . for lineage . . .

and there were lives which lacked these excellences . . . there was every possible combination of qualities . . . like wealth, poverty, sickness, and health, in extreme or moderate amounts" (618a-b). [Everyone one should aim to develop] the competence and knowledge to distinguish a good life from a bad one, and to choose the better life from among the possibilities that surround him (618c). [We have to decide] what are the effects of the various combinations of innate and acquired characteristics such as high and low birth, involvement and lack of involvement in politics, physical strength and frailty, cleverness and stupidity, and so on (618d).

[We then have to] make a rational choice, from among all the alternatives, between a better and worse life . . . this is the cardinal decision anyone has to make (618d–e).

The choice makes us the particular individuals we are. The Fates decide the time of our birth and death, and the contents of lives, but the choice of which life to live is up to each one of us. "Responsibility lies with the chooser, not with God" (617e).

In this metaphor, fate and autonomy are inseparably mixed. Fate determines the limits within which we must live; autonomy enables us to decide which of the possibilities we want to realize are available within the limits. The metaphor rightly suggests that both fate and autonomy have important and formative influences on how we live. Fate determines both the limits within which we must live and the possibilities that are available in a particular life. Autonomy enables us to decide which of the available possibilities we should try to realize. Optimistic defenders of our evaluative framework are right to stress the importance of autonomy, so long as they do not deny the importance of fate. Pessimistic defenders of the tragic view are right to stress the importance of fate, provided they do not neglect the importance of autonomy. The resolution of their conflict is to accept what they get right and reject what they get wrong. It follows from this proposed conflict resolution that there is reason for both optimism and pessimism about the extent to which we can live as we think we should.

The reason for optimism is that we can live as we think we should, provided we accept the limits fate imposes on us, make reasonable choices among the available possibilities, and do not pit ourselves against fate by pursuing possibilities beyond the limits set by fate. The reason for pessimism is that our evaluations are often mistaken about what our limits and possibilities actually are. We should, of course, question and, if necessary, correct our evaluations, but our efforts may also be frustrated by mistaken evaluations. That is why we are poised between optimism and pessimism about the sway of fate over our lives. I will now consider these mistaken evaluations.

Mistaken Evaluations

There is a suggestive but undeveloped, almost casual, remark in the myth of Er. Plato describes the many lives among which each soul has to choose one, and then says, in Shorey's translation, that "there was no determination of the quality of soul, because the choice of a different life inevitably determined a different character" (618b).[10] The suggestion is that autonomy and fate are inextricably interwoven. Autonomy enables us to choose, within the limits set by fate, what kind of life we live, but fate determines the character that goes with it. Do we, then, choose our character? Yes and no. Yes, because if we choose a life, we choose a character as well. No, because if we choose a life, we have no choice about the character that goes with it. Can we untangle this apparent contradiction?

I think we can. By choosing a life we choose, whether or not we know it, the character that would enable us, if we develop it, to do well in the chosen life. But whether we actually develop that character to a sufficient extent for our life to go as we think it should depends on further choices. We may or may not make those choices, and, if we make them, we may do so well or badly. With the possibility of choice comes the possibility of mistaken evaluations of the limits and possibilities of the life we choose and the character traits we need to develop if our chosen life is to go well.

It is not obvious what it means to choose a life. We are all born into some social setting, economic and political circumstances, a great variety of social conventions, and during the early years of life we are formed by our upbringing and education. The life we start out with is the result of these formative influences and our genetic inheritance and predispositions. They provide our initial limits and possibilities. This is our fate, our lot in life, our good or bad fortune. Autonomy has no foothold at this early stage in life. We have biological needs, and perhaps psychological and social ones as well, and we want to satisfy them. We have no choice about any of this. As we mature we acquire preferences, which may be sometimes stronger and sometimes weaker, sometimes compossible and sometimes conflicting, and with them comes the possibility of choice and the need for it. But making such choices is not enough for autonomy. The preferences we have, the alternatives among which we can choose, and the social conditions that impose limits on our possible choices are usually unavoidable parts of the context in which we live. It is our fate that the choices we can make depend on these limits and possibilities.

Choices become autonomous only when they are accompanied by some understanding and evaluation of the limits and possibilities, and having some overall attitude to the life we are living. Then, and only then, does it become possible to make an autonomous choice about whether to continue or change the life with which it is our fate to start. One outcome of the conclusion reached by autonomy is an overall sense of satisfaction or dissatisfaction with our life as a whole. As I claim in chapter 1, most of us are more or less dissatisfied with our life. If in doubt, ask yourself how many people you know, including yourself, who would not wish, reasonably or otherwise, that his or her life be different in important ways? Overall dissatisfaction with our life is one main reason for making autonomous choices about how our life should be changed so as to mitigate our dissatisfaction with it.

Such changes are rarely so radical as to involve the rejection of our entire life and the adoption of a completely different one. We cannot shed at will all the past influences that have formed us, abandon all our habits and preferences, alter our culinary, hygienic, sexual, musical, and other tastes, and leave behind all personal relationships and familiar comforts. We change our life, if we do, by changing in some important respects the one we have, while leaving it unchanged in some other respects. Autonomy typically involves both continuity and change.

Optimists think that autonomy is good, because it enables us to overcome dissatisfaction with our life. This is a dangerous half-truth. The other half is that autonomy may make our life worse by making us more dissatisfied. Optimists forget that the evaluations on which autonomy rests may be seriously mistaken about the limits and possibilities of our life. Is it a matter of fate—of unavoidable human fallibility—that we are doomed to make such mistakes, or does autonomy enable us to avoid them? This is a difficult question, as the case below shows.

Hiromichi Yahara

The last great battle in the Pacific during the Second World War was in Okinawa. The battle was the final stage of the island-hopping strategy of the Allies before the planned invasion of Japan. The battle was exceptionally fierce and bloody. It cost over 12,000 Allied and about ten times as many Japanese lives. The Japanese rejected repeated offers of surrender, and fought to the death. In the last hours of the battle, when the Japanese defeat was certain and the Allies were about to enter the caves where the Japanese headquarter was, all, except one, high-ranking Japanese officers committed suicide by hara-kiri, as was expected of them by the military code that guided how they lived. The one who did not was Colonel Hiromichi Yahara, who escaped, reached Japan, and lived to tell the story of the battle from the Japanese point of view. My discussion relies on his remarkable book.[11]

Why did Yahara not commit hara-kiri, as all his fellow officers did? Yahara was a professional soldier. He was trained at the Japanese military academy, played an important role in the strategic planning of the war, had a distinguished military record, demonstrated his courage and willingness to die on numerous occasions, was much decorated, and was indeed rightly recognized as one the best officers in the Japanese army. Given the Japanese military code, honor required that Yahara should commit hara-kiri together with his fellow officers. Honor was the highest value of their code, and acting contrary to it was the worst thing a Japanese officer could do. Yet that is what Yahara did. Why?

Yahara writes that he was ordered to escape by his superior and report the outcome of the battle to the Japanese high command in Tokyo. The order was implied rather than direct. High-ranking officers rarely gave direct orders to other high-ranking officers. They discussed what had to be done, and then did it. Orders were unnecessary. The context in which Yahara received what he believed was the implied order was fraught. They all knew that the war was lost and the consequences were disastrous for their way of life. They were about to kill themselves; Japan was going to be invaded; and they expected the victors to treat the losers as brutally as the Japanese treated those they had defeated. They were thinking of their children, families, and country; they believed that the worst was coming; their emotions were desperate; and the code by which they lived left them no choice but to kill themselves. Yahara was one of them, and yet he acted on another possibility. After much difficulty he reached Tokyo and reported on the battle. His fellow officers there doubted that he had received the order he claimed he was given, and Yahara was disgraced. He published his book more than thirty years after the war, when the military code had been abandoned, and he and his supposed disgrace were forgotten. He makes clear in the book that he, together with most Japanese, had come to reject the military code.

Now ask: was it fate or autonomy that dictated Yahara's actions? The answer, I think, is that they were inextricably mixed and it is impossible to say even approximately what their relative importance was. And it is impossible not only for us who are considering Yahara's actions from the outside, many years after the event, on the basis of his testimony. It would have been impossible also for Yahara himself, if he had tried to understand retrospectively the relative extent to which fate and autonomy dictated his actions. Pessimists will say that it was in that context largely a matter of fate how autonomous he could be. Optimists will say that if he was not sufficiently autonomous in that context at that time, he could have become more so by understanding, evaluating, and forming an attitude to the available possibilities and the unavoidable limits, and then acting accordingly. But even if that were true, it would not follow that becoming more autonomous would have made Yahara's life better. It is far more likely to have made it worse whatever he did. For if he had accepted the military code, he would have had to see himself as disgraced. And if he had rejected it, he would have had to see his whole life up to that point as misdirected. Doing either would have made his life even worse than it already was in the uncertain state in which he could not have told, had he asked himself, whether it was mainly fate or autonomy that dictated his actions.

Let us go back to the myth of Er. Yahara lived the life of a Japanese military officer until close to the end of the war. It was not a matter of autonomy what character was required by that life. But it required lifelong autonomous efforts to develop that character sufficiently to make him excel at that life. Are optimists right in supposing that such efforts made his life better? Surely, the answer is that it depends on the life and the character. Autonomy is good if it is directed toward good ends and bad if directed toward bad ends. Yahara arrived at the retrospective evaluation that military life and the character it required were directed toward bad ends. If that retrospective evaluation were correct, then, contrary to the optimistic view, autonomy toward that end would

not have been good for him. When he lived the life of a military officer, he evaluated his life one way. When he looked back on that life, he
came to evaluate it another way. Whether autonomy is good, as optimists claim, depends on the reliability of the evaluation of the possibilities and limits of a life. If the evaluations are mistaken, then autonomy
based on them is misdirected. If the evaluations are correct, then autonomy based on them is rightly directed. That is why the optimistic
insistence on the importance of autonomy is a dangerous half-truth.

Autonomy may make life better only if it is based on correct evaluations of the available possibilities and limits. I say may, not will, because
it may make life worse if correct evaluations reveal that the possibilities
and limits available in a context are so bad as to make life miserable. It
is useless to say that we should make the most of whatever possibilities
and limits there are in our context, if the limits make a civilized life impossible and the possibilities are unacceptable choices between death
and dishonor, slavery or starvation, self-sacrifice or the betrayal of all
that we cherish. That is just what happened to the Japanese officers who
killed themselves. The optimistic celebration of autonomy rests on the
mistaken assumption that one of the available possibilities will usually
make life better, and it is just a matter of finding it and acting on it.
Given the miserable conditions in which countless human lives had to
be and still have to be lived, the assumption can be sustained only by
ignorance or self-deception.

Pessimists, however, are also mistaken. The limits fate imposes on us
are not so stringent as to exclude the possibility of autonomy. Although
autonomy can lead to mistaken evaluations, it can also lead to correct
ones and make life better. Pessimists are partly right: fate makes us fallible, prone to mistaken evaluations, and renders our efforts to distinguish between correct and incorrect evaluations also liable to mistakes.
But pessimists are also partly wrong because sometimes we can we
identify and correct such mistakes. Let us now consider that possibility.

Correcting Evaluations

Aristotle thinks that it is possible but very difficult to correct mistaken
evaluations. It is not enough for correcting them to develop the appropriate character traits to a sufficient extent and reliably act on them.
"Any one can get angry—that is easy—or give or spend money, but

to do this to the right person, to the right extent, at the right time, with the right aim, and in the right way, *that* is not for every one, nor is it easy" (1109a26–29).[12] Why is it not easy? Aristotle's well-known and much-discussed answer is that we often fail through excess or deficiency. Then we cannot control our natural desires for pleasure, avoiding danger, getting what we deserve, and so on. That is why we need moderation, courage, and justice. But we often go wrong even if we have the necessary character traits because the emotions we need to control are strong and escape control. They may become too strong and fear turns us into cowards, desire makes us obsessed with food or sex, or envy and jealousy leads to begrudging when others get what they deserve. Or our emotions may be deficient, and we become blind to danger, ascetic, or collude in injustice. Guided by faulty emotions we cannot or will not control, our evaluations of the available possibilities are often mistaken.

All this is likely to be familiar to readers of Aristotle. I repeat it because Aristotle presupposes it as he goes on to say something less familiar, but no less important, about how we might correct the resulting mistaken evaluations. He says that

> of the extremes one is more erroneous, one less so; since to hit the mean is hard . . . we must as a second best, as people say, take the least of the evils. [And the way to do that is to] consider the things towards which we ourselves also are easily carried away; for some of us tend to one thing, some to another. [Then] we must drag ourselves away to the contrary extreme; for we shall get into the intermediate state by drawing well away from the error (1109a34-b2–6).

If we find this difficult, it indicates that our evaluations are at risk. Only if we reach the point at which we begin to take pleasure in controlling our unruly emotions will we evaluate them correctly. We can say then with Aristotle that we can correct our evaluations by controlling the tendencies that mislead them. Cowardice and foolhardiness, self-indulgence and self-denial, greed and resignation to the unjust distribution of desert corrupt our perception of the conditions in which we have to act and may make our evaluations of the available possibilities mistaken.

This Aristotelian approach to correcting evaluations takes us some way from a pessimistic view of the extent to which fate determines how we live and toward an optimistic view of the possibility of autonomy. Two considerations, however, show that the possibility it opens up is very limited. In the first place, the extent to which we can control our unruly emotions depends on whether we see our particular emotions as excessive or deficient. Excessive fear may seem to us as prudent response to danger; we may see our obsession with food or sex as healthy appetite; and our greed may appear to us as the desire to get what we deserve. The ever-present temptation is to make such mistakes through self-deception, selfishness, self-satisfaction, and so on. We can try to guard against them, but our evaluations of the success of these attempts is also vulnerable to the same self-serving mistakes. We attach exaggerated importance to the little control we exert, ignore our selfish motives for many of our actions, and make ourselves satisfied with little improvement. The Aristotelian approach makes autonomy possible but does not guarantee its success. Its success depends on our capacity for understanding, the reliability of our evaluations, the strength of the emotions we need to control, and on the prevailing conditions in our context. All of which, pessimists will say, are matters of fate.

The second consideration is that our evaluations do not depend only on our personal capacities and the extent to which we develop them. They depend also on the evaluative framework that guides our evaluations of how we should live and what we should do. It often happens that our evaluations are correct, given our evaluative framework. But they are nevertheless mistaken because the evaluative framework from which they follow is indefensible. This is just what happened to the Japanese officers who committed hara-kiri as prescribed by their awful military code: the samurai ethic.[13]

The samurai were fighters who dedicated themselves to serving a lord. They were fabled swordsmen who fought in whatever cause their lord chose, and were ready to die. Their ethos was the willingness to die rather than accept defeat. The rule that guided them was "the Way of the Samurai is Death." They prided themselves on being different from and superior to other men, not to mention women. They were distinguished by their legendary fighting skill and by valuing their life much less than whatever the causes were for which they happened to be fighting. Causes were only the means that allowed them to fight for victory or die. Their dominant motive was the morbid risking of death, in terms of which they saw honor, pride, and valor. And they held in contempt the multitudes who did not share their morbidity.

If their cause was defeated, usually by other samurai, they routinely committed ritual hara-kiri, which means "belly-cutting." It involves excruciatingly painful self-mutilation by denuding their torso and cutting themselves open from stem to stern. By this means they showed courage, willing endurance of pain, and contempt for life they regarded as disgraced by defeat. Their manner of death was thought to redeem the honor they lost by losing the battle. They were celebrated as heroes throughout the history of Japan. Their example infused the Japanese military code. It explained the willingness of even the lowliest Japanese troops in the Second World War to fight to death, the contemptuous cruelty with which the Japanese treated prisoners of war who allowed themselves to be taken alive, and why the Japanese officers in Okinawa committed hara-kiri. I mention in passing that it explains also why Mishima, the author of *The Way of the Samurai* and of many novels, killed himself in 1970 (!) by committing hara-kiri.

This was the evaluative framework that guided Yahara throughout his life leading up to the Japanese defeat first in Okinawa and then in the war. And it was the evaluative framework that dictated the evaluations of Japanese military officers, as well as Yahara's. Given that framework, the evaluations they had made were correct, and Yahara had indeed disgraced himself by not committing hara-kiri. But Yahara came to question that evaluative framework and the evaluations that followed from it, although he does not say what led him to do it. I think it is not implausible to suppose that it was the trauma of defeat in war, of the enormity of the bloodshed he witnessed throughout the war, the dissolution of the evaluative framework that fostered the military code, and his own disgrace. They jointly explain, I am supposing, why he questioned and rejected the evaluative framework that guided him until the end of the war.

What happened to Yahara is important in the present context for several reasons. One is that it shows that the cause of mistaken evaluations may be personal or social. It is personal if it is caused by defective character traits; social if it is caused by a defective evaluative framework.

In the first case, correcting mistaken evaluations depends on correcting the defective character traits. In the second case, it depends on correcting or abandoning the evaluative framework. Yahara's character traits were well developed, given the evaluative framework of the samurai military code, but they were nevertheless defective because that evaluative framework was defective. It would have been easier for

Yahara to correct his character traits, had they been defective, because he could have relied on the resources of his evaluative framework. But his mistaken evaluations followed from his defective evaluative framework. He drew from it all the evaluative resources he had, so it took an exceptionally traumatic series of events to make him question the evaluative framework itself.

Another reason why what happened to Yahara is important for understanding the connection between fate and autonomy is that it shows that autonomy is possible even if fate imposes severe limits on it. It was Yahara's fate to be imbued with the evaluative framework of which the Japanese military code was an essential part. His fate would normally have made it impossible for him to question it. The traumatic events that unavoidably influenced him, however, were exceptional and created exceptional circumstances. In those circumstances the normally impossible questioning became possible, and with it came the possibility of autonomy. Fate does not make autonomy impossible, only dependent on the stringency of the limits set by it in particular circumstances. That is why it is a mistake to agree with the pessimists that fate makes autonomy *always* impossible and a like mistake to agree with optimists that autonomy makes it *always* possible to overcome fate. There is no *always* about either. The extent to which our lives depend on fate and the extent to which we can overcome our fate both depend on our context, on the control we have over our character traits, and on how faulty our evaluative framework is.

How well we can cope with the necessity and adversity that significantly affect our lives depends on our evaluations of our possibilities. But those evaluations are affected by the necessities and adversities with which we want to cope. And they may lead us to make the wrong evaluations of the possibilities and limits of these necessities, adversities, and our possibilities of coping with them. Fate and autonomy coexist, and sometimes one, sometimes the other is dominant. Our evaluations and efforts to avoid or to correct them if they go wrong depend on whether fate or autonomy is, at that time, in that context, dominant. How much optimism or pessimism is warranted depends on these complexities. They exclude optimism about the human predicaments that permeates our contemporary evaluative framework and they exclude also the corrosive pessimism of the tragic view of life. The way we live now is dominated neither by fate, nor by autonomy. It is dominated by the complexity of our conflicts, choices, and predicaments.

5   Fear of Meaninglessness

Fear

Fear in general is a normal, natural, universally experienced emotion elicited by what we take to be a danger of some kind. The danger may be real or imagined, more or less threatening; the emotion may be more or less unpleasant and strong, and, if it is quite strong, it may disrupt life, threaten to turn into panic and overwhelm reasonable efforts to control it. The emotion is complex, typically combines beliefs and feelings about the danger with the desire to face or flee it and to express, control, or suppress the reaction to it. I say typically, because fear is possible in exceptional cases even if one or another of the usual beliefs, feelings, or desires is absent. Fear is a warning of the physical, psychological, or social dangers we believe we face.[1] Fear is reasonable if it is a response to real danger and its strength is commensurate with the danger, neither excessive nor deficient. This is roughly the Aristotelian view, and I accept it.[2] Tweaking a little what he says about the good, fear in general is reasonable if it is directed toward the right object, to the right extent, at the right time, with the right aim, and in the right way.[3] It is unreasonable if it is misdirected in one of these ways or if one or more of its constitutive beliefs, feelings, and desires is mistaken.

The particular kind of fear I will discuss is of the collapse of the evaluative framework of our society. The evaluations that follow from it and the evaluative framework itself may be entirely or partly mistaken, insufficiently supported by reasons, and thus arbitrary. If they were arbitrary, nothing we value would be valuable. All our evaluations would be mistaken. We could not rely on them to protect the possibilities that enable us to live as we think we should. The evaluative distinctions we draw, for instance, between meaning and meaninglessness, good and bad, art and kitsch, order and disorder, wisdom and folly, justice and injustice, sacred and secular, nobility and depravity would become untenable. We could not say what is valuable, nor what is more and what less valuable. All our customary evaluations would become arbitrary and we would not know how we should live and act. This is a danger that is reasonable to fear.

We would still have basic physiological needs and would want to satisfy them, but we would not be able to say about any possibility beyond that primitive level whether acting on it would be better or worse than not acting, or which way of acting would be better than any other. We would have no reason to value anything beyond the satisfaction of our basic needs, no reason to think that it is better to be Socrates dissatisfied than a pig satisfied. No way of life, no action would be worthwhile. It would also follow that our condemnation of ideological or religious fanaticism, human sacrifice, slavery, child prostitution, murder, rape, and so forth, would be as arbitrary as the practices we used to think of as reasonable. We would be left without any guide to how we should live and act beyond that barely human level. This would be a very serious danger indeed. It is reasonable to fear it and to do what we can to avoid it.

This is as yet an abstract possibility. In order to make it concrete, consider a thought I take from Pascal's *Pensées*. He writes:

> when I consider the short duration of my life, swallowed up in the eternity before and after, the little space I fill, and even can see, ingulfed in the infinite immensity of spaces of which I am ignorant, and which know me not, I am frightened, and am astonished at being here rather than there; for there is no reason why here rather than there, why now rather than then. . . . The eternal silence of these infinite spaces frightens me.[4]

If the infinite spaces were indeed eternally silent, then they would just be an immense collection of facts in constant flux without a beginning or an end. If the world were like that, nothing in it would have any value. And that is how I interpret what Pascal would have found frightening. I say "would have" because in fact he did not. He was a Catholic of the Jansenist persuasion, and he thought that the world is infused with a providential order. Our evaluations ought to conform to that order. We know what they are because it has been revealed to us. The world appears silent, he thought, only to those who do not listen.

Russell was certainly not a Catholic, but he had the same thought:

> Man is the product of causes which had no prevision of the end they were achieving . . . his origin, his growth, his hopes and fears, his loves and his beliefs are but the outcome of accidental collocations of atoms. . . . All the labours of the ages, all the devotion, all the inspiration, all the noon-day brightness of human genius, are destined to extinction in the vast death of the solar system, and that the whole temple of Man's achievement must be inevitably buried beneath the debris of a universe in ruins.[5]

Both Pascal and Russell thought that the fact-value distinction can be sharply drawn, that there could be a world in which there are only facts but no values. Much has been written in criticism of the sharp fact-value distinction, some of it by myself. Here, however, I am not concerned with the distinction but how it would affect human lives if our evaluative framework were to collapse.

Pascal wrote in the seventeenth century, Russell at the beginning of the twentieth. Much has changed since. We have learned a great deal from cosmology and other sciences about those infinite spaces. But none of that changes the fact that if we do not have faith in a providential order, then it is possible that the world contains only facts and we have no reasonable way of evaluating them. Perhaps we only think that our evaluations are reasonable because we rely on an arbitrary evaluative framework. If that were true, then all our evaluations would rest on a faith that differs only in detail from Pascal's. Perhaps our entire evaluative framework is an absurd fairy tale we tell ourselves to fend off our fear of the eternal silence of the infinite spaces in which for a passing moment we occupy a minuscule spot?[6]

Bernard Williams says about our evaluative framework that "to see the world from the human point of view is not an absurd thing for human beings to do."[7] This is not quite true. It is true that there is no other point of view from which we could see the world. That, however, is not our only option. We could refuse to form any systematic point of view of the world and just live from day to day, like the lilies of the field do, as has been recommended by you know who. But this is very difficult.

Those of us who are less innocent than Jesus reportedly said we should be are committed to an evaluative framework that guides how we live, and it cannot be anything but a human framework. But saying with Williams that this is not an absurd thing for us to do is not nearly enough. It could be ours and yet be arbitrary and unreasonable. If we do not have a better reason for it than that it is ours, then we face the questions I am asking: Is the evaluative framework that guides how we live no more than a fairy tale we tell ourselves? Is it more than the product of our fear of the eternal silence of those infinite spaces? Are it and its evaluations wistful noises we make to counter the ominous silence of the world of facts? Is it possible that none of our evaluations that guide how we live beyond the most primitive level is reasonable?

The questions I am asking cannot be reasonably answered by claiming that science has been and continues to give us more and more knowledge of facts. What we need reason for is not what we take to be facts but the evaluative framework on which we rely to evaluate the significance of all these facts from the point of view of how we should live and act. Science is not meant to and cannot provide that reason. Omniscience about the facts, were it possible, would only enable us to know what our evaluations are and what leads us to make them, but not whether they are reasonable. Nor is it a reasonable answer to rely on the supposed success of civilized societies to provide conditions that enable us to live as we think we should. Whether we are in fact successful depends on some standard by which success and failure can be judged. But all the standards we have or could have come from the only source they could, namely, the very evaluative framework in question. To rely on a standard derived from it is to assume that we already have the reasons we need. By that strategy anything could be made to seem reasonable.

Furthermore, even if we rely on some standard internal to the evaluative framework, it is by no means obvious that we have been practically successful in its own terms. Hegel has rightly said that

> when we contemplate this display of passions and the consequences of their violence, the unreason which is associated not only with them . . . when we see arising therefrom the evil, the vice, the ruin that has befallen the most flourishing kingdoms which the mind of man ever created, we can hardly avoid being filled with sorrow at this universal taint

of corruption. And since this decay is not the work of mere nature, but of human will, our reflections may well lead us to a moral sadness, a revolt of the good will—if indeed it has a place within us. Without rhetorical exaggeration, a simple truthful account of the miseries that have overwhelmed the noblest nations and polities and the finest exemplars of private virtue forms a most fearful picture and excites emotions of the profoundest and most hopeless sadness, counter-balanced by no consoling results.[8]

If in doubt about Hegel's words, watch the news, or remember the endless wars, violent crimes, immense and avoidable suffering that have been and are inflicted on innocent victims in the name of moral, political, religious, and other evaluations derived from an evaluative framework. Our supposed success is called into question by the multitude of problems that present serious difficulties for our evaluative framework—the failed policies, sufferings, and atrocities—that we know from anthropology, history, personal experience, and the media. We are, therefore, left with the possibility that the evaluative framework on which we rely to guide how we live and act is unreasonable. And that is a possibility we have reason to fear.

A possibility, however, is just a possibility. We have to decide how likely it is that it may become actual. We have reasons for taking it seriously and fearing it, but we also have reasons against it; these reasons conflict, and we have to make difficult choices between them. The reasons for it are the familiar problems of which Hegel reminds us. The reasons against it are that, although these problems have existed in one form or another throughout human history, life has gone on and the various evaluative frameworks of many different societies have enabled their participants to cope with the problems they have faced.

If we think that the reasons for this fear are much stronger than the reasons against it, then consistency requires us to take a pessimistic view of human existence, see it as insecure and vulnerable to contingencies we cannot foresee or control. That would undermine our confidence and make us uncertain about our evaluative framework on which how we think we should live depends. We would see ourselves as Pascal did, forever on the brink of an abyss into which we may blindly stumble at any moment. The pessimistic view, however, is nowadays a minority one. Our evaluative framework has been strongly influenced by the Enlightenment, secularization, and the great benefits we have and are deriving from science. The resulting optimism permeates the majority view. And those who share it make the difficult choice in favor of reasons against making too much of the fear. But if that is our view, then we must think that we have sufficient control over our lives to cope with present and future problems, as we have coped with past ones. We must then have some strategy for coping with our these problems, especially since they persist, lead to our conflicts, and present a continuous challenge to our evaluative framework. I now turn to a strategy on which we often rely.

Prudence

Prudence, among other things, is a strategy for coping with this kind of fear. As a first step toward understanding what it involves, I draw on Mary Douglas's celebrated theory of pollution,[9] but express it in my terms. Douglas thinks of what I am calling an evaluative framework as a system of classification. It often happens that something does not fit into it, and that presents a problem for participants in the evaluative framework. The problem may be something quite new, or an ambiguous case that does not fit any of the modes of evaluations, or having to choose between conflicting responses to it, or something whose very existence offends against prevailing sensitivities, or it is a result of changing conditions. If frequent, the problems strain the evaluative framework, as ours is strained by globalization, multiculturalism, the sexual revolution, secularization, and terrorism. If we are committed to the strained evaluative framework we must cope with its problems. Prudence is one strategy for this. It involves acknowledging the problem, de-emphasizing its urgency, tacitly denying that it presents a serious threat to the evaluative framework, and, for the time being, postponing any drastic changes to the evaluative framework on which so much depends. This strategy may or may not be reasonable.

It may seem at first as an unreasonable evasion of problems, but matters are more complex. To begin with, the strategy is not one that recommends itself to uncommitted observers of an evaluative framework from the outside, but one that is followed by us who are committed to our evaluative framework to which the resulting conflicts present a problem. We have reasons for our commitment to it. The evaluative framework enables us satisfy our basic needs. We could abandon it in favor of another framework if we thought that it might be better, but we stick to what we have. We think that it is open to reform that would help us cope with our conflicts, choices, and problems. And we make sense of our life in terms of the evaluative framework. So we have reasons for our continued participation in it.

Our prudent shelving the problem aims to conserve what we reasonably value. It is compatible with recognizing that our evaluative framework often needs reform to accommodate problems, but we think that even when reforms are necessary they should involve only changes that are needed for coping with the problems, while leaving the rest as unchanged as possible.

Whether changes are needed, and, if so, how extensive they should be force us to make difficult choices. We are likely to be conflicted about what the right choice is, because there are strong reasons both for and against changing and not changing the evaluative framework. It is a matter of judgment how serious the problems are, how likely it is that a proposed change would be effective, what unintended consequences might the proposed change have, and so forth. There are reasons for the prudent postponement of making hasty changes that might or might not cope with the problems, but there are also reasons against it. These reasons for and against following the prudent strategy are often, but not always, inconclusive, and lead to conflicts. If problems are frequent, if they threaten the deep assumptions on which the entire evaluative framework rests, then the reasons against the prudent strategy are stronger than the reasons for it. But if problems are isolated episodes and the evaluative framework is on the whole acceptable, then the weight of reasons favors the prudent strategy. The cases that follow are intended to make concrete some circumstances in which the prudent strategy seems reasonable.

Prudential Strategies

The first case in point is derived from Evans-Pritchard's discussion of Azande beliefs and practices.[10] Witchcraft occupies a central place in Azande life. They mostly conduct their affairs in commonsensical ways, but common sense is sometimes not enough. Accidents, illness, bad luck, or failure may befall individuals. Then the Azande attribute the mishaps to the malignant power of witches. They believe that witchcraft is hereditary. If someone is a witch, then everyone in a witch's family is a witch. Evans-Pritchard lived with the Azande and learned to converse freely with them. He pointed out to Azande elders that it follows from the frequency with which people are found to be witches that all families, and consequently all Azande, must be witches. The reaction of the Azande elders to this wicked piece of reasoning was indifference. They simply ignored the problem. They were not in the least disturbed by it, and continued to identify witches as before. They maintained a prudent disinterest in the matter. We want to know: why did this not make them doubt their beliefs about witches and witchcraft?

Evans-Pritchard's answer is that the Azande have

> no incentive to agnosticism. All their beliefs hang together. . . . In this web of belief every strand depends upon every other strand, and a Zande cannot get out of its meshes because it is the only world he knows. The web is not an external structure in which he is enclosed. It is the texture of his thought and he cannot think that his thought is wrong (194).

Evans-Pritchard had found a serious problem with the Azande evaluative framework, but the Azande prudently ignored it. And they had a good reason for it. Their situation was not that they could opt for one of several evaluative frameworks and they opted for one whose serious problem they have unreasonably evaded. They knew of no other evaluative framework. If they had abandoned it, their entire way of life would have collapsed. Instead, they ignored the problem and concentrated instead on coping with the pressing practical problems of everyday life, which they regarded as far more important than worrying about the theoretical question Evans-Pritchard raised.

What the Azande did is what we ourselves do when we do not know what caused a particular event. We do not give up our basic commitment to causal explanation. We tacitly assume that the event had a cause, even if we cannot now say what it was. We, like the Azande, "have no incentive to agnosticism." We may be aware that there is no good reason for assuming that the future will be like the past. We may know that Hume has found a serious problem with causal explanation, yet ignore doubts about our assumption. As Hume said, and as the Azande might have said to Evans-Pritchard,

I can only observe what is commonly done; which is, that this difficulty is seldom or never thought of; and even where it has once been present to the mind, is quickly forgot, and leaves but a small impression behind it. Very refin'd reflections have little or no influence upon us.[11]

The second example comes from Robin Horton's work. It concerns a reaction of the Kalabari, a tribe that when the episode had occurred, lived close to the subsistence level under inhospitable conditions in sub-Saharan Africa. The episode concerns the reaction of the Kalabari to first encountering a white man.

The first white man, it is said, was seen by a fisherman who had gone down to the mouth of the estuary in his canoe. Panic-stricken, he raced home and told his people what he had seen: whereupon he and the rest of the town set out to purify themselves — that is, to rid themselves of the influence of the strange and monstrous thing that had intruded into the world.[12]

The Kalabari needed to protect their evaluative framework that had no way of accommodating this strange and monstrous problem. They did not have the luxury of an open and inquiring mind. All their energies had to be concentrated on eking out a living. They did not see the first white man as a reason for questioning their evaluative framework that knew nothing of such monstrosity, but as a threat to their survival. And they dealt with it by the prudent strategy of acknowledging the problem it presented and did nothing to cope with it. They assumed, not unreasonably, that their survival was more important than seeking additional reasons for or against the evaluative framework on which their survival depended.

We do not have to go to distant lands to find examples of the same strategy. Montaigne was for many years a magistrate whose duty was to administer the laws. He wrote:

Consider the form of this justice that governs us: it is a true testimony of human imbecility, so full it is of contradiction and error. . . . [The laws] are sickly parts and unjust members of the very body and essence of justice (819). . . . There is nothing so grossly and widely and ordinarily faulty as the laws (821).[13]

He sees that in a corrupt society, such as his own,

> the justest party is still a member of a worm-eaten maggoty body. But in such a body the least diseased member is called healthy. . . . Civic innocence is measured according to places and the times (760). . . . Our morals are extremely corrupt, and lean with a remarkable inclination toward the worse; of our laws and customs, many are barbarous and monstrous; however, because of the difficulty of improving our condition and the danger of everything crumbling into bits, if I could put a spoke in our wheel and stop at this point, I would do so with all my heart (497).

Montaigne, like the Azande and the Kalabari, wanted to protect his evaluative framework, faulty as it was, by acknowledging and putting up with its problems as less dangerous than making radical changes to it. Montaigne feared that radical changes might lead to "everything crumbling into bits." He preceded Hume, the Azande, and the Kalabari in following the prudent strategy of ignoring the problems as preferable to endangering the evaluative framework on which French lives in the sixteenth century depended.

It might be thought that Montaigne and the others had a dubious commitment to reason. So consider Descartes whose commitment to reason was certainly not dubious. In the *Discourse on Method*, as every philosophy student knows, he questioned everything and accepted nothing until he had found sufficient reasons for it—well, almost everything and not quite nothing.

> Lest I should remain indecisive in my actions while reason obliged me to be so in my judgments, and in order to live as happily as I could during this time, I formed for myself a provisional moral code consisting of just three or four maxims, which I should like to tell you about. The first was to obey the laws and customs of my country, holding constantly to the religion in which by God's grace I had been instructed from my childhood, and governing myself according to the most moderate and least extreme opinions—the opinions commonly accepted in practice by the most sensible of those with whom I should have to live.

As Descartes was laying the foundation of modern science, he not only left the evaluative framework unquestioned, but explained that while he was doing his revolutionary work, he told himself and he tells us, that "you must also provide yourself with some other place where you can live comfortably while building is in progress."[14]

Like the Azande, the Kalabari, and Montaigne, Descartes realized that he needed a safe haven from which to venture out to change how we think of the world of facts. The evaluative framework of his society was that safe haven. It would have been easy for him to question it with the same relentlessness as he questioned the commonly accepted view of the facts, but he did not. He had prudently ignored problems with it. He must have been aware of them, yet he did not extend his questioning from facts to evaluations. He saw that the demands for reasons can go only so far, that not everything can be up for grabs, and that while he can question much, he must keep something unquestioned, if for no other reason than to protect himself and the conditions in which questioning can go on.

The last case is perhaps the most likely to be familiar. Hume concludes his examination of skepticism about reason by observing that

> we have, therefore, no choice left but betwixt a false reason and none at all. . . . Most fortunately it happens, that since reason is incapable of dispelling these clouds, nature herself suffices to that purpose, and cures me of this philosophical melancholy and delirium. . . . I find myself absolutely and necessarily determin'd to live, and talk, and act like other people in the common affairs of life.[15]

As the others I have cited, Hume followed the prudent strategy of ignoring the problem that has been with us since Pyrrhonian skeptics first called attention to it.

Are the Azande, the Kalabari, Montaigne, Descartes, and Hume guilty of unreasonable evasion? Is it unreasonable for us to be like them and continue to depend on our evaluative framework to guide how we live, even though we know that there are problems with it? What more is needed to make it reasonable to follow the prudent strategy of ignoring the problems, continue to participate in our evaluative framework that by and large enables us to live as we think we should, allows us to make sense of our lives, and is open to reform? These are genuine, not rhetorical, questions. The answer to them, I think, is that there are good reasons both for and against the prudent strategy, they conflict, and we have to make a difficult choice between them. What then are these reasons and why do they make the choice difficult?

Reasons for Prudence

I begin with a metaphor that has been used more than once. We sail a vast sea with no known port. Storms come and go, our supplies have to be rationed and replenished from the sea. We pick up from the flotsam of wrecks we encounter what we think we might be able to use to keep our ship afloat. Occasionally someone falls overboard and is destroyed by sharks. The ship is uncomfortable, leaks, and we have to keep repairing it. We have many problems, and no one is sure what we should do about them. We have no map and no clue what direction we should sail in. We could abandon the ship, but we dismiss that out of hand. Even a bad ship is better than no ship. So we prudently ignore questions about reasons for or against what we are doing, and cope as well as we can with our problems. Is that unreasonable?

It will be said that this is a bad metaphor. Our evaluative framework is not a solitary ship, but one among many. We know from anthropology, history, and literature that there are others. We travel, read books, observe foreigners, and we can find reasons for or against our evaluative framework by comparing it with others. Unlike those on the ship, we can abandon our evaluative framework and opt for another. All this is true, but it does not make the metaphor bad.

In the first place, we have to decide whether some other evaluative framework would be better than the one we have. What reason could we have for making that decision? Any reason would have to come from the evaluative framework we have. We cannot consistently rely on it for some particular reasons and abandon it for those same reasons. And, of course, the same is true of any other evaluative framework from which we might derive reasons. Furthermore, among the things we learn from other evaluative frameworks is that they also have problems, just as ours does. Why should we abandon our evaluative framework for a far less familiar one that also has problems? It has been well said that

> if we wipe out the social world in which we live, wipe out its traditions and create a new world on the basis of blue-prints, then we shall very soon have to alter the new world, making little changes and adjustments. But if we are to make these little changes and adjustments, which will be needed in any case, why not start them here and now in the social world we have? It does not matter what you have and where you start. You must always make little adjustments. Since you will always have to make them,

it is very much more sensible and reasonable to start with what happens to exist at the moment, because of these things which exist we at least know where the shoe pinches. We at least know of certain things that they are bad and that we want them changed.[16]

If we abandon our evaluative framework and opt for another, we would not abandon our reliance on some evaluative framework. We still need a ship to keep afloat. We would merely have changed ships. If we are reasonable, we will recognize that we cannot live a civilized life without relying on some evaluative framework to distinguish between our good and bad, and better and worse possibilities. It can be said in favor of prudence that it is unreasonable to search for reasons beyond these, if the evaluative framework enables us to make crucially important evaluative distinctions about how to live. Civilized life depends on it. One main reason for the prudent strategy, then, is that even if we opt for another evaluative framework, we would still have to avoid the search for additional reasons for or against that one. It seems that there is no reasonable alternative to following the prudent strategy. Underlying these reasons for it is the fear of casting doubt on the entire evaluative framework that enables us to live as we think we should. The Azande, the Kalabari, Montaigne, Descartes, and Hume all had more reasons to protect their evaluative framework than to subvert it by an ill-advised search for more reasons than they obviously have.

The prudent strategy does not cast doubt on the distinction between good and bad, better and worse reasons for evaluations. It casts doubt on there being a strong enough reason for abandoning the entire evaluative framework from which we derive the evaluations that guide how we live. That is consistent with doubting some of the particular evaluations that follow from it. These reasons for the prudent strategy, however, do not entitle us to conclude that the strategy is reasonable because there are also reasons against it.

Reasons against Prudence

Reasons against the prudent strategy need not lead to a drastic decision to abandon an evaluative framework. If it enables us to live as we think we should and to make sense of our lives in its terms, then fair-minded critics should acknowledge that we have reasons for it, even if we cannot cope with some of its problems. The most telling reasons against persisting with the prudent strategy make themselves felt more subtly. Reasonable defenders and critics of an evaluative framework are likely agree that the problem is that some of the evaluations that follow from it are now mistaken. They may have been reasonable in the past but contexts have changed. The evaluations may have become obsolete, like chastity, compulsory church attendance, thrift, or the prohibition of money-lending. Or their importance has become overvalued, as has happened, for instance, to our evaluations of physical bravery, religious faith, or wealth, or undervalued as may be the case with fidelity, honor, or modesty.

It may happen, however, that a particular mistaken evaluation is not merely one of many but basic to an evaluative framework. If it were mistaken, it would be a decisive reason against the entire evaluative framework. If the Aristotelian evaluation of eudaimonia, the Christian one of salvation, the Enlightenment one of human perfectibility, the Utilitarian one of happiness, or the Kantian one of reason were mistaken, then the evaluative framework that rests on them would be mistaken. The more subtle and more serious problems of an evaluative framework involve mistaken basic evaluations. Continuing the prudent defense of the evaluative framework, then, is reasonable only if the mistaken evaluation is not basic, or, if basic, then can be corrected in a way that does not endanger the entire evaluative framework. Consider now a case in point.

Thomas Reid was a clergyman, a philosopher, and a devout believer. He wrote:

> We acknowledge that nothing can happen under the administration of the Deity, which he does not see fit to permit . . . [yet] natural and moral evil is a phenomenon which cannot be disputed. To account for this phenomenon under the government of a Being of infinite goodness, justice, wisdom, and power, has, in all ages, been considered difficult to human reason.[17]

He went on to ask as a philosopher should:

> Since it is supposed, that the Supreme Being had no other end in making and governing the universe, but to produce the greatest happiness to his

creatures in general, how comes it to pass, that there is so much misery in a system made and governed by infinite wisdom and power (349)?

And he answered as a philosopher should not that

if it be asked, why does God permit so much sin in his creation? I confess I cannot answer the question, but must lay my hand upon my mouth. He giveth no account of his conduct to the children of men. It is our part to obey his commands, not to say unto him, why dost thou thus (353).

This is just the attitude, honest though it is, that gives a bad name to prudence. Critics will say that prudence is a name for the evasion of difficult problems to which defenders of an evaluative framework have no reasonable response. Reid may reply that even though he is unable to give a reasonable response, his inability affects only a particular evaluation that is not basic in Christianity. Reid acknowledged that the problem of evil is a problem indeed, but claimed that the evaluations that guide the Christian understanding of faith, hope, charity, miracles, revelations, and salvation are unaffected by the problem of evil.

Reid might have added that it is not at all unusual for there to be problems that defenders of an evaluative framework cannot cope with at a particular time. The problems should be acknowledged and it should be admitted that it is as yet unclear how they could be met. But they could go on to claim that it would be unreasonable to abandon the entire evaluative framework because of problems that affect some aspects of it. If Reid could have been familiar with Quine's holism, he might have said that

the totality of our so-called knowledge or beliefs . . . impinges on experience only along the edges. . . . A conflict with experience at the periphery occasions adjustments in the interior of the field. Truth values have to be redistributed over some of our statements. . . . But the total field is so underdetermined by its boundary conditions, experience, that there is much latitude of choice as to what statement to reevaluate in the light of any single experience. . . . Any statement can be held true come what may, if we make drastic enough adjustments elsewhere in the system.[18]

If Quine could say this about the evaluative framework of his kind of empiricism, then the same thing, *mutatis mutandis*, could be said about the Christian evaluative framework that Reid is defending. But this will not satisfy critics. For they will say that the problem of evil does not just affect a particular evaluation within the Christian evaluative framework. It affects a basic assumption on which the entire framework rests, namely that God is perfectly good, all-knowing, and all-powerful. They will say that the prevalence of evil is incompatible with the conception of God on which the entire evaluative framework rests. And that is a basic reason against the entire Christian evaluative framework.

In this disagreement both defenders and critics of the prudent strategy agree about the need to distinguish between problems with parts of an evaluative framework and basic problems that call into question assumptions on which the entire evaluative framework rests. But they disagree whether a particular problem is basic. The implications of this disagreement are crucial. For if the problem is not basic, then it is relatively minor, and all evaluative frameworks have such problems. But if the problem is basic, then it becomes a major problem that casts doubt on the entire evaluative framework. The prudent strategy may be reasonable in response to relatively minor problems, but it is unreasonable if the problem is basic.

This disagreement between defenders and critics affects many evaluative frameworks, not just the Christian one. Consider, for instance, the evaluative framework of the Enlightenment. It is a minor problem within it that human beings often act contrary to reason. But it is a major problem about the entire framework if it seems that there is something like the secular equivalent of original sin and people are basically ambivalent about living reasonably and morally. How else could we explain the constant presence throughout history of war, torture, ideological and religious atrocities, mass murders, and man's inhumanity to men and women? The minor problem is manageable within the evaluative framework of the Enlightenment; the major problem, however, indicates that a basic Enlightenment assumption—human perfectibility— is mistaken, since the undeniable facts of history and contemporary life are contrary to it. Perhaps there is also a secular problem of evil? Is there a reasonable way of resolving disagreements about whether or not a problem is basic?

There is, provided we are clear about what makes a problem basic. It is basic if it directly or indirectly affects all or most of the evaluations of an evaluative framework. The problem then calls into question the entire framework. In that case, the prudent strategy of shelving the problem is an unreasonable evasion. If the prevalence of evil shows that God is not perfect, then the Christian evaluations guiding the understanding of faith, hope, charity, redemption, salvation, and so forth that presuppose God's perfection are also mistaken. If the prevalence of evil shows that human beings are not perfectible, then the Enlightenment evaluations of liberty, equality, justice, and so forth that presuppose human perfectibility are mistaken. If the requirements of reason and morality diverge, then the Kantian views about good will, duty, kingdom of ends, and so forth are mistaken. If the dialectic of history does not lead to a just society, then the Marxist views of progress, a classless society without alienation, the justification of revolution, and so forth are mistaken. And so on. There is, therefore, a reasonable way of resolving disagreements about whether or not a problem is basic. It is basic in an evaluative framework if it affects all or most evaluations that follow from it. Otherwise, it is not basic.

It may be thought that one main reason against the prudent strategy is that if a problem is basic and defenders of an evaluative have no reasonable way of coping with it, then they ought, at the very least, acknowledge it rather than ignore it and evade the truth that all or most of their evaluations rest on a mistaken assumption. They should face the truth rather than obfuscate what they are doing by calling it prudence. It may be thought that civilized life, human dignity, and self-respect all require a commitment to facing the truth, even if it is unpleasant—perhaps especially then. How else could we improve our lives, make our society better, and cope with our problems? As Bernard Williams movingly put it close to the end of his last book—and his life—"the hope that a truthful story on a large enough scale will not cause despair is already hope."[19]

This hope is likely to be accepted by those who share the optimistic view held by the majority of participants in our evaluative framework.

Avoiding Extremes

There is, however, also Nietzsche's thought that expresses the pessimistic view held by a minority in our evaluative framework: "There is no pre-established harmony between the furtherance of truth and the well-being of mankind."[20] If this is so, then Williams's hope may well be a false hope. It is not unreasonable to ask: why should the commitment to facing the truth be unconditional, regardless of consequences? What if its pursuit makes us worse off than we were before we embarked on an endless quest for it? And what if the truth about our evaluative framework leads to despair? Is it so unreasonable to fear that danger, follow the prudent strategy, and keep the pursuit of truth within reasonable bounds?

Neither Williams's nor Nietzsche's thought is unreasonable. Perhaps in some contexts it is reasonable to fear more what the truth might reveal than to hope that it will bring good news? And perhaps in other contexts the opposite is reasonable. There may be reasons both for asking for reasons and for prudently refraining from it. If we face a dire economic crisis, epidemics, a foreign attack, natural disasters, or external or internal terrorism, or know of no alternative to the evaluative framework we have, then it is unreasonable to weaken our resolve by dwelling on the problems of the evaluative framework on which we rely to cope with the emergencies. If our society is affluent, secure, and views itself with smug self-satisfaction, then it is reasonable to focus on problems with it and demand additional reasons for its evaluative framework and thereby challenge the self-congratulating status quo.

The context-dependence of reasons we may have for or against fear and the prudent strategy is comparable to the context-dependence of the reasons we may have for or against getting a divorce, having children, changing jobs, committing suicide, emigrating, and so forth. Just so we may have reasons both for and against fear and the prudent strategy and searching for more reasons than we already have for or against our entire evaluative framework. It may be reasonable both to hope that the pursuit of truth will reveal that the evaluative framework is reasonable and to fear that it will show that it is unreasonable. Neither the hope nor the fear is contrary to reason in appropriate circumstances. But we may well be conflicted about how to make the difficult choice between these reasonable possibilities.

Suppose that it is pointed out to the Azande, the Kalabari, or to Montaigne, Descartes, and Hume that their prudent strategy is motivated by fear. Suppose they accept it and ask why should that make their fear and prudence unreasonable? Why could they not respond by saying that in their circumstances it is perfectly reasonable to fear the collapse of the evaluative framework on which how they live depends? I do not think that such a response is always unreasonable. But neither do I think that it is the only reasonable response. It is also reasonable in some circumstances not to allow fear to divert us from the pursuit of truth. Both may be reasonable in appropriate circumstances.

Fear, hope, and the pursuit of truth may all be unreasonable if they are excessive, much too weak, or directed toward wrong objects. However, fearing that our evaluative framework may collapse need not be unreasonable. What is unreasonable is to claim that reason requires all of us always in all circumstances to be guided by an unconditional commitment to the pursuit of truth regardless of any other consideration. Some people may live according to that commitment. Perhaps Nietzsche was one of them, and insanity may have been the price he paid for it. Others may be more fortunate. But it need not be unreasonable to refuse to make that unconditional commitment. That does not mean indifference to the truth. The truth certainly matters. However, there are also other things that matter, they may conflict with the pursuit of truth, and there are good reasons why any one thing that matters should not *always* override other things that matter. Fearing danger and pursuing truth may both be reasonable.

The evaluative framework of our society is the bulwark that stands between the eternal silence of the infinite spaces and the civilized world we have created. The evaluations that guide us in the interstices when the necessities to which we are unavoidably subject leave us some possibilities among which we can choose. These possibilities and choices among them is the luxury our evolutionary good fortune enables us to enjoy. We can make good or bad uses of it. Our evaluative framework enables us to distinguish between good and bad uses, opt for the good ones, and protect us from those who put them to bad uses. It makes civilized life possible. When we fear its collapse, we fear the collapse of civilized life. We fear that the bulwark between the world of facts with its eternally silent infinite spaces and the civilized world of values will be breached. This is a reasonable fear. And it is reasonable to adopt the prudent strategy of limiting the pursuit of truth if it threatens to lead to the collapse of the evaluative framework. Prudence is our strategy for coping with that fear.

Fear can get out of hand, like anything else we do, and the prudent strategy may be premature, overdue, or abused. We can be too fearful and see danger lurking behind every effort to cope with our problems, and correct the mistakes of some, perhaps many, of the evaluations that follow from our evaluative framework. No evaluative framework is perfect, and those known to us, including our own, have serious problems.

Our attempts to identify and correct these problems are also among the conditions of civilized life. Excessive fear is an obstacle to it. Just as the pursuit of truth must be kept within reasonable limits, so must be our fear. Our conflicts between pursuing the truth and fearing the danger to which it might lead makes the choice between them difficult.

How to make that difficult choice reasonably is for us a serious problem because whether the reasons are stronger for their fear or for their prudence depends on conditions that vary with times and contexts. As long as there are serious problems with our evaluative framework, we will have to face the conflict between fearing the loss of the evaluative framework on which living as we think we should depends and protecting the evaluative framework by prudently evading its problems. And then we will have to make a difficult choice. Unreasonably stressing either fear or prudence at the expense of the other is a mistake to which we in our evaluative frameworks are prone. That is why distinguishing between reasonable and unreasonable fear and excessive or deficient prudence is and will remain for us a serious human predicament.

6 The Contingencies of Life

The Counsel of Imperfection

Consider three worlds. The amount of good and bad things in them is exactly the same, but the worlds differ in whether they are distributed justly, that is, according to what is deserved.[1] In one world, their distribution is entirely haphazard. We cannot predict whether we ever get what we deserve, whether our actions will ever have their intended consequences, or whether our efforts will make success more rather than less likely. We would not want to live in such an unpredictable world. Intention, good will, planning, prudence would be useless in it. We would have no control over what happens to us, and be at the mercy of conditions we do not understand and can neither avoid nor change. In such a world, it would be pointless to try to act reasonably.

In the second world, good and bad things are unfailingly distributed according to divine justice. We all get exactly what we deserve — neither more, nor less — be it good or bad, depending on ineluctable laws we cannot change. Benefits and burdens, success and failure, rewards and punishments, praise and blame, satisfactions and frustrations are enjoyed or suffered in exact proportion to the goodness or badness of our actions, as ordained by the laws. We know that the consequences of our actions are determined by laws that allow no exceptions and from which there is no escape. If we act as the laws prescribe, we flourish; if not, we suffer. Yet the laws are mysterious, and we are only dimly aware of why desert is distributed as it is.

This world is certainly better than the haphazard one in which there is no justice, but, since in this divinely ordered world we are often unclear about what justice is, we are only a little better off than being entirely without justice. The difference between no justice and not knowing what justice is makes little practical difference to how we see the distribution of desert.

This divinely ordered world is the archaic world of Job, who intended to follow God's laws and yet lost all he valued, until, eventually, God replaced what He caused Job to lose. Job dared to complain, and

> the Lord answered Job out of the whirlwind" (Job 40: 6–7) Behold, the hope of a man is disappointed. . . . Who then is he that can stand before me? Who has given to me that I should repay him? Whatever is under the heaven is mine (Job 41: 9–11).

And this is also the world of Theognis:

> No man . . . is responsible for his own ruin or his own success: of both these things the gods are the givers. No man can perform an action and know whether its outcome will be good or bad. . . . Humanity in utter blindness follows its futile usages; but the gods bring all to the fulfillment they have planned" (133–36, 141–42).[2]

Much has been written about how life seemed to those who thought that they are living under archaic justice.[3]

Archaic justice is as relentless as the laws of nature. If we fall, we fall, regardless of why we fall. It is reasonable that perfect beings should live in a perfectly just world, but we are imperfect. If we had to choose between living in the haphazard world without justice and the archaic world with justice which we often do not understand, we would choose the latter, but not without hesitation. We certainly want to live in a just world, but no less certainly we want to understand its laws and the likely consequences of our actions.

This brings us to a third world. There is a connection in it between what we deserve and what we get, but it is uncertain. Sometimes we get it, sometimes not. And even if we get it, it may be disproportionate. This is our world in which justice is imperfect. Our system of justice gives us some control over the distribution of desert, but the control is imperfect. Justice in this world is a human construct, not divinely ordered, and often miscarries. We make the laws that define what justice is, but we are fallible and self-interested, to put it mildly, the laws we make reflect our faults, and we often do not get what we deserve.

But the laws are neither ineluctable nor mysterious. We can change and improve them, and we can distinguish between good and bad laws, and between culpable and non-culpable failures to act according to them. We can make allowances for our faults.

If we understand what the worlds of unpredictability and archaic justice are like, we would, I think, have more reason to live in our imperfect world than in either of the other two, even though justice in our world is imperfect and we do not always get what we deserve. However, the reason for living in our world is not that it is a good world to live in, but that it is the least bad of the three possibilities. We would be far from wholeheartedly in favor of it because various contingencies in it often prevent the just distribution of desert.

The counsel of perfection is to struggle against these contingencies and do all we can to remedy the imperfections of our world. This is the accepted wisdom that has guided the Western tradition for close to three millennia. In Aristotle's words,

> we must not follow those who advise us, being men, to think of human things, and, being mortal, of mortal things, but must, so far as we can, make ourselves immortal, and strain every nerve to live in accordance with the best thing in us; for even if it be small in bulk, much more does it in power and worth surpass everything.[4]

The way to live in accordance with the best thing in us is to formulate an ideal theory of justice that should guide the transformation of our world from its imperfectly just condition to approximate ever more closely the ideal of perfect justice as depicted by the theory. The aim of this chapter is to show, critically, that ideal theories of justice rest on illusions and, constructively, that we should follow the advice of those who think that imperfect human beings must live in an imperfectly just world. This is the counsel of imperfection that I will endeavor to defend. It follows from a deeper understanding first of contingency, then of justice, and then of the contingency of justice. If we reach that understanding, we realize that the conflicts between justice and contingency are not only social but also personal, because we will be conflicted about how to respond to the contingency of justice. We will realize also that coping with their conflicts requires us to make difficult choices and doing that reasonably is a serious human predicament.

Contingencies

It is necessary that we will die but it is contingent when we die. Both the necessity and the contingency significantly affect how we live. I propose a way of understanding necessity and contingency from the point of view of our evaluative framework. This, of course, is only one point of view and there are many others from which different ways of understanding necessity and contingency may follow. My proposal is to understand necessity as natural, dictated by the laws of nature together with specifiable conditions that jointly cause particular effects. If the causes and the conditions are present, the effects will follow. We may be ignorant or mistaken about the laws, the conditions, the causes, and the effects, but if we get them right, we can be as certain as it is possible for us to be about matters of fact that the causes will necessarily lead to the effects. The necessity follows from the way the world is regardless of what our logical or metaphysical principles, theories, or expectations happen to be.

Contingency is also natural. It exists within natural necessity, not apart from it. Natural necessity sets limits beyond which we cannot go, but within those limits there are some possibilities that allow us to change the conditions in which effects follow from causes and give us some control over the consequences of our actions. Changing these conditions is not always possible, but sometimes it is. If the laws and conditions are as we take them to be, then death sets a limit to human lives. It is a natural necessity that we will die. But it is contingent when we die because we can sometimes change the conditions in which we live. We can delay our death if we live in a healthy, prosperous, secure society and take advantage of its life-prolonging possibilities. We can also hasten our death by not taking advantage of them. (In the interest of brevity, from now on I omit the qualification that both necessity and contingency are natural.)

Contingency is neither uncaused nor a matter of luck. It depends on what our limits and possibilities are and on what we can make of them. These, in turn, depend on our own and others' actions or inactions. All of them are within the limits set by the conjunction of necessity, the physiological, psychological, and social characteristics of the kind of beings we are, and the conditions in which we live. It may be that there are contingencies other than natural, such as uncaused causes or supernatural interference with natural necessity, but I ignore their possibility. I am concerned with understanding the significance of what happens when necessity and contingency are parts of causal chains that have neither a beginning nor an end and are free of supernatural interference.

Significance is the sense we attribute to facts. Facts would have no significance if there were no human beings, or perhaps non-human beings, who attribute significance to them. I have no idea whether some other mammals, like chimpanzees, can do this. But we, human beings, certainly can. When we do it—which is by no means always, because we may be ignorant, indifferent, or have other concerns—we attribute some more or less important significance to them. We may also find some facts insignificant. I will be concerned with the significance we attribute to facts from the point of view of the limits they set to how we live, such as death, and the possibilities we have, like hastening or delaying when we die.[5]

When we attribute significance to facts of this kind, we typically have some personal attitude toward them. It is formed of some combination of our evaluative framework and preferences, experiences, beliefs, emotions, and desires. They give us reasons to act or not to act in certain ways. Each component of our personal attitude may be mistaken, and so may be the reasons we form on their basis. I repeat: we are fallible. The significance we attribute to facts, therefore, may also be mistaken. We are often wrong about the limits to which we think we are subject and the possibilities we think we have. Whether we are mistaken in these ways is also a matter of the contingency of our evaluative framework, natural endowments, education, circumstances, the various pressures on us, and so forth. These contingencies are among the causes of our problems.

Here is one kind of contingency. I am driving my car to keep an appointment and have to cross a bridge over a deep ravine. Suppose, first, that when I am in the middle of the bridge, it collapses, the car and me in it fall into the ravine, and I die. This would be a bad contingency for me. Suppose, second, that the bridge collapses only a few minutes after I crossed it. This would be, for me, a good contingency. In either case, the contingency is only apparent. My death or escape is the effect of two chains of causes. One leads to the collapse of the bridge; the other to my crossing. These causal chains have intersected either to my benefit or detriment. If we knew enough about the causes and the relevant conditions, we would understand that what happened was a matter of necessity. This kind of contingency, therefore, is only apparent because we do not know enough about the relevant causes and conditions. Many accidents, coincidences, and events are only apparently contingent. I say many, not all, because I want to avoid metaphysical entanglements that are irrelevant to the distinction I am trying to draw between understanding and misunderstanding contingency.

A second kind of contingency emerges if we recognize that the causal chains that have led to my death or escape are indifferent to what I deserve. I die, or not, regardless of whether I am on the way to inform the world of a great and beneficial discovery or to sell drugs to school children. The necessity to which we are all subject is what it is regardless of what we deserve. The good or bad effects that causes have on us are just facts. We attribute goodness or badness to them from the point of view of our evaluative framework. But that point of view is a human one, not, so to speak, the universe's point of view, assuming it could have one. Necessity does not lead to a distribution of good and bad facts according to what we deserve.

This kind of contingency is not an exception to necessity, but a consequence of it, one that *we* may find good or bad. It is real, not apparent, but it would not exist if it were not for human beings, or beings like us, who have an evaluative framework and evaluate the facts that affect us. We evaluate them as good or bad, even though the facts, in themselves, are just facts, neither good nor bad. The facts are what they are, regardless of whether we do or do not deserve their effects on us. This gap between what we deserve and what we get is the context of the second kind of contingency. It is from now on what I mean by contingency.

Contingency in our world is limited. Pessimists think that it is pervasive; optimists think that we can go a long way toward freeing ourselves from it. Regardless of what our view is, we all want our world to be less contingent and more just. Of course we often disagree about what is good or bad, and deserved or undeserved. I take it, however, that we agree that the connection between what we get and what we deserve should be less contingent than it is. What is the reason for this virtually universal agreement among those who think about such matters?

The reason is that we want a world in which we can reliably predict the consequences of our actions. One of these consequences is the distribution of desert, but we are inconsistent about wanting it. Few of us want to get what we deserve if it is bad, such as punishment or failure.

And we often want to get what we do not deserve, provided it is good, as shown by those given to impossible hopes, petitionary prayer, and gambling. What is the reason, then, for wanting a world in which we get what we deserve? The reason is that in such a world we have some control over what we get. We can sometimes act in ways that are more likely to have good than bad consequences, and refrain from actions that are more likely to have bad than good consequences. We want the distribution of desert to be less contingent.

The qualification that the connections between actions and consequences is only likely is important. If the consequences of our actions depend only on ourselves, then the likelihood of getting what we deserve and not what we do not deserve would be more predictable than it in fact is. Actually, the consequences depend also on others with whom we live. We are among the sources of the desert they get, and they are among the sources of the desert we get. Although we depend on each other to make it more, rather than less, likely that we get what we deserve, we are all, at least occasionally, undependable for regrettably familiar reasons. This is part of the explanation why our control over what we get is inadequate. We want to increase whatever control we have so that we could count on our actions having the consequences we expect. We have some control in our world, but clearly not enough. In the perfectly just world, we would have perfect control, provided we were perfect beings, but since we are not, we prefer our world. In the perfectly contingent world, we would have no control at all, and that is why we are not at all ambivalent about not wanting to live in it.

To sum up, in our world the connection between our actions and their consequences is contingent and we often do not get what we deserve. Part of the significance we attribute to this fact is that our control is inadequate. That we have the control we have is a consequence of the necessity within which we have some possibilities open to us. We cannot help knowing, however, that our control is inadequate. We cannot change our upbringing, experiences, education, and society; we cannot free ourselves from disease, accidents, and social changes; we are saddled with our native capacities and incapacities; and we will mature, have sexual preferences, get sick and with luck recover, and we will age and eventually die. All that and more is a matter of contingency we cannot alter. Justice is a way of making it more likely, within the limits set by contingency, that we get what we deserve and not what we do not deserve. It is a hard taskmaster because it often requires us to accept the bad things we deserve and reject the good things we do not deserve. No wonder we are not entirely consistent about wanting it.

Justice

How just a society is partly depends on its evaluative framework. If it is in good enough order, it is more likely that the distribution of what is deserved will be just. The evaluations that follow from it are intended to guide, protect, enforce, and settle disputes about how desert should be distributed. The particular forms of these evaluations are likely to be different in different societies, but without evaluations of this kind no society can be civilized. There are so many evaluations and they are so varied that it would be futile to try to enumerate them. I will proceed instead by sketching — no more than that — four areas of life which are likely to be present in all civilized societies that have a reasonable evaluative framework. The evaluations are of what is deserved. They overlap, sometimes conflict, and sometimes reinforce one another. Their variety has significant implications for a deeper understanding of contingency and justice.

One of these implications I mention now in order to avoid a common misunderstanding. There is a large volume of work on desert.[6] The general consensus among contributors to it is that the evaluation of who deserves what is and should be moral. Whether this is true depends on whether morality is understood in a wide or a narrow sense. In the wide sense, all evaluations are supposed to be moral. Then, of course, the evaluation of who deserves what is moral. But this is more confusing than clarifying. Economic, legal, medical, political, and religious evaluations are obviously often quite different from moral evaluations. If they are all supposed to be moral, then the appropriate distinctions among different modes of evaluations must be drawn within morality, and the force of the claim that the evaluation of who deserves what is moral becomes a truism since all evaluations about anything are supposed to be moral. In the wide sense of morality, the claim that the evaluation of who deserves what is moral adds nothing to saying that questions about who deserves what are evaluative.

If, however, morality is understood in a narrow sense in which moral evaluations are only one mode among others, then it is misleading to claim that the evaluation of who deserves what is or should be moral. Certainly, some such evaluations are moral. But no less certainly, some are economic, legal, medical, political, or religious. Clarity requires recognizing that evaluations of who deserves what are as various as the different modes of evaluations recognized in an evaluative framework. I stress this point now in order to call attention to the obvious consequence that follows from it, namely, that different modes of evaluations of who deserves what often conflict and how their conflicts should be resolved is often reasonably disputed by those whose modes of evaluation are different. This has significant implications for the contingency of justice, which I merely note now and discuss later.

One mode of evaluation concerns relationships. Lovers, competitors, friends, colleagues, parents and children, teachers and students, judges and defendants, physicians and patients, merchants and customers are connected by conventional ties. The relationships may be reciprocal, as between lovers, competitors, friends, and colleagues. Or they may be asymmetrical, because one party has authority over the other, or provides a service the other needs, or sells something the other wants to buy. In such relationships, the participants have different responsibilities and expectations. These evaluations are of whether those who are related in these ways treat each other as they deserve.

Another mode of evaluation concerns agreements, such as contracts, promises, loans, memberships in organizations, employment, political or legal representation, and so forth. Some of these agreements are formal. The responsibilities and expectations are written down and legally binding. Others are informal, such as those of tact and gratitude. What is deserved, then, rests on the tacit understanding of the parties. The force behind such informal agreements is a shared sense of trust and mutual good will that often prompt supererogatory actions that go beyond what is deserved. The evaluations, then, are of whether the parties treat each other as they deserve according to the terms of the formal or informal agreements.

A third mode of evaluation centers on actions that affect the security of others. A society cannot endure unless it protects the life and health of those living in it, but different societies have different laws, rules, and customs guiding how extensive and widespread their protection should be, what violations are permissible, excusable, or prohibited, how people outside of the society should be treated, what counts as cruelty, negligence, accidental injury, and, of course, how security should be understood. Take, for instance, homicide. All societies must regulate it in some way, otherwise they will fall into anarchy. But when homicide is murder, when it is excusable or justifiable varies greatly, as do the permissibility of abortion, suicide, revenge, euthanasia, capital punishment, infanticide, and so forth. What is and is not deserved, then, depends on how what people do or is done to them affects their own and others' security.

A fourth mode of evaluation concerns what is deserved as a result of participation in the evaluative framework of a society. Conduct that strengthens it — for instance by judicious decisions, exemplary actions, a lifetime of integrity even under difficult conditions, faithful service, and good judgment about when actions contrary to it should be condemned, excused, or justified — deserves appropriate praise. Actions that weaken the evaluative framework by crime, fraud, spite, hostility, prejudice, or selfishness are condemned.

Part of the significance of these different modes evaluation is that they specify what is deserved in a particular context. They are parts of our evaluative framework and establish the responsibilities and the expectations that those living in a society have to and of others. In our society, children normally deserve a decent upbringing from their parents, because that is part of how parenthood is understood by us. Incompetent physicians deserve to lose their licenses, because we expect physicians to treat illness and injury well. Murderers deserve to be tried and, if found guilty, punished, because that is how we safeguard security. Freeloaders who take advantage of others when they can get away with it deserve to be condemned.

Such evaluations specify what we do and do not deserve. They vary with societies, but the evaluative framework of a society is reasonable only if it specifies what is and what is not deserved. A society that systematically, rather than occasionally, fails to provide what is deserved would be on the road to disintegration. When we say, therefore, that we deserve this or that, what we are saying is that this is the particular way in which some of our basic interests are protected in our society. Justice makes it more likely that we get what we deserve by following the evaluations of our society's evaluative framework. As I will shortly argue, there are unavoidable limits to the extent to which we can get what we deserve. Because of these limits, it will remain forever a contingent matter whether we get what we deserve. At best, we can make its distribution less contingent, but the limits make it impossible to eliminate the unjust distribution of desert. That is why the distribution of desert is a serious problem. We can perhaps make the problem less acute, but we cannot escape it. We need to face it and try to cope with it as best as we can.

How reasonable a society's evaluative framework is depends on whether the evaluations that follow from it make it more likely that those living in it will get all and only what they deserve. This happy condition may be approximated, but there are several reasons why it will not be achieved. One is that its evaluations may rest on false belief, as was the case in the not too distant past in our society. (Those who disagree with the examples that follow should feel free to substitute their own. Examples of false beliefs are plentiful.) It is a false belief that sex outside of marriage is sinful, atheism is immoral, public nudity is obscene, homosexuality unnatural, suicide self-murder; and so on for a long list. The results are mistaken condemnations and the unjust distribution of desert.

Another reason why evaluations of what is deserved may be mistaken is that, although they are free of false beliefs, they are excessive in rewarding deserving actions or punishing undeserving ones. A novel that tells a good story deserves praise, but it is excessive to celebrate it as a great work of art. A robber deserves to be jailed, but not to have an arm cut off. Racial prejudice deserves to be condemned, but not be treated as a hate crime.

A third reason why evaluations of what is just may be mistaken is that, although they are factually correct and involve no excess, they fail to make it more likely that we get what we deserve. It is far from clear that imprisoning nonviolent criminals, especially together with violent ones, is a good way of protecting security. The protection of free press is important, but it is highly questionable whether it should be extended to investigative journalists whose job and income depend on publishing titillating information about the private life of public figures. Having a system of taxation is necessary for the distribution of desert, but it is absurd to have a tax code so complicated that only skilled specialists can tell what is a legitimate exemption.

Evaluations, therefore, can be and often are mistaken because they rest on false beliefs, are excessive, or fail to provide what we deserve. But such mistakes can, at least in principle, be corrected. We can learn from our past and present mistakes and perhaps correct them, even if the process is slow and beset with pitfalls and problems. However, even if mistaken evaluations were corrected, they would not guarantee that we get what we deserve. Some evaluations are better than others, often much better, but no matter how much better they are, no matter how close we get to correcting mistaken ones, it will remain an uncontrollable contingency whether we get what we deserve. The reasons for this are the problems of scarcity, incorrigibility, and conflicts to which I now turn.

Scarcity, Incorrigibility, and Conflict

Not even a perfect system of distribution could give us all we deserve, since the available resources are chronically scarce.[7] The reason for this is not that some people accumulate so much that not enough is left for others. That happens, but it is not scarcity. Scarcity is when the available resources are insufficient and not even a perfectly just society could distribute them so that we all get what we deserve. The equal distribution of scarce resources would not guarantee that we get what we deserve, because it may just increase the number of those who do not get all they deserve. Depriving some who got what they deserve in order to decrease by a fraction the plight of those who did not may just spread injustice more evenly.

The scarcity of resources affects much more than *materiel* and money, although, of course, both may be scarce. If resources are understood as widely as I think they should be, they will include human capacities, knowledge, skill, experience, and judgment. I will refer to them jointly as *competences*. Education and training can increase them, but it is impossible to increase them sufficiently to avoid their scarcity. The reason for this is not merely poor education and training, but the statistical necessity that the possession of all human competences is unavoidably unequal. Perhaps all human beings possess some of the same competences at least to some minimum extent, but how far they can develop them will vary according to statistical necessity. Most of us will develop them in a way that does not deviate much from the statistical mean. Some of us, however, will deviate a great deal by developing the relevant competence either well below or far above the mean.

This is just a fact of life, not a controversial evaluative claim. We all know that some of us excel and others are poor at finding imaginative solutions to difficult problems, organizing complex data, sympathetically entering into other people's point of view, being sensitive to nuances, not allowing personal likes and dislikes to influence our judgments, and so forth. These and countless other differences make it a statistical necessity that administrators, civil servants, judges, lawyers, nurses, physicians, politicians, scientists, teachers, and others on whose competences we rely to provide the services they are responsible for and we deserve to get will differ in whether they can do it well, middlingly, or poorly. Through no fault of anyone, it is a statistical necessity that the competences of a percentage of experts will be below average. Those who happen to have to rely on them will not get the service they deserve. This will be true regardless of what the expertise is and how conscientious the experts are.

An implication of this statistical necessity is that the distribution of desert is and will remain contingent and often unjust, since the competences of those on whom we rely will be unequal. This is not anyone's fault. It is a problem inherent in human nature and the world being what they are. It limits our possibilities and makes it impossible to increase whatever control we have sufficiently to overcome statistical limits. Within these limits, however, we still have some possibilities. One of them is to try to cope with the limits to which we are subject by doing what we can to correct the unjust distribution of desert and thereby diminish the gap between what we deserve and what we get. I now turn to this possibility.

In a civilized society there must be evaluations that guide the correction of the unjust distribution of desert. The injustice may range from slight to very serious matters. It is one thing if an appointment is forgotten, the repayment of a loan is a little late, or a child steals a chocolate bar. It is quite another if innocent people are murdered, mutilated, or tortured. Injustice can be corrected when it is slight and the injury is small. But if it causes lasting, undeserved, and incapacitating harm, then it often cannot be corrected. The more serious the unjust injury is, the less likely it is that anything could be done to correct it. Compensating the victims and punishing the perpetrators cannot undo the injury that has been caused.

Nothing can compensate innocent people who have been murdered, mutilated, or infected by some ghastly disease while being a patient in a hospital. The undeserved injuries need not be fatal and physical. They may be psychological traumas caused by long periods of torture, solitary confinement, or extreme humiliation. No amount of sympathy or monetary award can redress the injustice suffered by the victims. A long passage of time can sometimes heal psychological traumas, but sometimes not. In any case, no evaluation could possibly correct the injustice in such cases. The same is true of punishment. It cannot undo the injury that has been caused. The perpetrators may be punished as they deserve to be, but that cannot change the fact that their victims did not get what they deserve.

The unjust distribution of desert often cannot be corrected because it is impossible to change the past by changing the present or the future. We can try to improve the evaluative framework by correcting some of its mistaken evaluations and thereby make it more likely that we get what we deserve in the future, but the greater is the undeserved injury, the more its correction is needed, and the less likely is its possibility. It is often impossible for victims of serious injustice to do anything more than bear, with as much patience as they can muster, the burden of the serious injuries caused by past and present unjust distribution of desert. This is one of the problems we need to face.

A further problem is that the economic, legal, medical, moral, political, religious, and other modes of evaluation that specify what we deserve often conflict. Their conflicts could be resolved if one mode of evaluation would always have priority over all the others, perhaps because it aims at something that all reasonable people recognize as having greater importance than any other aim. It might be supposed, for instance, that this most important aim is the common good, or the rule of law, or a free and secure society, or living in conformity to a providential order.

If the overriding importance of one of these aims were generally accepted, reasonable people could agree that the mode of evaluation that best reflects that aim should have priority over the others. But the importance of these aims is as disputed as the priority of evaluations. There is no general agreement about what the common good excludes and includes, what laws should govern a society, whether freedom and security are more important than, say, justice or happiness, or whether there is a providential order. What actually happens is that those living together in a civilized society typically have conflicting aims and assign conflicting priorities to different evaluations. And they all claim that the aims and evaluations they favor are necessary conditions of the pursuit of other aims by means of other modes of evaluation. Conflicts about what is deserved, therefore, will remain problems so long as there are modes of evaluation that may come into conflict.

Another approach to conflict resolution might be based on epistemological requirements that are independent of the conflicting evaluations. Any reasonable evaluation must be logically consistent, take into account relevant facts, and be open to criticism and change. Meeting them, however, is not sufficient for assigning priority to one mode of evaluation. For most of the familiar economic, legal, medical, moral, political, and religious evaluations do conform to these epistemological requirements. It is very unlikely that evaluations that have been accepted for generations are followed voluntarily, and are responsive to prevailing problems and changing conditions would fail to conform to these elementary requirements.

Yet another possibility is to appeal to human interests and claim that one mode of evaluation offers better protection of them than any other. These interests may be identified as the basic physiological, psychological, and social needs whose satisfaction must be protected by any reasonable evaluative framework. It is perhaps obvious that there are such requirements. But it is far from obvious and often false that when the satisfaction of basic requirements turns out to conflict with requirements that follow, say, from deep moral, political, or religious commitments, then reason requires giving priority to the satisfaction of the basic need.

The protection of life and health is a basic need. In countless cases, however, legal, moral, political, or religious commitments lead us to risk our life and health. Soldiers, cops, and critics, among others, are honored for doing this if thereby they protect the evaluative framework of their society. And so are those who are led by love, integrity, or a sense of justice to risk their lives and health for others. Legal, moral, political, or religious commitments may be thought to have priority over the satisfaction of basic needs. The point is not that this is always or ever reasonable, but that there are and have been conflicting views about whether the satisfaction of basic needs should always have priority over other commitments.

It does not follow from such conflicts that there are no strong reasons for assigning priority to some consideration in determining the just distribution of what is deserved. There are strong reasons of this kind, but they depend on the context of a society, its evaluative framework, and the prevailing conditions. All of them are subject to contingent changes, and what strong reasons are changes with them. The recognition that strong reasons that guide the just distribution of desert are contingent, context-dependent, and particular does not call into question the possibility of having good reasons and acting on them. It calls into question the assumption that reasons can be strong only if they are context-independent and general. The just distribution of desert, therefore, always depends on contingent conditions whose changes are often beyond our control. And it depends also on the extent to which it is frustrated by scarcity, incorrigibility, and conflicts. The contingency of justice is a human predicament. We need to face and try to cope with it to the extent to which it is possible within the limits of necessity and contingency.

Imperfect Justice

There are several ways of responding to contingency. Trying to make the distribution of desert more just is one of them, but there are others. Another is to deny that life is contingent, believe that it is governed by a benign providential order, and say with Julian of Norwich that eventually "all shall be and all manner of things shall be well." Or opt for love, rather than justice, and "repay no evil for evil, but take thought for what is noble. . . . Do not be overcome by evil, but overcome evil with good" (Romans 12: 17 and 21).

Or follow

the image of the heroic individual . . . not as the crown of a harmonious cosmos, but as a being alienated from it, and seeking to subdue and dominate it. . . . The noblest things a man can do is to serve his inner ideal no matter at what cost. . . . The only principle which must be sacredly observed is that each man shall be true to his own goals, even at the cost of destruction, havoc, and death.[8]

Or be guided by the realization that

not having enough fortitude to endure the annoyance of adverse accidents to which we are subject . . . I foster as best I can this idea: to abandon myself completely to Fortune, expect the worst in everything, and resolve to bear that worst meekly and patiently. . . . Not being able to rule events, I rule myself, and adapt myself to them if they do not adapt themselves to me.[9]

If we realize that our response is one among many others, we come to a yet deeper understanding of the contingency of justice beyond recognizing its unavoidable imperfections as a result of scarcity, incorrigibility, and conflicts. We may come then to understand then that not only is justice contingent, but so are our responses to it. We become aware of possibilities of life other than our own. We do not have to adopt them. Our understanding is deepened merely by becoming aware of them and seeing them as possible alternatives to the usually unreflective context-bound responses we derive from our evaluative framework. If we compare other responses that follow from other evaluative frameworks with our own, we can ask ourselves whether we have better reasons for them than that they happen to be ours.

Our response to the unjust distribution of desert is to try to make our society more just. Ideal theorists of justice take this response for granted and then propose a way of coming closer to the ideal of justice. The reasons against ideal theories I will now discuss are not directed against any particular ideal theory, but against all of them. The dominant ideal theory in our present context is liberal. The reason against it is not that it is liberal, but that it is an ideal theory. For the record, I accept basic liberal values in our context. What I do not accept is that they should be accepted in all contexts regardless of great differences in cultural, economic, historical, legal, moral, political, and technological conditions.

The doyen of ideal theorists in our context starts with the assumption that "justice is the first virtue of social institutions . . . laws and institutions . . . must be reformed or abolished if they are unjust."[10] He does not ask, Why there is there so much injustice? Why social institutions have to have a first virtue, rather than many important virtues? Why the first virtue is justice rather than order, peace, prosperity, or security? or Why conflicts among the so-called virtues of social institutions must always be resolved in favor of justice rather than in favor of other things we value no less than justice? He takes for granted the assumption on which his ideal theory rests.

It cannot be reasonably denied that justice is important. But there are also other things that are important. The assumption needs to be justified that justice is always, in all circumstances more important than, say, compassion, education, loyalty, moderation, peace, prosperity, security, self-reliance, or social harmony. Ideal theorists should not blithely start with an unquestioned assumption, but ask why the response to injustice they take for granted is more reasonable than these other responses. They should first ask the questions that need to be asked, give reasonable answers them, and realize that only after that can their theories get off the ground. Since they prescribe how our society should be arranged and how we should live, they should give reasons why their prescriptions are preferable to alternatives to them. But they do not ask such questions, give no such reasons, and show no awareness of alternatives.

Those who are more thoughtful than these ideal theories may pay attention to the great variety of life-enhancing and life-diminishing possibilities of life available from anthropology, history, and literature, to the complexities of human motivation, and to the ubiquitous presence of irrationality and ill will in all societies known to us. They may realize then the futility of constructing ideal theories of justice that ignore these possibilities and complexities. And if they realize them, they may become aware of the importance of other things that may conflict with justice. They may realize that whether or not such conflicts should be resolved in favor of justice is contingent on the prevailing conditions, on what it is that conflicts with justice, and on the different modes of evaluation that form parts of different evaluative frameworks. More thought, however, brings with it more problems.

Instead of facing and struggling with these conflicting complex possibilities, ideal theorists formulate abstract requirements of ideal justice. These requirements are theoretical artifacts that cannot cope with the pressing practical problems of scarcity, incorrigibility, conflict, contingency, and the unjust distribution of desert. The reason for this is that ideal theories are by their very nature abstract and general, whereas the problems with which they are meant to cope are particular and context-dependent. It is always particular resources and competences that are scarce; particular acts of injustice that need to be corrected in some particular way; and particular conflicts that must be resolved. These problems are caused by the particular historical, scientific, and technological conditions of a society at a particular time. And the possible ways of coping with them depend on the particular economic, legal, medical, moral, political, religious, and other evaluations that follow from the modes of evaluation of an evaluative framework of a particular society at a particular time. Since ideal theories are abstract and general, while the problems of injustice with which they are meant to cope are particular and context-dependent, the theories cannot possibly succeed.

Furthermore, even if it were possible to apply an abstract and general ideal theory to particular and context-dependent contingencies, and even if reasons could be found that make it preferable to alternative responses to injustice, ideal theories would still be inadequate responses. Contingencies affect much more than the just distribution of desert. They also affect evaluative frameworks and personal attitudes on which the distribution of desert depends. Ideal theorists do not realize that the contingencies to which they are responding pervade also their responses. How we think of justice, desert, scarcity, incorrigibility, and conflict depends on the contingencies of our upbringing, experiences, and the possibilities of our evaluative framework. If we understand how far contingency extends, we will recognize that what purports to be an ideal theory is as much vulnerable to contingency as the unjust distribution of desert. Ideal theories are just theories. They deal with contingencies by ignoring them. It is unreasonable to assume that ideal theorists could transcend contingencies to which they are as much subject as we all are.

I conclude that if we question the assumption on which ideal theories of justice rest, then we will face the fact that contingency and injustice are human predicaments. If we realize that our efforts to make the distribution of desert more just are themselves contingent, then what should we do about the prevalent injustice in the distribution of desert? The answer is obvious. We should do what we can about the particular episodes of injustice we encounter in our context, while bearing in mind the fallibility and contingency of our efforts and the prevailing conflicts between justice and other things we do or perhaps should value.

There is no blueprint for what in particular we can or should do. Certainly, we should try to distribute scarce resources to deserving rather than undeserving recipients; correct unjust distribution to the extent we can; and be as reasonable as we can be about reconciling conflicts among the evaluations that guide the distribution of what is deserved. But doing these fine things depends on the particular problems of scarcity, incorrigibility, and conflict with which we try to cope. In civilized societies, there are usually several conflicting ways of trying to cope with them. The choice between them is difficult, and much depends on how we make it. But no ideal theory could possibly free us from having to face the conflicts and make difficult choices. We can refuse to accept that and continue the futile search for an ideal theory. But we should have learned after millennia of failed attempts that it cannot be found because it is not there. We should understand that we can only try, and keep trying in our particular context, while knowing that we will often fail. Understanding this is the counsel of imperfection.

7   The Divided Self

The Self

We all have a self, our one and only self, but it is divided, makes us conflicted, and forces us to make difficult choices. A divided self may be pathological, if it has multiple personalities or beset by schizophrenia. But the divided self I will discuss is an everyday condition that is not normally pathological. Its division is between our present self with which we are, at least to some extent dissatisfied, and a future self, which we want to make better than the present one. We may think, for instance, that we care too much about unimportant matters and too little about important ones, or neglect those we love, or under or overestimate our capacities or talents, or fail to live as we think we should, and so forth. We want to have a better future self that would not make such mistakes.

The fact remains, however, that we evaluate both our present and supposedly better future self in the only way we can: by relying on the evaluations of our present self, since we have at any given time nothing else we could rely on. Even if we follow the guidance of some authority, we do so only because our evaluations lead us, rightly or wrongly, to accept its guidance. We want a better future self because we want to avoid the mistakes made by the present one. If we recognize the mistakes we have made, we will distrust our present self that has led us to make the mistakes. But we will distrust also our supposedly better future self, because our idea of what it would be is formed by our mistake-prone present self. We are conflicted because we do not know whether we can trust either our present or future self. And the conflicts force us to make difficult choices between following one or the other. If we choose instead to get on with life, ignore the conflicts, and do as well as we can, we in effect choose to follow our present self with which we are dissatisfied. The faults of our present self, however, will not disappear just because we choose to ignore them.

I approach this problem in terms of T. S. Eliot's suggestive discussion of the dissociation of sensibility.[1] I follow him in asking why our sensibility is dissociated and what we could do about it. This leads to considering the lives of Hernan Cortes and Simone Weil whose self was undivided and sensibility unified. They trusted the self they had, and the consequences were disastrous. This should alert us to dangers inherent in the pursuit of an undivided self. There are strong reasons both for and against wanting to have an undivided self. That is why our conflicts between these reasons force us to make difficult choices, and why making them is a serious problem for us. The resulting uncertainty encourages the cultivation of negative capability, another pregnant phrase of literary origin. I borrow it from John Keats,[2] adapt it to the present purposes, and show why it may be a reasonable response to the human predicament presented by our divided self.

Dissociation of Sensibility

Writing about poetry, Eliot says that "in the seventeenth century a dissociation of sensibility set in, from which we have never recovered."[3] Eliot thinks that before the seventeenth century, the metaphysical poets — Donne, Cleveland, Cowley — had a unified sensibility, but it was subsequently lost. Eliot does not say, but obviously thinks that what had been lost is the unified evaluative framework of Roman Catholicism that dominated Europe for more than a millennium. It was shattered by the growing influences of the emerging scientific view of the world, the Renaissance, the Reformation, the Thirty Year War, and the Enlightenment. There were, of course, disagreements within the Catholic evaluative framework before the seventeenth century, but they were largely family quarrels about how its various elements should be interpreted. Doctrinal disputes were about interpretation, not basic challenges to Catholicism. There always were those who acted contrary to the prevailing modes of evaluation, but they were seen, and, except a few incorrigible ones, saw themselves as weak or willful sinners. There were also minorities — Jews, Muslims in Spain, and Byzantine Catholics — but they did not seriously threaten Roman Catholicism in most of Europe. After the seventeenth century, European sensibility became dissociated because the challenges to it became fundamental. It was eventually replaced by a plurality of religious and secular alternatives among which Catholicism was only one. That plurality is still with us. That is why, following Eliot, it may be thought that the sensibility of so many of us is now dissociated and our self is divided.

The basic assumptions of the Catholic evaluative framework are that there is a providential order; a hierarchy of values follows from it; the hierarchy is rational and prescriptive to the extent to which it conforms to that order; and the Roman Catholic Church is the authoritative interpreter of what the hierarchical evaluative framework should be. Individual salvation depends on living as closely to it as the moral and cognitive faults of individuals allow. Those who do not, and there are many, have only themselves to blame for their perdition that ineluctably follows. The lives of the vast majority in Europe before the seventeenth century were informed by these basic assumptions, and that gave them a unified sensibility. Skeptics, both before or after the seventeenth century, had to live as well as they could with the dissociated sensibility that resulted from their doubts.

Eliot is right about the subsequent plurality of evaluative frameworks and why the sensibility of so many of us is now dissociated and our self divided. We have become aware of evaluative frameworks of the *Iliad*, the Book of Job, Sophocles, Pyrrhonian skepticism, Zen Buddhism, Hobbes, empiricism, Spinoza, Rousseau, Kant, the utilitarians, and so forth. We can rely on history, anthropology, philosophy, literature, and non-Western religions to compare our contemporary evaluative frameworks with very different alternatives to them. We can think and feel our ways into sensibilities quite different from our own. This enormously enriches what we may come to recognize as the possibilities of life. But with that enrichment comes the problem of how we should live, resolve our conflicts, make difficult choices, and unify our divided self.

The sources of our problems are not the familiar conflicts between facts and values, reason and emotion, autonomy and authority, tradition and change, optimism and pessimism, secular and religious orientation, classicism and romanticism, realism and idealism, and so forth. All but the most simple-minded evaluative frameworks have some such conflicts. The deep sources of our dissociated sensibility are the conflicting reasons and evaluations that guide how we think we should live. Of course we value beauty, conscientiousness, goodness, happiness, imagination, law, love, reason, rectitude, truth, and so forth. Of course we think that art, history, law, literature, morality, politics, religion, science, and so forth are important. But we disagree about the relative importance of the conflicting reasons and evaluations that follow from them.

Our contemporary evaluative frameworks lack a clear standard to which we could appeal to resolve such conflicts. That standard is what had been lost when our sensibility became gradually dissociated after the seventeenth century. Whatever we may think of the Catholic evaluative framework, it had the sort of standard we now do not have. Being without it makes our self divided, sensibility dissociated, reasons conflicting, choices difficult, and problems about how we should live serious.

The Ideal of an Undivided Self

It is an acute observation that an evaluative framework

> as it advances toward maturity, produces its own determining debate over the ideas that preoccupy it: salvation, the order of nature, money, power, sex, the machine, and the like. The debate, indeed, may be said to *be* the culture, at least on its loftiest levels; for a culture achieves identity not so much through the ascendancy of one particular set of convictions as through the emergence of its peculiar and distinctive dialogue.[4]

In our evaluative framework, part of the distinctive dialogue is, what Isaiah Berlin has described making use of Archilocus' fable, between hedgehogs who know one big thing and foxes who know many small ones. Berlin says that

> the words can be made to yield a sense in which they mark one of the deepest differences which divide writers and thinkers, and, it may be, human beings in general. For there exists a great chasm between those, on one side, who relate everything to a single vision, on system . . . in terms of which they understand, think and feel—a single universal, organizing principle in terms of which alone all they are and say has signifi-

cance — and, on the other side, those who pursue many ends, often unre-
lated and even contradictory . . . without, consciously or unconsciously,
seeking to fit them into . . . [a] unitary vision.[5]

Hedgehogs are committed to the pursuit of the ideal of an undivided
self. They believe that we should do our best to come as close as we can
to having it. If we succeed, our self will no longer be divided, our sensibility will not be dissociated, we will not have conflicts between our
present and future self, and we will not be beset by problems.

One of the most articulate contemporary hedgehogs is Charles Taylor. He says about his collected essays that they are "the work of a mono-
maniac; or perhaps better, what Isaiah Berlin has called a hedgehog."[6]
Being a hedgehog is to be committed to strong evaluation that "is concerned with the qualitative *worth* of different desires." It is to eschew
the consummation of some desire because we judge that it is "bad, base,
ignoble, trivial, superficial, unworthy, and so on."[7] There are "standards,
independent of my own tastes and desires, which I ought to acknowledge."[8] How do we know what these standards are? Taylor's answer is
that we begin with "an inner impulse or conviction which tells us of the
importance of our natural fulfilment." But it is not merely a subjective
one but "the voice of nature within us" (369–70).

> My claim is that fulfilling my nature means espousing the inner élan, the
> voice or impulse. And this makes what was hidden manifest both for my-
> self and others, But this manifestation also helps to define what is to be
> realized (374–75). If nature is an intrinsic source, then each of us has to
> follow what is within (376).

Taylor's view is that our individual nature is part of the nature of the
world. Implicit in the world is the standard by which we can distinguish
between good and bad. We can do so by listening to our inner voice,
which is the voice of nature speaking through us. Strong evaluation enables us to satisfy our

> craving for being in contact with or being rightly placed in relation to
> the good [which] can be more or less satisfied in our lives. [This is not] a
> matter of more or less but a question of yes or no. And this is the form in
> which it most deeply affects and challenges us. [It dictates] the direction

of our life, towards or away from it (45). We cannot do without an orientation to the good [and] this sense of my life having a direction towards
what I am not yet (47).

Strong evaluation makes our self undivided, unifies our sensibility, and
helps us avoid problems that prevent us from living as we think we
should. Taylor says that this can be captured by seeing our life "as a
quest for the good" (48).

Taylor's view is a restatement of the basic assumptions of the evaluative framework that existed before the seventeenth century, except that
he, unlike Eliot, leaves out of it the authority of the Catholic Church.
He uses the language of an inner voice, but his point does not depend
on it. We can substitute for the inner voice the categorical imperative,
conscience, faith, intuition, self-control, self-knowledge, or, indeed,
strong evaluation. The point remains that it comes from within us,
guides how we think we should live, and we distinguish between good
and bad, better and worse possibilities by its deliverances. If we fail to
follow it, we fail ourselves.

Taylor does not think that what the inner voice tells us is self-
generated. It certainly speaks to us from within us, but it expresses the
inspirational force of some ideal we have internalized from the evaluative framework of our society. It articulates the ideal of an undivided
self and a way of life, and we can and should become wholeheartedly
committed to it. The ideal strikes us with compelling force. We may
grow up already possessing it because it was part of our upbringing and
education which we share with others in our evaluative framework.
Or we may encounter it in later life, and then experience it as conversion, being born again, or, less dramatically and without religious con-
notations, as the articulation of something that we have inarticulately
sensed for a long time without realizing what it was. We come to see
in terms of the ideal our previous self as divided, as lacking unity, as
having had a floundering, uncertain existence, or, in religious terms,
as having lived in sin. But the ideal that we have made our own shows
us the way in which we should aim at an undivided self, and live as we
should. We see our life in terms of what it was before and what it became after we have been overpowered by the ideal.

It makes no difference to the compelling force of the inner voice of
the ideal how we have come to it. It may have been as a result of the in-

fluence of some authority, dogma, education, faith, ideology, morality, miracle, religious experience, upbringing, or something else. It may have been our encounter with a work of art, the corruption of our society, the experience of great evil, witnessing the life and actions of an admirable person who may not even know of our existence, and so forth. What matters is not how we became dedicated to the ideal, but that it is now our own, it overpowers us, commitment to it is our deepest response that overrides all else, and, if we listen to it, it guides how we should live. Novalis described Spinoza, wrongly I think, as a God-intoxicated man. Intoxication with an ideal, however, is an apt way of characterizing its overpowering influence on those who come to be possessed by it. The ideal is not merely a passive, contemplative point of view from which we interpret and evaluate our experiences. It compels us to make our life a quest for coming as close as we can to living and acting according to the ideal. The quest aims to make our divided self undivided.

This account of the ideal of an undivided self is too abstract and general. To make it less so, I will now consider two remarkable people. Each had an undivided self, unified sensibility, certainty undaunted by adversity, and the life of each was a quest. Each believed, in Walter Pater's words that "to burn with this hard, gem-like flame, to maintain this ecstasy, is success in life."[9] Hernan Cortes's ideal was conquest; Simone Weil's was self-transformation. Each trusted an inner voice, and each had disastrous consequences.

Hernan Cortes[10]

Cortes was a Spanish conquistador who achieved a military feat the like of which has not been seen since Alexander's conquest of much of Asia. Cortes arrived from Cuba to Vera Cruz in 1519 with a ragtag troop of about 400 mercenaries, a few pieces of light artillery, sixteen horses and a few dogs, both bred and trained for war. The distance from Vera Cruz to what is now Mexico City, then called Tenochtitlan, is about 200 miles. The way to it was over high mountains, uncharted, and narrow mountain passes guarded by tens of thousands of hostile local troops. Cortes's aim was to conquer the Aztec Empire, which had a population of about 25 million. Tenochtitlan was the Aztec capital. It had about

200,000 inhabitants. It was then the largest city in the world, but Europeans did not know of its existence until a few years before Cortes's arrival. The Aztecs had an affluent agrarian economy, a flourishing and highly developed culture with elaborate religious rituals, keen aesthetic sensibility, skilled craftsmen, finely wrought gold and silver works of art, a sophisticated method of writing and calendar-keeping unheard of by Europeans, festivals in which everyone participated, aristocratic warrior and priestly classes, and millions of people under their rule whom they have conquered in wars and from whom they extracted tributes. Their religious rituals involved extremely cruel sacrifices of thousands of people (to which I will return in chapter 11). Their Empire was rich, sophisticated, unified, and without serious rivals, not unlike the Roman Empire was at its zenith. Montezuma was then the absolute political, religious, and military ruler of the Aztec Empire.

Cortes crossed the mountains, massacred (this is not a figure of speech) tens of thousands of hostile tribal warriors along the way, and eventually arrived to Tenochtitlan. The city was surrounded by a lake. It was accessible only by three causeways, and was defended by a well-trained army of seasoned warriors. For reasons that have not been fully explained, Montezuma allowed Cortes and his troops to enter Tenochtitlan. Soon thereafter Cortes repaid Montezuma's hospitality by taking him hostage. He then secured Montezuma's compliance by threatening him with the same ghastly tortures as Cortes had inflicted on Montezuma's courtiers and with the devastation of his Empire. Montezuma crumbled, and by using him as his mouthpiece, Cortes assumed command first of Tenochtitlan and later of the Empire. He then destroyed their sacred religious objects, killed their priests, melted down the plentiful gold and silver artifacts, and arranged to ship to Spain the immense fortune of an estimated 180 tons of gold and 16,000 tons of silver. Eventually the Aztecs revolted and tried to expel Cortes and his troops. Cortes killed Montezuma, defeated the vast army the Aztecs had assembled, and reduced Tenochtitlan to rubble. He did all this with a few hundred men.

In the course of approximately two years that elapsed between landing in Vera Cruz and conquering the Aztec Empire, Cortes faced enormous odds against him, overcame obstacles with treachery and undaunted personal courage, showed unyielding determination, mercilessly killed all who opposed him, constantly strengthened the weakening resolve of his Spanish followers, and was not known to have felt, not even at the worst moments, the slightest uncertainty about continuing his quest and the eventually succeeding in conquering the Aztec Empire. One result of his triumph was that between 1520 and 1600 the population of what used to be the Empire was reduced from 25 to 2.5 million. Another result was the destruction of the flourishing Aztec culture. The cost in Spanish lives was a few hundred. These figures put Cortes in the company of Stalin, Hitler, and Mao. He did burn with hard gem-like flame. The enormity of Cortes's crimes, however, should not blind us to the inhumanity of the Aztec Empire. Nevertheless, the crimes of the Aztecs claimed perhaps tens of thousands of victims, while those of Cortes claimed millions.

Why did Cortes do all this? Why did he embark on the conquest? What made his self undivided, his sensibility unified, and his certainty untouched by conflicts, difficult choices, and problems? I turn to Elliott, the outstanding English-speaking historian of Spain (see Note 10), for answers to these questions. Cortes lived from 1469 to 1527. He came from a Castilian family of minor nobility. Throughout his life he was fiercely loyal to the Catholic Church and the Spanish King, who then was Charles V.

> Charles V embraced the imperial theme and [saw himself] . . . as being on the way to achieving universal empire . . . in which in the words of Saint John's gospel [John 10:11] "there shall be one flock and one shepherd." Here . . . was the providential mission, of the union of all mankind beneath the government of a single ruler, foreshadowing the return to universal harmony (4).

It is not a mistake if these words bring to mind the lamentable chant of "Ein Volk, Ein Reich, Ein Fuhrer." In any case, this was the ideal whose chosen instrument Cortes conceived himself as being. This is what motivated him as well as all those Castilians who took part in the conquest of what is now South America.

> The Roman Empire became a model and a point of reference for the sixteenth-century Castilians, who looked upon themselves as the heirs and successors of the Romans, conquering an even more extended empire, governing it with justice, and laying down laws which were obeyed

to the farthest ends of the earth. . . . The sixteenth-century Castilians saw themselves as a chosen, and therefore a superior people, entrusted with a divine mission which looked to universal empire as its goal. This mission was a higher one than that of the Romans because it was set into the context of Catholic Christianity. The highest and most responsible duty of Castile was to uphold and the extend the faith, bringing to a civilized and Christian way of life . . . to all those benighted peoples who, for mysterious reasons, had never until now heard the gospel's message (9).

The source of this vision were the Franciscan advisers of Charles V, some of whom accompanied Cortes and acted as his spiritual guide throughout the conquest. They

provided Cortes with an enlarged vision, not only of the new church and the new society to be built in Mexico, but also of his own special role in the providential order. He had . . . been careful to insist that God had arranged the discovery of Mexico in order that Queen Juana and Charles V should obtain special merit by the conversion of its pagan inhabitants. It followed from this that he himself, as the conqueror of Mexico, enjoyed a special place in the divine plan. The attitude of the Franciscans was bound to encourage him in this belief, for to them he inevitably appeared as God's chosen agent at a vital moment in the ordering of world history—the moment at which the sudden possibility of converting untold millions to the Faith brought the long-awaited millennium within sight (39).

Cortes never deviated from his quest. Nor did Charles V who used the immense wealth Cortes looted from the Aztecs and shipped back to Spain to finance his wars aiming at the establishment of a universal Catholic empire of united Europe under Spanish rule. The many millions of people—not just Aztecs but also Peruvians and Europeans—who were killed in the wars, epidemics, and starvation, and the ruin of hitherto flourishing empires was, in the view of those possessed by this vision, a negligible if regrettable price to pay for the success of their quest. However, that quest, as all others in human history, came to nothing. Millions of eggs were broken, but no omelet was baked. All this was made possible by the undivided self, unified sensibility, and utter certainty of people like Cortes.

Simone Weil

She was also on a quest, but the only person she killed was herself at the age of thirty-four. She was born in 1909 into an affluent, secular Jewish family in Paris, and died in 1943 in London during WWII. She graduated in philosophy from the École Normale Supérieure, whose mission was to educate the future intellectual elite of France. Throughout her life she was frail, sickly, and suffered from frequent headaches. At the age of sixteen she had a religious experience, became intoxicated with God, wanted to convert to Catholicism, but moral scruples prevented her. She could not reconcile the immense compassion she felt for human suffering with God's supposed goodness and she could not accept the authority and the sacraments of the Catholic Church. She had no doubt whatsoever that the fault was hers: insufficient faith, understanding, and moral commitment—in a word, her imperfections. She expressed these sentiments in a series of letters to a Dominican priest, Father Perrin, on whom she relied for spiritual guidance throughout her life. The passages I quote come from her letters to him.[11] Her life was a quest whose aim was to make herself less imperfect. This was her ruling passion, the source of her terrible opinion of herself, and of her unwavering commitment to the quest directed inward toward overcoming her imperfections.

She writes about her religious experience that

> we experience the compulsion of God's pressure, on condition we deserve to experience it. . . . God rewards the soul which thinks of him with attention and love, and he rewards it by exercising a compulsion upon it which is strictly and mathematically in proportion to this attention and love (2). The idea of purity, with all that this word can imply for a Christian, took possession of me at the age of sixteen (18)

She concluded that since she had not felt the compulsion strongly enough to accept the sacrament, her attention to and love of God must be insufficient. For this reason, she wrote,

> I consider myself to be unworthy of the sacraments. This idea . . . is due . . . to a consciousness of very definite . . . and even shameful faults. . . . The kind of inhibition which keeps me outside the Church is due . . . to my state of imperfection" (3–4). "I have the germs of all possible crimes,

or nearly all, within me. . . . The crimes horrify me, but they did not sur-
prise me . . . they filled me with such horror" (5). "I am an instrument
which is all rotten" (46) and "I think when I consider things in the cold
light of reason that I have more just cause to fear God's anger than many
a great criminal (48).

She wrote all this by way of a spiritual autobiography at the age of
thirty-two, shortly before her death. She castigates herself although
she had lived, by ordinary evaluations, not only a completely blameless
life, but one of Christian purity, service, compassion, self-denial, while
suffering from various illnesses and severe recurrent headaches. She
was a dedicated high school teacher, took leave from it to do manual
work and thereby express solidarity with working people, went to Spain
in 1936 to join the Republican forces, she was passionately concerned
with social reform, wrote books and articles about it, lived simply on
her meager earnings, barely ate, dressed shabbily, had no love affairs,
and, apart from her family, Father Perrin, and one other Catholic ad-
viser many years her senior, she had no close friends.

In the midst of all this she undeviatingly and unquestioningly per-
severed in her quest. She writes that "I have never even once a feeling
of uncertainty" (26), that her "particular vocation demands that my
thought should be indifferent to all ideas without exception" (35) since
that would interfere with her quest for overcoming her imperfections
because she wanted to free herself from her "painful spiritual state" because her "eternal salvation was at stake" (9–10). [All references are
to Letters except the last, which is to Last Letter]. Her unwavering certainty, sense of vocation, and her conviction that her eternal salvation
was at stake made her a terribly difficult person. Her hagiographic biog-
rapher writes that she

> was sometimes absurdly intransigent . . . arguing *ad infinitum* in an in-
> exorable monotonous voice . . . and Father Perrin . . . confesses that, in
> spite of her desire for truth and enlightenment, he never remembers her
> to have given way in a discussion.[12]

She writes with absolute conviction that

> all the texts [of the Old Testament] . . . are, I think, tainted with funda-
> mental error (14), all peoples at all times have always been monotheistic
> (15), our civilization owes nothing to Israel and very little to Christianity;

it owes nearly everything to pre-Christian . . . Germans, Druids, Rome, Greek Aego-Cretans, Phoenicians, Egyptians, Babylonians (19), Heraclitus recognized a Trinity . . . The Persons are: Zeus, the Logos, and the divine Fire of Lightning (25), it shows a lot of presumption to suppose that the apostles misunderstood Christ's commands, I can only answer that there is no doubt at all that they did display incomprehension (30) [References are to *Last Letter*].

Remarks such as these have led people to describe Simone Weil variously "as a victim of spiritual delusion, a social prophet, a modern Antigone or Judith, and a new kind of saint."[13] Having read her books and letter, I attribute all this to spiritual delusion. I ask, however, why others have regarded her as a modern saint? Largely, I think, because of her death, which was of a piece with her life.

She died in London in 1943. She was there to support the Free French Forces. She was as frail and sickly as ever, but was then rapidly becoming emaciated. She insisted on eating no more than the rations the Germans officially allowed to those in occupied France. Not surprisingly, she contracted tuberculosis. She struggled on untreated but was eventually hospitalized. Her physicians repeatedly told her that unless she eats more she will die. Nevertheless, she absolutely refused, and did die. She was thirty-four. She harmed no one but herself and those few who loved her. Her self was undivided, sensibility unified, and she was absolutely certain that she was not worthy of the God she worshipped and that she must make herself worthy by making herself less imperfect. But an undivided self may be deluded, a unified sensibility may be destructive, and certainty may be baseless. Her quest to overcome her imperfections led to the deliberate decision to die rather than to deviate from her certainty about how she ought to live. She was intransigent and deluded. If that makes her a modern saint, then she was that. I find it impossible, however, to share that opinion.

Reasonable Doubt

In their very different ways, and for very different reasons, the lives of Hernan Cortes and Simone Weil should make it obvious that a divided self, a dissociated sensibility, conflicts, and difficult choices are preferable to the quests of Cortes and Weil, as well as to the like quests of religious fanatics, political ideologues, terrorists of various persuasion, and murderous scourges of the supposed enemies of a race, nation, ethnic group, or tribe. They all do what they do because their inner voice tells them. And some of them burn with hard gem-like flame.

My point is not that all quests have disastrous consequences. They may be those of dedicated statesmen, scientists, artists, and other bene-factors of humanity. My point is that living such a life involves great risks both for those who embark on it and those who are affected, for good or ill, by their consequences. Quests can go horribly wrong. Whether or not they do does not depend on the dedication of the quest-ers to following their inner voice, nor on the strength and constancy of their efforts, but on the consequences to which they lead and the means by which the consequences are brought about. Our inner voice is no more reliable than the outer voices that may guide how we live. It is reasonable for both individuals and evaluative frameworks to recog-nize that there are reasons both for and against pursuing the ideal of an undivided self, unified sensibility, and certainty about the overriding importance of whatever our quest happens to be. However, if we recog-nize it, we will face conflicts, have to make difficult choices, and come face to face with a human predicament.

If we compare our contemporary evaluative framework with the Christian one that had dominated Europe for more than a millennium, we realize that ours is a result of contingent historical developments that might have been different. We realize that our art, economy, his-tory, laws, literature, morality, politics, religion, and science would have been other than they now are if other conditions had formed them. We realize that the reasons and evaluations we derive from the modes of evaluations that guide how we should live are as contingent as the modes of evaluations from which we derive them. Their contin-gency does not undermine the importance they have for us. Contin-gent or not, they provide the possibilities whose realization, we believe, would enable us to live as we think we should. We are often dissatisfied with some possibilities, but their importance does not diminish even if our dissatisfactions run so deep as to make us question our entire evaluative framework. We can question it, or indeed anything else, only in terms of the reasons and evaluations we derive from our evaluative framework and personal attitude formed of our beliefs, emotions, and desires.

We could abandon our evaluative framework and immerse ourselves in another. But the reasons and evaluations that guide our choices must have some basis, and that must be some evaluative framework and personal attitude from which we could derive our reasons and evaluations. If we opt for another evaluative framework, radically change our personal attitude, and derive our reasons and evaluations from them, we will still have the problem that the fit will be imperfect between how we think we should live and how we can live in the circumstances in which we find ourselves. We will then face the same problem as we now have with our present evaluative framework, and we will have gained nothing by abandoning it and choosing another.

Alternatively, we may abandon all evaluative frameworks, since they all lead to the same problem. That means, however, abandoning all modes of evaluation, all bases from which we could derive our reasons for evaluating the possibilities of our lives. We could not, then, distinguish between good and bad, better or worse possibilities, beyond the primitive necessity of having to satisfy our most basic needs. We could not live a recognizably human life without some evaluative framework whose guidance we accept—and chafe under. We are therefore saddled with conflicts, choices, and problems that we have to face when we realize that the fit between our evaluative framework and personal attitude is always imperfect, the prevailing modes of evaluation always yield conflicting evaluations, and changing conditions always require us to evaluate again and again the changing possibilities of life. This is not a peculiarity of our evaluative framework. The same is true of the Christian one, as well as of those of Homer, Sophocles, Plato, Zen Buddhists, Hobbes, Spinoza, Kant, and any other we might think of. It is a human predicament.

However, it is a characteristic feature of our evaluative framework that its modes of evaluations are many, and that there is no generally agreed hierarchical order in which their relative importance could always be arranged. The reasons and evaluations that follow from them often conflict, make us conflicted, and we cope with such conflicts by giving precedence to one mode of evaluation in one context and to another in another context. The reasons by which we evaluate our possibilities are plural and context-dependent. That does not cast doubt on the reliability of some of the reasons that may guide us, but it makes us realize, if we are thoughtful enough, that the search for an ideal theory of a dominant, hierarchical system of reasons and evaluations is doomed to fail, even though it has ruled many evaluative frameworks in the past.

Something like the creed of Rousseau's Savoyard Priest has motivated the search for an ideal theory in the past and continues to do so in the present. Those devoted to it want to be able to say to themselves: "what I feel to be right is right, what I feel to be wrong is wrong" (249). Conscience! Divine instant, immortal voice from heaven . . . infallible judge of good and evil, making man like God (254)."[14]

It would be a great comfort to convince ourselves of this. But we cannot reasonably do that. We have or should have learned from history to distrust the supposed authority of an inner voice. Cortes and Weil believed otherwise, and their lives stand as warnings of how dangerous are quests like theirs. We have come to doubt that there is, or that we can reliably discern the nature of, a providential order from which we could derive a hierarchical system of values. And even if we are unable to give up the search or the hope for such an order, we cannot be confident that any religion, ideology, or metaphysical system can be an authoritative guide to what it is. The widespread contemporary experience of the divided self, dissociated sensibilities, conflicts, and difficult choices are unavoidable consequences of our evaluative framework being what it is. I do not think that these consequences are simply good or simply bad. There are reasons both for and against welcoming them.

One important reasons for welcoming them is that they help us to avoid the doomed quest for an ideal theory. They help us to accept the plurality of reasons and evaluations, their conflicts, our fallibility, and that we lack a universal standard to which we could appeal to evaluate our reason, resolve their conflicts, and guard against our fallibility. We have many defects, but the failure to find a universal standard is not one of them. It is not there to be found. The quest for it is misguided and often disastrous. One no less important reason against welcoming them is that we now each have to cope with our divided self, the dissociated sensibility, conflicts, difficult choices, and problems that follow from it. I now turn to negative capability as a possible way of coping with these problems.

Negative Capability

If Keats's famous letter had not been written a little more than hundred years before Eliot lamented the dissociation of our sensibility, negative capability could be thought of as a response to dissociated sensibility—a response that Eliot must have known but, oddly, ignored. Keats's words were:

> Several things dove-tailed in my mind, & at once it struck me what quality went to form a Man of Achievement, especially in Literature, and which Shakespeare possessed so enormously—I mean *Negative Capability*, that is, when a man is capable of being in uncertainties, Mysteries, doubts, without any irritable reaching after fact and reason.[15]

In his fine biography of Keats, drawing on all that is known about Keats's thoughts, letters, and poems, Bate paraphrases these much-quoted sentences as follows:

> in our life of uncertainties, where no one system or formula can explain everything—where even a word is, at best, in Bacon's phrase, a "wager of thought"—what is needed is an imaginative openness of mind and heightened receptivity to reality in its full and diverse concreteness. This, however, involves negating one's ego. . . . To be dissatisfied with such insights as one may attain through this openness, to reject them unless they can be wrenched into a part of the systematic structure of one's own making, is an egoistic assertion of one's identity.[16]

The great religions, metaphysical systems, and the poetry of Homer, Virgil, Dante, Spenser, Milton, and Donne are alike in presupposing an evaluative framework in terms of which everything can be ultimately evaluated. They are also alike in not having survived the crucial test of giving a convincing explanation of why it is more reasonable to accept one of these evaluative frameworks than other, no less consistent and systematic attempts at ultimate evaluations. Historical, anthropological, literary, and philosophical comparisons between these all-embracing evaluative frameworks enable us to understand and perhaps even to admire the different visions that animate them. But that is not an adequate reason for accepting any of them in preference to the others and for dedicating our life to wholeheartedly following them.

An adequate reason would have to establish that one of these evaluative frameworks is more reasonable than competing ones. The reason defenders of the supremacy of an evaluative framework need to give does not depend on adducing facts that confirm it and disconfirm the competing ones. Enduring religious, metaphysical, and ideological evaluative frameworks can rarely be faulted for getting the facts wrong. Their sophisticated defenders can readily accommodate well-known commonsensical and newly discovered scientifically accredited facts, and they can agree with their critics about what the facts are.

What defenders of an evaluative framework cannot provide is a reason that would convince their critics of the supremacy of their evaluative framework that the relative importance they attribute to the facts is more reasonable than what is done by their rivals. They would need to provide a reason why conflicts between aesthetic, economic, historical, legal, medical, moral, political, religious, scientific, and other modes of evaluation and reasons should always, in all circumstances, be resolved in favor of the one among them that should always override conflicting evaluations. They would have to give a convincing answer to the question of why one of the undoubted values of beauty, compassion, conscientiousness, faith, happiness, health, justice, law, liberty, peace, prosperity, truth, and so forth should always, in all circumstances, be so important as to override the conflicting claims of the others. The search for such a reason has been going on for millennia, but has not been found. And the reason for that is that it is not there to be found. It has been well said that

> The conviction, common to Aristotelians and a good many Christian scholastics and atheistical materialists alike, that there exists . . . a single discoverable goal, or pattern of goals, the same for all mankind—is mistaken; and so, too, is the notion bound up with it, of a single true doctrine carrying salvation to all men everywhere, contained in natural law, or the revelation of a sacred book, or the insight of a man of genius, or the natural wisdom of ordinary men, or the calculations made by an elite of utilitarian scientists set up to govern mankind.[17]

Negative capability is to accept this fact and to give up the illusion that if we look hard enough, we can arrive at an evaluative framework that can accommodate all known facts, provide a standard by which we can evaluate their relative importance for how we should live, resolve our conflicts, make difficult choices easy, and enjoy having an undivided self, unified sensibility, and face no serious problems about how we should live. Negative capability is to know, when we leave childish things behind, that there is no Garden of Eden to which we could return, that we have eaten the apple and cannot undo our knowledge of the good and evil we encounter in the world and perhaps even in ourselves, and that we must live with the resulting problems to which our conflicts and difficult choices lead.

Negative capability, however, is negative. It tells us that we should not expect that our life will be a long blissful picnic with loving family, friends, and lovers in the cool shade of a well-tended garden as our children, dogs, and cats joyously cavort in the benign sunshine. It does not tell us how we might cope reasonably with our divided self, dissociated sensibility, conflicts, and difficult choices that result from abandoning the hopeless quest for the realization of an impossible dream. What, then, can we do? How, then, should we live?

We should acknowledge the obvious fact that our evaluative framework is an unstable compound of often conflicting modes of evaluations and of reasons that follow from them. We should accept that their conflicts are unavoidable consequences of our pluralistic evaluative framework and that life in our society can be civilized only if we find reasonable ways of coping with these conflicts and make the choices. We can take comfort in the fact that we have found such a way: a way that is context-dependent, not universal; concrete, not abstract; and particular, not general. We can normally find a more reasonable way of coping with a context-dependent, concrete, and particular conflict than any of the alternatives to it. But finding it takes experience, good judgment, and objectivity, all of which are in short supply both in us and in our society. And even if we find the most reasonable way of coping with a conflict and making a difficult choice, it will not carry over to other conflicts, choices, times, and circumstances. Our problems will remain.

The key to coping with our problems is to recognize that the protection of our entire evaluative framework is more important than the protection of any of the conflicting modes of evaluations and reasons that are parts of it. The evaluative framework and its parts are interdependent. Coping with conflicts among the parts requires subordinating one part to another, but its subordination is only temporary. It is based on the evaluation that in a particular context one of the conflicting parts is more important for the protection of the entire evaluative framework than the other parts. In another context, however, the evaluation may be to favor the temporarily subordinated part. That is why coping with conflicts is context-dependent.

It is also concrete and particular because the evaluation depends on what the conflicting parts are. The conflict is always between particular modes of evaluation and reasons. In one context, when truth conflicts with peace, justice with compassion, law with liberty, health with prosperity, then perhaps the first in these pairs is more important than the second. But in another context the reverse may be the case. If the conflict is between the true historical account of the origin of a war and making peace depends on ignoring the true account, then the latter may be reasonably regarded as more important. If the severity of just punishment is extenuated by compassion, then compassion may rightly override the severity of just punishment. If the law conflicts with liberty of conscience, or if prosperity is diminished by the protection of public health, then the reasonable evaluation may favor the second alternatives over the first.

There will likely to be conflicting evaluations also of the relative importance of these conflicting evaluations. But if the evaluations are reasonable, conflicts between them will not be intractable. Their defenders could agree that protecting the evaluative framework they share is more important than resolving conflicts in favor of their own evaluation. They can agree then that the reasonable way of making the difficult choice they face is to ask whether in their context, at that time, in those circumstances, concerning that conflict, which is more important for protecting their shared evaluative framework: Truth or peace? Justice or compassion? Law or liberty? Health or prosperity? And given their agreement, it will transform their conflict from a deep disagreement about modes of evaluation and reasons into a practical disagreement about finding the best means to the shared end of protecting their evaluative framework.

This assumes that it is reasonable to want to protect the evaluative framework. Perhaps its problems are so deep as to undermine commitment to it. This could happen, and if it does, it leaves those who used to be committed to it with two options. One is to make radical changes to the aspects of the evaluative framework that are the sources of the problems. This is, for better or worse, what the French tried to do in 1789, the Russians in 1917, and the Chinese and Japanese, in very different ways, after WWII. Although the problems of the contemporary Western evaluative framework are many, they are not as deep as these others were. We can protect our evaluative framework by reforming some of its aspects, while relying on its other aspects. The other option is to abandon the entire evaluative framework. This is perhaps the worst thing that could happen to a society, short of extermination by enemies they cannot resist, as the Aztecs could not resist Cortes. But we have not yet come to so sorry a pass as to have to choose between these options. And the difference between our context and these others strengthens the case I have been making for the coping with our problems by treating them as context-dependent, particular, and concrete. If we cultivate negative capability will be able to seek and often find a *modus vivendi*. And that is surely preferable to the destructive consequences of the doomed quest for an illusory ideal.

8   The Complexities of Problems

The Problem

Legal obligation and personal loyalty, truthfulness and ambition, discipline and comfort, social harmony and deep conviction, impartiality and love are familiar conflicts in everyday life. We consider what we should do when we face them, and find that sometimes we have much stronger reasons for acting on one of the alternatives than on the other. Such conflicts are simple. Sometimes, however, we have strong reasons for acting on both alternatives and we cannot decide which are stronger. Then the conflict is complex. One source of complexity is that one set of reasons follows from the prevailing modes of evaluation in our society, the contrary reasons follow from our personal attitude, formed of our beliefs, emotions, and desires, and both sets of reasons guide how we think we should live. I will call evaluations that follow from the prevailing modes of evaluation social, and those that follow from our personal attitude personal.

Coping with simple conflicts is relatively easy because our society's modes of evaluation and personal attitude to some extent coincide. Our personal attitude is unavoidably influenced by the social evaluations to which we are exposed in the course of our upbringing, education, and contacts with others. But the extent to which social and personal evaluations coincide vary. Complex conflicts occur when they diverge. And the more they diverge, the more frequent complex conflicts between social and personal evaluations become. These conflicts are always wrenching because they indicate that we are uncertain about how we should live. If we resolve the conflict in favor of personal evaluations, it puts us at odds with our society. If we resolve it in favor of social evaluations, it stifles our personal evaluations. What, then, should we do when they conflict?

A tension in John Stuart Mill's thought—I do not say contradiction—illustrates how this complex conflict affected his works. It follows from *On Liberty* that personal evaluations should override social ones because

> the free development of individuality is one of the leading essentials of well-being . . . it is not only a co-ordinate element with all that is designated by the term civilization, instruction, education, culture, but is itself a necessary part and condition of all those things. . . . The evil is that individual spontaneity is hardly recognized by the common modes of thinking as having any intrinsic worth, or deserving any regard on its own account.[1]

In *Utilitarianism*, however, he wrote that

> laws and social arrangements should place . . . the interest of every individual as nearly as possible in harmony with the interest of the whole; and . . . establish in the mind of every individual an indissoluble association between his own happiness and the good of the whole (17) . . . [and] this feeling of unity [should] be taught as a religion, and the whole force of education, of institutions, and of opinion directed . . . to make every person grow up from infancy . . . by the profession and practice of it (32).[2]

Like Mill, we certainly have strong reasons for living in harmony with the social evaluations we share with others. And no less certainly, we have strong reasons for following our personal evaluations of how we should live. We need to find a reasonable way of coping with such conflicts. As we will see, there is much that we can learn from Montaigne about how we can do that reasonably.

If we are undamaged adults, we rely on our personal evaluations. They are personal in that they are our own evaluations, but they are not personal in the quite different sense that the rightness or wrongness of our evaluations depends only on what our beliefs, emotions, and desires are. Our beliefs may be false, emotions excessive, deficient, or misdirected, and desires ill-advised. Personal evaluations may be corrected by social evaluations and social evaluations may be criticized if they stifle personal evaluations. They are at once interdependent and conflicting. That is why their conflicts lead to complex problems.

Personal evaluations that neglect social evaluations are seriously defective. And so are social evaluations that ignore personal evaluations. It adds to the complexities of the resulting conflicts that both personal and social evaluations change, but in different ways and for different reasons. Personal evaluations change because we learn from experience, failure, and other people, and, as a result, may revise how we think we should live. Social evaluations change in response to the changing conditions of our society. These changes may or may not be connected. We may change how we think we should live in response to social changes, or we may change it as a result of coming to a deeper personal understanding of the prevailing social evaluations. In trying to grapple with the complex problems caused by the conflicts and interdependence of personal and social evaluations, we must begin with avoiding several misunderstanding of both kinds of evaluation.

Avoiding Confusion

First, social evaluations need not be public, a personal evaluations need not be private. Personal evaluations are public, if they are based on well-known and widely shared legal, moral, political, religious, or other evaluations we have derived from our society. And social evaluations are private if they concern how reasonable or realistic are our personal evaluations, for instance, of the significance of death, health, salvation, sexual preferences, success or failure, or wealth.

There can be no simple way of deciding whether the reasons are stronger for or against conflicting social and personal evaluations. If in doubt, consider whether our evaluations of addiction, raising children, pornography, shame, or suicide are or should be thought of as social or personal. Social and personal evaluations are historically conditioned and context-dependent, just as the distinctions are between what is legal and illegal, prudent and imprudent, and important and unimportant.[3]

Second, personal evaluations may or may not be self-centered. They certainly reflect our personal attitude, but that typically involves the evaluation of our relationships with others who are committed to the same institutions and practices in which we do or might participate.

Personal evaluations are concerned with living as we rightly or wrongly think we should. But they are seriously impoverished if they ignore other people and the society in which we live. We usually share at least some of our personal evaluations with others who are committed to the same legal, moral, political, religious, or other modes of evaluation. Personal evaluations are personal because we are voluntarily committed to living according to them without being compelled to do so by social forces. It does not make them less personal if we have derived them from the prevailing modes of evaluation. The voluntariness of our evaluations is crucial, not their origin.

The evaluations that follow from different modes often conflict, and then we have to choose between them. Such choices may or may not be personal, depending on whether one of the conflicting legal, moral, political, or religious evaluations is generally accepted in our context. If there is no generally accepted way of deciding the relative priority of conflicting social evaluations, then the choice between them must be made personally by those who face the conflict. It adds to the complexities of coping with such conflicts that personal and social evaluations may both be mistaken. The first because how we think we should live may be based on our mistaken personal attitude, and the second because the modes of evaluation may be defective.

Lastly, none of us is the only one who has access to our personal evaluations. Our intimates may know as well as we do what our personal evaluations are or should and would be. And they may know it better than we do if we happen to be thoughtless, inarticulate, preoccupied, or under much pressure. Personal evaluations are our own, we have the authority and responsibility for making them, but we are not always the only ones who know, or know best, what they are.

Personal and social evaluations often conflict. Then the more we cultivate one, the less we can rely on the other. We know from daily experience that living as we think we should is curtailed by social evaluations we have accepted. And we know also that we have accepted them partly because they protect the conditions that enable us to live as we think we should. But they conflict in countless ways and we often have strong reasons to be guided by both because they are evaluations we accept. Whatever we end up doing then will be contrary to living as we think we should. This makes the choice between them difficult. And the question is how we should make them.

Difficult Choices

Hobbes thought that we should make them in favor of social evaluations because

> there is in men's aptness to Society, a diversity of Nature, rising from their diversity of Affections; not unlike that we see in stones brought together for building an Edifice. For as that stone which by the asperity, and irregularity of Figure, takes more room from others, than itself fills; and for the hardness, cannot be made plain, and thereby hindered the building, is by the builders cast away as unprofitable and troublesome: so also, a man by that asperity of Nature will strive to retain those things which to himself are superfluous, and to others necessary; and for the stubbornness of his Passions, cannot be corrected, is to be left, or cast out of Society, as cumbersome thereunto.[4]

According to this way of thinking, the conflict between social and personal evaluations is only apparent. Social evaluations are presupposed by the personal ones, so they cannot conflict:

> What we call an individual man is what he is because of and by virtue of community, and that communities are not mere names but something real. . . . He is what he is because he is born and educated social being, and a member of an individual social organism. . . . If we suppose the world of relations, in which he was born and bred, never to have been, then we suppose the very essence of him not to be [168] . . . He appropriates the common heritage of his race, the tongue that he makes his own is his country's language, it is . . . the same that others speak, and it carries into his mind the ideas and sentiments of the race . . . and stamps them indelibly. He grows up in an atmosphere of example and general custom. . . . If he turns against this he turns against himself; if he thrusts it from him, he tears his own vitals; if he attacks it, he sets his weapon against his own heart [172].[5]

A sociological and an anthropological argument for the same point is in note 6.[6]

The possibility that social evaluations might override personal ones was anathema to the Mill of *On Liberty*, as well as to his many followers:

He who lets the world, or his own portion of it, choose his plan of life for him has no need of any other faculty than the ape-like one of imitation . . . it is so much done toward rendering his feelings and character inert and torpid instead of active and energetic.[7]

As Hayek put it in the title of his early book, this is the road to serfdom.[8]

But if personal evaluations override social ones, then what stops us from regressing into the barbaric state of nature from which living in our society was meant to rescue us? According to Hobbes,

during the time men live without a common power to keep them all in awe, they are in that condition which is called Ware; and such a Ware, as is of every man, against every man. . . . To this ware of every man, this is also consequent; that nothing can be Unjust. The notions of Right and Wrong, Justice and Injustice have there no place. Where there is no common Power, there is no Law; where no Law, no Injustice. . . . In such condition, there is no place for Industry; . . . no Culture of the Earth; no navigation . . . no Arts; no Letters; no Society; and which is worst of all, continual feared, and danger of violent death; And the life of man, solitary, pore, nasty, brutish, and short.[9]

A contrary argument for defusing the conflict between social and personal evaluations is that social evaluations presuppose personal ones, rather than the other way around. Human actions are unavoidably the actions of individual human beings. We may join together and act collectively, of course, but whether we do so depends on our personal evaluations. In fact, whatever we do, whatever strong or weak reasons we have for doing it, depends on our evaluations of our reasons we should or should not follow. Such evaluations need not be conscious, articulate, or reasonable, but they motivate all human actions that go beyond merely instinctive responses to our surroundings.

This remains so even when our actions are based on social evaluations. For we will act only if motivated to act, and social evaluations can motivate us only if our personal evaluations prompt us to follow them. We may follow them because we are forced, manipulated, deceived, or just stupid, but unless we follow them, we will not and could not act. This is not the consequence of a theory or a principle, nor the peculiarity of a society at a particular time. It is a fact about all human beings, like having a head or aging. Social evaluations must presuppose personal evaluations because personal evaluation is a necessary condition of all, but the most primitive action. This is a matter of fact, not of evaluation. What is a matter of evaluation is why and how well or badly, reasonably or unreasonably we act. And even if that evaluation were always social, its acceptance would reflect our personal evaluations. Of the many evaluative implications of this view I cite one:

> among the duties of self-perfection is the conscientious man's commitment to live without evading any issue—to seek out and weigh what cogent reasons would lead him to do, and to submit himself without self-deception or evasion to their determination. One cannot derive that one ought to live in this manner from one's special obligations towards others. For one may never duly confront any of one's special obligations unless one is already willing to live that way. . . . And this commitment has the most intimately personal reason. It rests on an individual's inmost concern to preserve himself intact as a living and functioning self: mentally in possession of himself and of his world, able to look at himself and what he is doing without having to hide himself from himself.[10]

Social evaluations, then, are thought to presuppose personal ones because personal evaluations of how we should live are necessary conditions of any social evaluation we might follow. All subsequent personal and social evaluations depend on this most basic evaluation.

This argument for personal evaluations being presupposed by social ones is no more persuasive than the reverse. Any reasonable personal evaluation of how we should live must be based on something. And whatever that is partly depends on satisfying our needs and avoiding injuries by relying on social evaluations of what possibilities are acceptable. Our unavoidable dependence on social evaluations is just as much a universal fact of human life as that human actions must be the individual or collective actions of human beings. The salient point is that they are interdependent and we have strong reasons for being committed to both social and personal evaluations.

Conflicts

Social and personal evaluations, however, are not just interdependent but also conflicting, and therein lie the complexities of the problem.

If resolving their conflicts in favor of social evaluations threatens with despotism and resolving them in favor of personal evaluations threatens with anarchy, then what should we do? The first step toward an answer is to understand that the source of their conflicts is not an aberration for which we or our society could always be blamed. No doubt, we and it are often blameworthy. But it is far too simple to suppose that their conflicts are always caused by avoidable mistakes. Social and personal evaluations would conflict even if they were as free of mistakes as they could possibly be.

The society in which we live must coordinate and thus limit the ways in which we can live. We are unavoidably subject to legal, moral, political, religious, and other limits to what we can do, regardless of how we think we should live. The limits curtail our possibilities. That is a fact of social life that would remain unchanged even if we and our society were both perfect. Of course, we and it are and have always been imperfect, and that is one source of human predicaments. We want to have more or different possibilities than our society provides and fewer or different limits to which we are subject. These problems, however, are always context-dependent and historically conditioned because they are caused by the particular possibilities and limits of our context. Social evaluations will defend existing possibilities and limits; personal evaluations will oppose at least some of them. Bradley and Hobbes are certainly right to stress the formative influence of the social on the personal. And Mill and Hayek are no less right to stress the importance of the personal to the social. But both fail to recognize that

> neither in the social order, nor in the experience of an individual, is a state of conflict the sign of vice, or defect, or a malfunctioning. It is not a deviation from the normal state of a city or of a nation, and it is not a deviation from the normal course of a person's experience. To follow through the ethical implications of these propositions about the normality of conflict . . . a kind of moral conversion is needed, a new way of looking at all the virtues, including the virtue of justice.[11]

Underlying their failure is

> the optimistic view . . . that all good things must be compatible, and that therefore freedom, order, knowledge, happiness . . . must be compatible, and perhaps even entail one another in a systematic fashion. But

this proposition is not self-evidently true, if only on empirical grounds. Indeed, it is perhaps one of the least plausible beliefs entertained by profound and influential thinkers.[12]

Abandoning the optimistic view that has persisted in the face of contrary historical evidence that again and again falsified the latest restatement of it, and giving up the hope for a life that is free of conflicts, in which all problems have a solution, and no choices are difficult is only a first step. It enables us to avoid misunderstanding the conflicts between our social and personal evaluations, but it will not tell us what we should do about them. I now turn to the help we might get from Montaigne's *Essays*. His proposal is that we should cope with our conflicts and make difficult choices by balancing the claims of social and personal evaluations without assigning overriding importance to either of them.

Michel de Montaigne

There is a long philosophical tradition whose aim is to resolve conflicts between social and personal evaluations by proposing one or a small number of principle(s) or value(s), base a theory on it, and claim that reason requires everyone to accept its priority to any consideration that may conflict with it. Hobbes, Locke, and Rousseau, among numerous others, start with a hypothetical state of nature; Hume begins with sympathy as the master motive; Mill proclaims a simple principle in *On Liberty*, and the greatest happiness for the greatest number in *Utilitarianism*; Kant postulates the categorical imperative; Rawls says that justice is it; Nozick thinks that it is rights; Dworkin claims that it is equality; according to Hayek it is liberty; Habermas thinks that it is an ideal speech community; and so endlessly on.

I follow Machiavelli who presciently rejected all such theories, regardless of their content.[13] He thought of them as

> waste of time with a discussion of an imaginary worlds . . . that have never existed and never could; for the gap between how people actually behave and how they ought to behave is so great that anyone who ignores everyday reality in order to live up to an ideal will soon discover he has been taught how to destroy himself.[14]

Montaigne agreed.[15] He proposed no theory, no authoritative principle, no highest value, and he did not deduce anything from anything else. He began with everyday life, told stories, reflected on examples, and offered suggestive metaphors. For contemporary readers like myself, his approach is a refreshing breeze in the arid, scholastic, ahistorical, abstract domain presided over by theorists who prescribe how reason requires everyone to live. Montaigne treats his readers as intelligent grown-ups "who live in the world and make the most of it as [they] find it" (774). For reasons that will soon appear, I begin with a brief sketch of his life.

He was born in 1533 into a Gascon Catholic family of lesser nobility, residing not far from the city of Bordeaux. He was educated at home, where he learned Latin before French, and later at one of the best schools of France. He was trained in the law, and, at twenty-four, became a Councillor in the Parlement of Bordeaux, where his duties required him to participate in legislation and act as something like a magistrate. During this period he married, had six children, all but one of whom died in infancy, and formed the most significant relationship of his life: a friendship with La Boetie, who died from a painful illness four years later. In 1570, after thirteen years of service, Montaigne retired to his estate "long weary of the servitude of the court and of public employments . . . where in . . . freedom, tranquility, and leisure" (ix–x). He intended to read and reflect, and began to record his thoughts in a form that eventually resulted in the *Essays*.

But two years later he was called out of retirement to act as a mediator between the warring Catholics and Protestants of France. As a moderate Catholic and an experienced man of affairs, he was acceptable to both parties. He was intermittently engaged in this for four years. In 1580, when he was forty-seven, the first edition of the *Essays*, containing Books 1 and 2, appeared. It was well received. Montaigne, then, traveled for almost two years in Switzerland, Germany, and mainly in Italy. In his absence, he was elected Mayor of Bordeaux, a prestigious office he did not seek and was reluctant to accept. But he was prevailed upon, and, when his two-year term came to an end, he was given the rare honor of a second term. After this, like Cincinnatus, he once again took up residence at his estate, finished Book 3 of the *Essays* and kept revising the first two books. The three books were first published together in 1588, when he was fifty-five years old. He continued revising them until the end. He died in 1592, a few months before his sixtieth birthday.

He was rightly honored as a wise, eminent scholar, and a distinguished public servant. This no doubt pleased him, but what he most deeply cared about was the *Essays*. He said of it that it is

> a book consubstantial with its author. . . . I have no more made my book than my book has made me. . . . [It is] concerned with my own self, and integral part of my life . . [and that] in modeling this figure upon myself, I have had to fashion and compose myself so often to bring myself out, that the model itself has to some extent grown firm and taken shape (504).

He lived and acted, but he also reflected on it, wrote it all down, and through his writing constructed a model for himself. Thus he came closer to being as he wanted to be.

My present interest in the *Essays* is the light it sheds on Montaigne's thinking about the relation between social and personal evaluations. One of his metaphors is:

> He who walks in the crowd must step aside, keep his elbows in, step back or advance, even leave the straight way, according to what he encounters. He must live not so much according to what he proposes to himself but according to what others propose to him, according to the time, according to the men, according to the business (758).

Civilized life is possible only if we live in a society, but then we must learn to walk in a crowd. Otherwise, we will be "cast out of Society, as cumbersome thereunto," as Hobbes succinctly put it.[16] Learning it consists in learning to be guided by social evaluations. We live in our society and thus have to walk in a crowd because we want to get to somewhere. But where we want to get depends on our personal evaluations, and that, Montaigne thinks, is up to us. How we might get to wherever we want to go must be adjusted to what we encounter along the way, and that is largely beyond our control. This raises the obvious question of how we can be guided by social evaluations and yet retain enough of our personal evaluations to enable us to live as we think we should, not as social evaluations dictate. The beginning of Montaigne's answer is that

> there is no one who, if he listens to himself, does not discover in himself a pattern all of his own, a ruling pattern (615). [Finding that pattern is] the greatest task of all . . . to compose our character . . . not to compose books, and to win, not battles and provinces, but order and tranquility in our conduct. Our great and glorious masterpiece is to live appropriately [according to that pattern]. All other things . . . are only little appendages and props, at most (850–51).

This may seem at first like the familiar romantic illusion that we can leave society behind, turn inward, and concentrate on the fine-tuning of our soul. But this is not Montaigne's view. He knows that we cannot opt out of society because we have basic physiological, psychological, and social needs that we either satisfy or come to a bad end. We need to earn a living, have some companionship and protection of our security; and, short of being brutish troglodytes, we need some contact with other people and the institutions and practices of our society. Montaigne knew all this; struggled with the conflict between social and personal evaluations, and offered the influential answer of an experienced, reflective, worldly person.

> We must live in the world and make the most of it such as we find it (774). [Doing that, however, is corrupting] whoever boasts, in a sick age like this, that he employs a pure and sincere virtue in the service of the world, either does not know what virtue is . . . or if he does know, he boasts wrongly, and, say what he will, does a thousand things of which conscience accuses him (759).

So wrote Montaigne in the imperfect sixteenth century, and so we may say, even if only *sotto voce* and less honestly than he did, in our century whose imperfections have not appreciably diminished since then.

> The justest party is still a member of a worm-eaten maggoty body. But in such a body the least diseased member is called healthy. . . . Civic innocence is measured according to the places and the times (760).

Civic innocence is a paltry thing. Montaigne supposed, however, that we need to compromise only our social evaluations, which are the bulwark protecting our "strategic retreat into an inner citadel," as Berlin put it about the pursuit of positive freedom.[17] Montaigne thought that the wise man should withdraw his soul within, out of the crowd, and keep it in freedom and power to judge things freely; but for externals, he should wholly follow the accepted fashions and forms. Society in general can do without our thoughts; but the rest—our actions, our work, our fortunes, and our very life—we must [only] lend (86).

As for personal evaluations,

we must reserve a back shop all of our own, entirely free, in which to establish our real liberty and our principal retreat and solitude. Here our ordinary conversation must be between us and ourselves, and so private that no outside association and communication can find a place (176–77).

It is now beginning to look as if Montaigne sided with those who claim that when they conflict, personal evaluations should have priority over social evaluations. This would make him liable to the criticism I mentioned earlier that personal evaluations unavoidably depend on the prevailing social evaluations for resources required for our sustenance, protection, and daily life. But Montaigne avoided this problem. He knew that we must live in the world and cannot have a civilized life apart from other people and the prevailing institutions and practices. The prevailing modes of evaluation are also *our* modes of evaluation, even if we are critical of some of them, and even if we some of our personal evaluations conflict with them.

It is very easy to accuse a government of imperfection, for all mortal things are full of it. It is very easy to engender in people contempt for their ancient observances; never did a man undertake that without succeeding. But as for establishing a better state in place of the one they have ruined, many of those who have attempted it have achieved nothing for their pains (498).

What, then, are we to do if we see the faults of the prevailing social evaluations for what they really are, as Montaigne saw the faults of those in his time and context. We know that we depend on faulty social evaluations for living as we think we should. But how can we reasonably depend on conditions we know are faulty and withdraw from them into our back shop? If depending on them is reasonable, then withdrawing from them must be unreasonable. And if withdrawing from them is reasonable, then what could we withdraw to that is left untainted by the corrupting influences of the faulty social evaluations that had formed our personal evaluations through upbringing, education, and daily contact with others? Nothing could escape what Montaigne much too sanguinely calls mere imperfections. Montaigne's answer is that

> I do not want a man to refuse, to the charges he takes on, attention, steps, words, and sweat and blood if need be. . . . But this is by way of loan and accidentally, the mind holding itself ever in repose and in health, not without action, but without vexation, without passion. . . . But it must be set in motion with discretion. . . . I have been able to take part in public office without departing one nail's breadth from myself, and to give myself to others without taking myself from myself (770).

Has he forgotten his own words that "whoever boasts, in a sick age like this, that he employs a pure and sincere virtue either does not know what virtue is . . . or boasts wrongly" (759)?

Doubts

We can understand and sympathize when Montaigne recognizes that both social and personal evaluations are essential to living as we think we should. It may be true that all personal evaluations, except the most primitive ones, had been in some way derived from social evaluations. And it may also be true that we would find social evaluations unacceptable unless they coincide with at least some of our personal evaluations. He may be right: personal evaluations without social ones would have no content and social evaluations unsupported by personal ones would not be acceptable. The two kinds of evaluation are interdependent and living as we think we should depends on balancing their conflicting claims. But none of this comes even close to acknowledging the problem that if the modes of evaluation from which we derive our personal evaluations are faulty, then so are the personal evaluations we cultivate in the back shop to which Montaigne advised us to retire. Montaigne did not face the implications of his recognition of the interdependence of social and personal evaluations. That recognition was one of his great achievements. Not facing its implications was his failure.

Montaigne's announced aim was to face and record facts, warts and all, about himself and the world as he found it. He did this in the *Essays* in great detail. It may seem perverse to claim then, as I will now do, that he stopped short sooner than he should have. But that is what he did. He did not ignore facts that were available to him. He ignored the obvious implication of facts of a certain kind, namely the bad ones, that is, facts that are bad from the human point of view. He certainly did not shy away from registering them. He saw the sickness of his age, the imbecility of the laws, the injustice and cruelty of much punishment, the intolerance that spawned the religious war that was tearing France apart, the venality of the people he encountered, as well as his own faults. And he saw also, as we know from the many historical examples he cites, that bad facts, allowing for local variations, were pervasive throughout history. How could he have gone further? By asking obvious questions: why are bad facts as pervasive as he rightly claimed? What do they imply about human beings and societies? How is it possible that the bad facts all reasonable people deplore nevertheless exist and persist?

All we know about Montaigne suggests that he must have been aware of these questions. Yet he does not discuss them. I can only speculate why he did not. Perhaps he was afraid of the Church or secular authorities, or his temperament was too sanguine to dwell on the dark side of life, or he was more interested in other matters. The fact remains that he does not discuss and certainly does not answer these questions. But if we are interested in the conflicts between social and personal evaluations, it becomes unavoidable to ask whether the causes of bad facts are mainly personal evaluations that have been corrupted by social evaluations, which, in turn, have been corrupted by the faulty modes of evaluation of our society? Or, are the causes of bad facts mainly our personal evaluations that have been corrupted by our stupidity, irrationality, or vices? Bad facts are obstacles to living as we think we should. And we need to answer the question of whether surmounting the obstacles depends on correcting our personal or our social evaluations.

It adds force to these questions if we bear in mind that there are also good facts. Are their causes mainly personal or mainly social evaluations? And when good and bad facts conflict, as we all know they do, how should we resolve their conflicts if they are both caused by one or another of our evaluations? Are the social or personal evaluations that lead us to cause them not our own evaluations? And what could or would motivate us to act contrary to our own evaluations? We should not shy away from asking these questions because we cannot understand why the choices we have to make are difficult unless we, at the very least, face and discuss their difficulty.

Toward Realism

In order to do so, I return to the optimistic view that I argued earlier is presupposed by both parties in the conflict between social and personal evaluations. Both parties assume that ultimately one or another kind of evaluation should have priority over the other and the conflicts between them should be resolved in favor of the one that has priority. This assumption is based on the optimistic view that the conflicts between them can be resolved once and for all and the problem is only to find that final solution. Ultimately, one kind of evaluation will have priority over the other when they conflict, and we should be guided by that one. If we are not, the assumption is, it is only because we are mistaken about which should have priority.

I have already argued that this assumption is mistaken. There is no way in which the relative priority of social and personal evaluation could be established once and for all, since it varies with contexts, depending on the contents of the social and personal evaluations, and the changing conditions of our society. One will have priority in a particular context, but contexts change, and their relative priority will change with them. Furthermore, even if there were a final resolution of the conflict between social and personal evaluations, the conflict between good and bad motives within each of us would persist. The assumption, therefore, would remain mistaken.

Defenders of the optimistic view would deny this. They would say that if we were aware of the goodness or the badness of our motives, we would resolve conflicts between them in favor of the good ones. What is the justification of this assumption? Why would we not resolve conflicts between good and bad motives in favor of the bad ones, or sometimes in favor of one and other times in favor of another depending on our shifting preferences, rather than on their goodness or badness? I can think of only one justification for this assumption: human beings are basically good. If that were true, then, if we understood the goodness or badness of our motives, we would indeed tend to resolve conflicts between them in favor of the good ones.

This assumption has been and continues to be widely held by many influential thinkers, even though they disagree about a great many other matters. Perhaps Montaigne is one of them. I have no textual support for this, but it would explain what would otherwise be unexplained: he did not ask the deeper questions about the implication of the bad facts he described because he thought that the answers were obvious. He thought, I am supposing, that bad facts are pervasive because basically good human beings are corrupted by their society and its defective modes of evaluation. Whether or not I am right about Montaigne's acceptance of the belief that human beings are basically good, other distinguished thinkers certainly accepted it: Hume thought that

> it requires but very little knowledge of human affairs to perceive, that a sense of morals is a principle inherent in the soul, and one of the most powerful that enters into the composition. But this sense must certainly acquire new force, when reflecting on itself, it approves of those principles, from whence it is deriv'd, and finds nothing but what is great and good in its rise and origin.[18]

According to Rousseau, "man is naturally good; I believe I have demonstrated it".[19] In Kant's words, Man is

> not basically corrupt (even as regards his original predisposition to good), but rather . . . still capable of improvement" and "man (even the most wicked) does not, under any maxim whatsoever, repudiate the moral law. . . . The law, rather, forces itself upon him irresistibly by virtue of his moral predisposition.[20]

Mill held that

> The leading department of our nature . . . this powerful natural sentiment . . . the social feeling of mankind—the desire to be in unity with our fellow creatures, which is already a powerful principle in human nature, [is] happily one of those which tend to become stronger, even without inculcation.[21]

In Rawls's view,

> men's propensity to injustice is not a permanent aspect of community life; it is greater or smaller depending in large part on social institutions, and in particular on whether they are just or unjust.[22]

If human beings were basically good, then the prevalence of bad facts would have to be explained by something interfering with the motivational force of our basic goodness. And that something must be the society—what else could it be—in which live. It is our defective social evaluations that corrupt our personal evaluations, and motivates us to cause the bad facts. That is why in the passage above Rawls attributes injustice to unjust social institutions.

This optimistic view has been and continues to be immensely influential. It acknowledges the dark side of life, the horrors of past and present atrocities, and yet allows those who hold it to rhapsodize with Rousseau about our idyllic pastoral existence before we have been despoiled by civilization; to say with Hume that the sense of morals is inherent in the soul; with the faith of Kant that we are not basically corrupt; and with Rawls' attempt to theorize as if the horrors of the past and the present did not contradict his rosy picture of humanity. They all believe that although we may be corrupted, we remain perfectible because our basic goodness is ineradicable. That is why our personal evaluations, the carriers of our basic goodness, take priority over our corruptible, or corrupted, social evaluations. There is, therefore, hope for the future. We can correct our bad motives. The key to it is to pursue policies that abolish or reform corrupting social institutions and practices. This optimistic view is the animating force of contemporary morality and politics. It has been growing in strength at least since the unsilenced Pelagian heresy.

I must now say, not without heartache, that it is untenable. This becomes obvious if we ask what made the corrupting social institutions and practices corrupting. Social institutions and practices exist because human beings create and maintain them. If the institutions and practices are corrupting, it is because those who create and maintain them make them corrupting. Their corruption is the effect of corrupting causes, and those causes are human beings. The optimistic view is untenable because it explains causes by their effects. Human beings are the causes. The institutions and practices we create and maintain are the effects. The causes come first and the effects can only follow. We are the corruptors of corrupt institutions and practices.

It is a subterfuge to say that we corrupt institutions and practices only because we ourselves have been corrupted by other institutions and practices. For the identical question must be answered about those other corrupting institutions and practices: how did they become corrupt? Defenders of the optimistic view, if reasonable, must sooner or later acknowledge that we are the causes that corrupt institutions and practices. And if many institutions and practices are bad—and who can reasonably deny that?—then the unavoidable consequence is that many of us are bad. And that makes the optimistic view untenable. This much seems to me undeniable.

There is, however, more that needs to be said to avoid jumping to the equally implausible pessimistic view that we are *only* bad. Some institutions and practices are good and they are made good by human beings who create and maintain them. And that means that we are also good. Since there are both good and bad institutions and practices, we who create and maintain them are both good and bad.

I conclude that we are neither basically good, nor basically bad, but much of the time ambivalent. This leads to one, among the many and various kinds, of difficult choices we have to make between our possibly mistaken social and personal evaluations. We often have strong reasons for attributing greater importance to both of them, but we cannot do that simultaneously and reasonably. And we often have strong reasons to suspect both our social and personal evaluations because it is unlikely that they are free of the ambivalence that seems to be inherent in our nature. Ultimately, after we have done all we reasonably could, we will continue to have to cope with the resulting conflicts and make difficult choices. This is what "our nurse-maids try to appease with their lullaby about Heaven."[23]

9   Unavoidable Hypocrisy

Hypocrisy[1]

Dictionary definitions give us a starting point. According to the *OED*:

> Hypocrisy. The assuming of a false appearance of virtue or goodness, with dissimulation of real character or inclination, esp. in respect of religious belief, hence in general sense, dissimulation, pretense, sham.

Random House defines it as:

> Hypocrisy. 1. A pretense of having a virtuous character, moral or religious beliefs or principles, etc. that one does not really possess. 2. a pretense of having some desirable or publicly approved attitude.

Hypocrisy involves the misrepresentation of our personal attitude to how we think we should live. It is formed of our beliefs, emotions, desires, experiences, and history. There may be many reasons for misrepresenting it: haste, stress, ignorance, self-deception, or the deliberate intent to deceive others. The last is necessary but not sufficient for hypocrisy, because the misrepresentation may be harmless or even benevolent words or acts of politeness, reticence, tact, or white lies. It is hypocritical only if it is self-interested, deliberate, and aims to make us appear in a more favorable light than we would be if the truth were known.

Hypocrisy is when a corrupt politician tries to be reelected by accusing opponents of corruption, or when a manufacturer, bent on maximizing profit by fraudulent practices, accuses his competitors of fraud. Hypocrisy, therefore, is not only the failure to live up to our responsibilities, but to contrive to give the false impression that we are living up to it in order to promote some self-interested aim. The misrepresentations of hypocrites are deliberately pursued means to self-interested ends.

It is virtually impossible not to act hypocritically at least sometimes. The demands of our personal attitude and of the variety of social positions we occupy as parents, colleagues, citizens, neighbors, sons or daughters, workers, friends, lovers, teachers, and so on often conflict. Each imposes on us responsibilities that we are expected to live up to and we often find that an onerous task. We may believe that some people do not deserve what we are responsible for according them. We may rightly or wrongly resent, envy, or be jealous of them. We may be tired, bored, judgmental, ache to turn inward away from the pressure of obligations to others, or just to take a brief holiday from the responsibilities imposed on us by the often unchosen social positions we occupy in our society.

If we let on that we have more important things to do than to take our child to see a promised movie, or to waste time exchanging trivial conversation with a neighbor, or are impatient with unresponsive students, or find it hard to be polite to unpleasant people, then we fail in the responsibilities of parenthood, neighborliness, pedagogy, or politeness. We do not want to be seen as defaulting on what we ought to be or do and pretend to do willingly what we in fact begrudge doing. We do it to appear in a better light than we would be if we were truthful about our unsocial, self-interested inclinations. If we misrepresent in these and other ways our personal attitude in order to appear in a more favorable light than we would be without misrepresentation, then we are hypocritical.

Who among us is not hypocritical at least sometimes? Even Flaubert mitigated his heartless portrayal that unmasks Madame Bovary's hypocrisy by owning up to: "Madame Bovary, c'est moi." And there is the same cynical relish with which sociologists, like Erving Goffman and Pierre Bourdieu, and ever so clever deconstructionists, like Derrida, hypocritically pretend to perform a service by doing what Burke rightly condemned:

> All decent drapery of life is to be rudely torn off. . . . All the super-added ideas . . . necessary to cover the defects of our naked shivering nature, and to raise it to dignity in our estimation, are to be exploded as a ridicu-

lous, absurd, antiquated fashion. . . . This barbarous philosophy, which is the offspring of cold hearts and muddy understandings, [is] void of solid wisdom.[2]

Many of the hypocrisies these unmaskers castigate are not momentous and do not reflect on us too badly. But the conflicts between our personal attitude and social responsibilities may concern weightier matters, such as protecting our loved ones, livelihood, or career. Our self-respect, ambition, living standard, social acceptance, security — generally, success in life — may depend on being hypocritical about our beliefs, emotions, desires, and about our past and present words or actions.

There may be strong reasons both for and against being hypocritical. In Hume's words:

By our continual and earnest pursuit of a character, a name, a reputation in the world, we bring our own deportment and conduct frequently in review, and consider how they appear in the eyes of those who approach and regard us. This constant habit of surveying ourselves, as it were, in reflection, keeps alive all the sentiments of right and wrong, and begets, in noble natures, a certain reverence for themselves as well as others, which is the surest guardian of every virtue.[3]

Hume's point is that how we evaluate ourselves and how others evaluate us are connected. What makes us care about how we seem to others is partly that how we seem to ourselves is strongly influenced by it. I have been arguing throughout the book that this is not surprising if we bear in mind that we and many others in our society participate in and have been formed by the same modes of evaluation. We evaluate ourselves and others by relying on the evaluations that follow from them. Our hypocrisy sometimes conflicts with the requirements of our evaluative commitments, but in many cases hypocrisy may indicate our acceptance of the requirements. In those cases, we may recognize that there can be strong reasons both for and against hypocrisy, and the reasons for it may be stronger than the reasons against it, as in criminal investigations, counterinsurgency, national security, diplomacy, and the protection of our privacy.

Another reason for it may be that by hypocritically misrepresenting our personal attitude we may improve it. This may happen if the misrepresentation motivates us to live up to our misrepresentation of it. We become better by endeavoring to live and act in ways we would if we were better than we in fact are. Consider an autobiographical report as a case in point:

> I did once command a ragged platoon of low-grade infantry that was pretty much left on its own over a couple of days, directly facing a larger and far more heavily armed enemy unit that seemed to be preparing to attack us. Had I been rational, I would have run away. Because I was too cowardly to flee, I had to pretend that I was filled with confidence — had to act as if I had something up my sleeve. Because the soldiers also resisted the impulse to run away, they had to accept my entirely spurious confidence as if it was soundly based. So we did not budge, and the enemy did not advance.[4]

As the commander's testimony makes clear, he deliberately misrepresented his self. His misrepresentation was self-serving because, as he says, "I was too cowardly to flee," and yet, assuming his platoon was fighting in a just cause, what he did was good rather than bad. He had strong reasons for doing it, his reasons were self-interested, but they also served other interests. Such cases are not rare. Hypocritical politicians who deceive the electorate in order to get reelected may champion much better policies than their authentic opponents. Hypocritical manufacturers who lie about their corruption in order to maximize their profit may actually produce much-needed and better goods than their authentic competitors.

What follows is that the wholesale condemnation of hypocrisy is much too simple. It is certainly true that if a worthy aim can be achieved both hypocritically and non-hypocritically, then there are strong reasons against being hypocritical. But it is also true that the choice is often unavailable. The hypocritical pursuit of self-interest may also serve the interests of others.

My interim conclusion is that whether hypocrisy is good or bad, whether the reasons for or against it are stronger depends on the context, on what the reasons actually are, and on the nature and importance of the requirements of the purposes served by hypocritical misrepresentations. These are often, although certainly not always, difficult matters of evaluation about which there can be reasonable disagreements. I will return to these problems after discussing authenticity.

Authenticity[5]

In its primary meaning, authentic is an adjective indicating that an object, often a work of art or an antique is genuine, not a fake, imitation, or a copy of the original. In its secondary, derivative meaning it is predicated of people whose words and actions are truthful, not hypocritical, representations of their personal attitude. The words and actions of authentic people are of a piece with how they are. What they say and do reveal what they are genuinely believe, feel, or desire to do. Unlike the deceptive words and actions of hypocrites, authentic people do not intend to deceive anyone. They genuinely are as they are shown by their words and actions. And they are authentic not as a means to something else, but because they think or feel that being truthful about themselves is intrinsically valuable, regardless of how others may judge it.

According to Rousseau, perhaps the most influential champion of authenticity, the conviction is what he puts in the mouth of the Savoyard Priest: "I need only to consult myself with regard to what I wish to do; what I feel to be right is right; what I feel to be wrong is wrong."[6] This is echoed by Charles Taylor:

> There is a certain way of being human that is *my* way. I am called upon to live my life in this way, and not in imitation of anyone else's. But this gives new importance to being true to myself. If I am not, I miss the point of my life, I miss what being human is for *me* . . . . Being true to myself means being true to my own originality, and that is something only I can articulate and discover. In articulating it, I am also defining myself. . . . This is the background that gives moral force to the culture of authenticity (28–29).

The widely felt force of authenticity is the importance attributed to being true to our personal attitude, to following its light, to being truthful about it regardless of social pressures and the great weight of tradition, convention, and public opinion exacting conformity to the prevailing modes of evaluation.

Thus understood, authenticity is obviously indefensible. The personal attitude to which we try to be true may be vicious, or inconsistent, fickle, or confused, and we may be mistaken about what we take it to be. The pursuit of authenticity may have consequences that no reasonable person could accept.

Consider first the possibility that the personal attitude is vicious. A case in point is Frantz Schmidt. We know about him from the diary he had kept throughout the many years during the sixteenth century when he was the official executioner in the city of Nuremberg.[7] Harrington, the author of book on which I rely, discovered the diary in which Schmidt recorded what he did and why.

> Overall, during his first decade of work for the city of Nuremberg, Meister Frantz performed 191 floggings, 71 hangings, 48 beheadings, 11 wheel executions, 5 finger choppings, and 3 ear-clippings. On average he put to death 13.4 people annually during this period and administered 20 corporal punishments (135).

He did this to those who have been tried and duly convicted crimes.

> Frantz Schmidt was not only a willing executioner but also a passionate one. His outrage at the atrocities committed by robbers and arsonists appears genuine and his commitment to restoring social order likewise heartfelt, not grudging or calculated. . . . Rather than suppressing or denying his emotions . . . Meister Frantz chose to channel them, providing the only relief he could to the victims of crime—legal retribution (122–23).

What did he do to the convicted people?

> During their slow procession to the execution site, Frantz administered the court-prescribed number of "nips" with red-hot tongs, ripping flesh from the condemned man's arm or torso. . . . Upon their arrival at the execution scaffold, Frantz then forced the weakened and bloody [man] . . . to strip down to undergarments, then lie down while the executioner staked his victim to the ground, meticulously inserting slats of wood under each joint to facilitate the breaking of bones. The number of blows with a heavy wagon wheel or specially crafted iron bar was also preordained by the court as was the direction of the procedure. If the judge and the jurors had wished to be merciful, Frantz proceeded "from the top down" delivering an initial "blow of mercy" (coup de grace) to [the victim's] neck or heart before proceeding to shatter the limbs of his corpse. If the judges deemed the crime especially heinous, the procedure went "from the bot-

tom up," prolonging the agony as long as possible, with Frantz hefting the wagon wheel to deliver thirty or more blows before the condemned men expired (47–48).

The office of the executioner was well-paid and coveted. Schmidt was trained to it by the executioner who preceded him and whom he succeeded. Nuremberg was then a Lutheran city and its laws and practices had the imprimatur of Luther himself who explicitly endorsed executioners and what they did:

> If there were no criminals, there would also be no executioners. The hand that wields the sword and strangles is thus no longer man's hand but God's hand, and not the man but God hangs, breaks on the wheel, beheads, strangles, and makes war.[8]

What are we to make of these horrors? Schmidt was a genuine and devout Lutheran. There is no doubt whatsoever that he truthfully represented his personal attitude and that his actions as an executioner were authentic. He genuinely believed that he was doing God's work. And his beliefs and actions, as well as his social position, were endorsed, respected, and well paid by the authorities in Nuremberg.

Nor is there any doubt that his actions were vicious regardless of how he and his society evaluated them. It is not just actions but also societies and their modes of evaluation that can be vicious. If in doubt, bear in mind Hitler's Germany, Stalin's Russia, Mao's China, and numerous other awful societies and their practices. That murderers and torturers may be authentic, that their atrocities are genuine representations of their personal attitude does not make their actions less vicious. Their actions, just as the Schmidt's, may be endorsed or even prescribed by the vicious modes of evaluation of their society. Perhaps if their modes of evaluation had been different, so would have been the perpetrators of these atrocities, including Frantz Schmidt. But that does not make his actions less vicious. How we judge the perpetrators is one thing, how we judge their actions is quite another. We may even excuse the perpetrators. But if we do, it must be because excuses are needed for their vicious actions.

However we judge the perpetrators of these atrocities, it is clear that there are overwhelmingly strong reasons against their authentic actions. It would have been far better if they had hypocritically refrained from what they authentically did. Perhaps criminals should be punished, perhaps even executed, but it is vicious to torture them before their execution. If it is hypocrisy that makes would be torturers refrain from authentically torturing them, then what they may hypocritically do is preferable to their authentic actions. It cannot be reasonably supposed, therefore, that authenticity is always preferable to hypocrisy. It would surely be much better if people whose personal attitude is vicious hypocritically misrepresent it and act contrary to its dictates than to be authentic and vicious.

Defending Authenticity

Taylor knows that authenticity may be vicious. What he says about it, however, gives a bad name to toleration:

> Authenticity can develop in many branches. Are they all equally legitimate? I don't think so. I am not trying to say that these apostles of evil are simply wrong. They may be on to something, some strain within the very idea of authenticity, that may pull us in more than one direction . . . even potentially to what we recognize as immorality (66).

Taylor, of course, deplores this strain within authenticity, but he owes an answer to the obvious question of how commitment to authenticity could avoid it. I turn now to his attempt to specify an ideal of authenticity in a way that excludes viciousness. As we have seen, Taylor thinks that

> there is a certain way of being human that is *my* way. I am called upon to live my life in this way. . . . If I am not, I miss the point of my life, I miss what being human is for *me*. This is the powerful moral ideal that has come down to us (28–29).

If this were all, it would follow that those who are hypocrites, or confused about what their personal attitude motivates them to do, or imitate others, or live in obedience to some authority, or frequently change their minds about how they should live and act are all authentic, just so long as they are consistently and genuinely hypocritical, confused, imitative, obedient, or fickle. No one could then fail to be authentic because we all live in some way, which is our way of living, and thus authentic, according to Taylor's odd interpretation of the ideal of authenticity.

It makes matters worse that Taylor claims that "the ethic of authenticity is something relatively new and peculiar to modern culture. Born at the end of the eighteenth century" (25).

This cannot be right because people obviously had many different ways of living even before the glorious eighteenth century supposedly bequeathed us the ideal of authenticity. As far as I can see, the only way to avoid the absurd consequences of this ideal of authenticity is to specify the content that would make a personal attitude authentic. And Taylor does try to specify it. In being authentic, people

are not left with just the bare facts of their preferences. . . . [In order] to understand better what authenticity consists in . . . the general feature of human life that I want to evoke is its fundamentally *dialogical* character. We become full human agents, capable of understanding ourselves, and hence defining an identity, through our acquisition of rich human languages . . . we are inducted into these in exchange with others who matter to us (32–33).

This, however, does not help to avoid the indefensible view that just about everybody is authentic. For all of us, being language-users, are engaged in what Taylor calls dialogue with some others who matter to us. We are all influenced by our parents, teachers, friends, legal, moral, political, or religious authorities through agreement or disagreement with them. What Taylor calls the dialogical character of authenticity still leads to the indefensible view that virtually everyone is authentic, because everyone is influenced by talking to others. Moreover, authentic viciousness is still not ruled because the modes of evaluation we and our dialogical interlocutors follow may itself be vicious, and so may we and the others be with whom we are having a dialogue. Something essential is still missing that would make Taylor's defense of authenticity reasonable.

Taylor says in *Sources of the Self*[9] that what is missing are

standards, independent of my own tastes and desires which I ought to acknowledge (4). [These standards are] the voice of nature within us

(369–70). My claim is that the idea of nature is an intrinsic source. . . . Fulfilling my nature means espousing the élan, the voice or impulse. And this makes what was hidden manifest for both myself and others. But this manifestation also helps to define what is to be realized (374–75). [Authenticity, then, is to follow this voice.] And since we cannot be indifferent to our position relative to this good . . . the issue of the direction life must arise for us (47).

Taylor claims then that authenticity involves the voice of nature within us. It is oriented toward the good, and that is why authenticity excludes viciousness.

I must now say that although I looked hard, I have not found any reason that Taylor gives for accepting that there is a voice of nature within us, that it, in some no doubt metaphorical sense, speaks to us, that what it says is manifest, and that it orients us toward the good rather than the bad. He does not say why the voice we supposedly hear is of nature, rather than of our upbringing, instinct, indoctrination, malevolence, fear, envy, or, indeed, viciousness? Why is it intrinsic rather than acquired? Why good rather than bad? Taylor does not say. He repeats, in a complicated way, laden with unsupported metaphysical assumptions and unnecessary jargon, what I have already quoted Rousseau's Savoyard Priest say simply:

> I need only to consult myself with regard to what I wish to do; what I feel to be right is right; what I feel to be wrong is wrong.

The authentic executioner and numerous other vicious ideologues and religious fanatics were doing what they felt was right, what they took the voice of nature within them to be saying to them, and they perpetrated atrocities. Taylor's defense of the ideal of authenticity fails to exclude the possibility that authentic people and actions are vicious. The hypocritical misrepresentation of a vicious personal attitude by non-vicious actions is surely far better than acting authentically and viciously.

Suppose, however, that viciousness is somehow avoided. Would that make authenticity a reliable guide to how we should live? It has been known and emphasized throughout the millennia, that we should be very skeptical about what we take to be the voice within us. What we mistakenly take to be the voice of nature may be self-deception, wishful thinking, ignorance of or denial of our real motives, the result of ideological or religious indoctrination or manipulation, rather than the authentic expression of our genuinely personal attitude.

Taylor's insistence that authenticity must be dialogical does not help to avoid such mistakes. Our dialogical partners, those we care about, talk to, and are influenced by may be as much mistaken about what they take to be the voice of nature as we are. And we care about our dialogical partners because we think that they are worth caring about. That thought, however, may be as mistaken as those we take home with us from the dialogue. It does not help Taylor's case that both we and our interlocutors follow the evaluations of our modes of evaluation. All of them may also be badly mistaken, as we know from the history of countless societies that produced, not just vicious monsters, but also deluded miserable humans who made their own lives and those of others miserable.

Such were those who heard the voice of nature tell them that masturbation, theater attendance, money lending, homosexuality, divorce, wine and coffee drinking, having a child outside of marriage, working on Sunday, atheism, polygamy, and countless other abominations are contrary to the voice of nature that authentically reveals what is good and bad. Taylor is much too civilized and tolerant to believe such nonsense. But the nonsense follows from trusting the voice of nature, and he gives no reason why anyone should share his trust.

He and like-minded champions of authenticity should bear in mind Sophocles' tragedy of Oedipus the King who never failed to follow what he took to be the voice of nature and to act authentically. Doing so brought great grief on everyone, himself included, who were affected by his authentic actions. He acted authentically in leaving behind his supposed parents who were not his parents; in killing the man who injured his pride who was his real father; in marrying the woman who was his mother; in trying to protect the city he ruled and upon which he brought the plague; in scorning Tiresias who told him the truth; in passionately pursuing the knowledge that ruined the lives of his wife/mother and of his daughters/sisters; and in swearing to punish the killer who was himself. Sophocles shows the untrustworthiness of authenticity.

Consider as another example the authentic life of Arthur Koestler who was neither vicious, like the authentic executioner, nor unaware, as Oedipus was, of the importance of skepticism about what his inner voice told him. Koestler was led by just such skepticism to become authentic again and again. He rejected his bourgeois upbringing and became an authentic communist; abandoned communism and became an authentic anticommunist; then he authentically turned to Zionism; then came close to being executed for being an authentic fighter against the Falangists in Spain; then he authentically immersed himself in psychoanalysis; then into being an authentic novelist; then into being an iconoclastic historian of science; then into an authentic scientist beguiled by psychic research, extrasensory perception, and clairvoyance; and no doubt he would have been led by skepticism to be authentic in other ways, if his authentic act of suicide had not put an end to his many different sequentially authentic activities. He was certainly authentic, but his authenticity was inconstant and fickle.

Some of his authentic activities were inconsistent with others, but even those were sequential and explainable by his frequent changes of mind. What was odd about his authenticity is the constant shift in what he thought mattered. He typically did not repudiate his earlier authentic activities, only lost interest in them. There is no reason to doubt that his many talents and interests led him from one authentic activity to another, but his authentic activities could be said to have represented his personal attitude only in the sense that his personal attitude was always changing according to what he temporarily regarded as important.

Taylor thinks that authenticity has to do with being true to our personal attitude. This assumes that there is an enduring personal attitude to be true to, an attitude that may be authentically represented or hypocritically misrepresented by our actions. Were Koestler's numerous activities authentic? Could it be reasonably said that his activities represented his personal attitude when he was forever changing the importance he had attributed to his activities? When do often changing representations of our personal attitude become misrepresentations? I am not sure. But I am sure that Taylor's assumption that authenticity depends on doing what we suppose the voice of nature tells is mistaken. It is more than a little odd to say that people know what the voice nature tells us them is important if they keep changing their minds about what is important, or that it tells the truth if they keep changing their minds about what the truth is.

I conclude that authenticity may be bad because authentic actions may be vicious, badly mistaken, inconsistent, or fickle. If authentic actions conflict with hypocritical ones, as they often do, either may be reasonably preferred to the other, in some cases, for some persons, at some times. If this context-bound conflict occurs, which is not always, then the choice between hypocrisy and authenticity becomes difficult because there are strong reasons for and against both. I will now discuss a context close to home in which this conflict does occur.

The Value of Life

In our society, a virtually universally shared attitude toward human life (simply life from now on) is that its protection is a basic value. The agreement may be expressed in various ways. The protection of life may be a human right, a primary good, prescribed by natural law, a necessary condition of human well-being, a requirement of reason or morality, and so forth. Theists, agnostics, and atheists agree on this point, and so do all those who are situated somewhere on the political spectrum between right and left.

There is also general, although not universal, agreement that there may be exceptional cases in which life can be justifiably or excusably taken (e.g. in self-defense, just war, or in order to save numerous other lives). The value of life is agreed to be basic, even if not absolute. But it is basic enough to make it universally agreed that there is a presumption in favor of protecting it and that the presumption can be overruled only rarely and in dire emergencies.

There are passionate disagreements about when the presumption in favor of protecting life can be justifiably overruled. This is the crux of the controversies about abortion, capital punishment, euthanasia, national security, suicide, and so forth. But those on opposite sides agree that life has basic value and disagree only about what is a justifiable or excusable exception to the presumption in its favor. This appears to be an authentic attitude toward life that expresses one of the most fundamental legal, moral, political, and often religious evaluative commitments of those living in our society.

The appearance, however, is misleading. A quick search on the web yields the information that in the U.S. in 2012 34,080 people died in motor vehicle accidents, and the figures are not significantly different in other years; there are approximately 88,000 deaths every year traceable to alcohol; and obesity is a significant contributing factor to roughly 300,000 deaths per annum. This information is widely available and no moderately intelligent adult in our society could fail to know that legislation lowering the speed limit, say, to forty miles per hour, outlawing alcohol, and prohibiting the sale of particularly fattening food and drinks would save many thousands of lives every year. Yet it would be politically impossible to enact such legislation. If it were nevertheless enacted, it could not be enforced. And if it were enforced, it would provoke at least widespread civil unrest, and, more likely, revolution. The widely proclaimed attitude to the basic value of life is contrary to the widespread habits of fast driving, drinking beer, wine, or hard liquor, and keeping an unhealthy diet.

These actions are contrary to the prevalent attitude to life as a basic value, so those who proclaim the attitude and act contrary to it are hypocritical, not authentic, regardless of how passionately they proclaim the basic value of life. Their lip service to the basic value of life seems to be sanctimonious verbiage that misrepresents the truth about themselves in order to cut a morally fine figure and thus appear to others in a favorable light. They are no different from politicians who take bribes and condemn bribery or from manufacturers who fraudulently maximize profit and accuse their competitors of doing the same. Are we to say then that the virtually universal attitude to life as a basic value is hypocritical, and that it should be unmasked and rejected?

No! Although it is hypocritical to claim that life is a basic value while acting contrary to it, there are also reasons for the claim. The strongest reason is that the protection of life is a minimum requirement of any civilized society. Of course there always have been and continue to be disagreements about how far the protection of life should extend, under what conditions could taking a life be justified or excused, and, as a result of new technology, what counts as life. But these disagreements presuppose that however life is defined, it is a basic value and that taking it needs to be justified or excused. It is true, and always has been, that those who claim to accept life as a basic value often hypocritically act contrary to it. That, however, does not call into question the importance of protecting it.

I have repeatedly argued that hypocrisy may sometimes be good, and authenticity may sometimes be bad. The reason for hypocritically protecting life is stronger than the reason for authentically denying its importance. A society that pays lip service to protecting life, while failing in various ways to protect it, is still better than one that authentically treats life as having no more value than education, peace, prosperity, security, and so forth. The reason for this is that the protection of life is a necessary condition of these other values. That is why there are strong reasons for thinking that life is a not just one value among others, but a basic one.

These reasons, however, are not conclusive, because there are also strong reasons against regarding the value of life as basic. One is that the mere fact of being alive is not a basic value. Prolonging life in a coma without the possibility of recovery, or a brain dead life, or a life of excruciating pain cannot be reasonably regarded as a *basic* value, even if it is still thought to have value. Life is a basic value provided it has certain qualities and possibilities, and meets at least some elementary conditions. The other strong reason against life having basic value is that just as life is presupposed by other values, so life presupposes other values. A life lacking the possibility of some choices, at least minimal resources, or one that is subject to unrelieved persecution and terror is not a recognizably human life. This is recognized by those who put an end to their miseries. There is a strong reason against claiming that a life devoid of these other values has basic value.

The strong reasons for and against life as a basic value conflict. Hypocrisy about it is supported by one set of strong reasons. Authentic denials that the bare fact of being alive has basic value is supported by another set of strong reasons. These reasons conflict and the choice between hypocrisy and authenticity, given these two sets of strong reasons, is difficult. I will shortly argue that the choice can nevertheless be made reasonably. But first I need to say more about what makes the choice between hypocrisy and authenticity difficult, not just about the value of life, but between hypocrisy and authenticity as overall evaluative commitments.

Hypocrisy or Authenticity?

The distinction between our personal attitude and the evaluations that follow from our modes of evaluation is not sharp. Our personal attitude is partly formed by these evaluations. Although there is considerable overlap between them — how considerable it is varies with individuals and contexts — they nevertheless differ. We cannot entirely lack a personal attitude because a fully human life requires more than an embryonic self that is only a grammatical subject to which character traits could be ascribed. The context of hypocrisy and authenticity, and of the conflicting strong reasons for and against each, is whatever the difference happens to be between our personal attitude and the modes of evaluation of our society.

The authentic expression of our personal attitude to others, especially if it is adverse and ambivalent, would often be destructive of our relationship with them. We can rarely tell others that we regard them as untrustworthy, stupid, vulgar, or motivated by spite. We hide from them that we are jealous or envious of them. Our various social positions often impose on us conflicting responsibilities and the authentic expression of our struggles with these conflicts would prevent us from living up to the responsibilities.

We cannot listen patiently to the confidences of a friend or the triumphs of our child unless we inauthentically disguise that we are impatient with hearing about yet another episode in a familiar pattern. We cannot be effective in politics or teaching if we authentically tell our supporters or students what we think of them. We want to fulfill the responsibilities of our various social positions, but can often do so only by being hypocritical about the expression of our personal attitude toward them. The strong reason for hypocrisy and against authenticity is that if we all became scrupulously authentic, we would make living with others impossible and destroy our personal relationships. As Molière's Philinte rightly says:

> In certain cases it would be uncouth
> And most absurd to speak the naked truth;
> With all respect for your exalted notions,
> It's often best to veil one's true emotions.
> Wouldn't the social fabric come undone
> If we were wholly frank with everyone?[10]

The strong reason against hypocrisy and for authenticity is that if we made hypocrisy a lifelong and pervasive policy of never expressing our personal attitude, our self would atrophy and be gradually transformed into a tool for pursuing forever changing opportunistic ends. Both the means and the ends would constantly shift in response to changing external conditions, our evaluative distinctions between good and bad, better and worse, possibilities would disintegrate, and we would be left without any constancy of motivation and purpose. We would be adrift in life. If we were systematically hypocritical, our self would disappear and be replaced by endless self-interested instrumental deceptions. We would become inconsistent poseurs through and through without a lasting core of genuinely held personal attitude.

But there is a strong reason also against following authenticity as a systematic policy: it would alienate us from others and make us into outcasts. Molière's Alceste accepts that:

> I fall into deep gloom and melancholy
> When I survey the scene of human folly,
> Finding on every hand base flattery,
> Injustice, fraud, self-interest, treachery. . . .
> Ah, it's too much; mankind has grown so base,
> I mean to break with the human race.

And his friend, Philinte, replies:

> The world won't change, whatever you say or do;
> And since plain speaking means so much to you,
> I'll tell you plainly that by being frank
> You've earned the reputation of a crank,
> And that you're thought ridiculous when you rage
> And rant against the manners of the age.[11]

What, then, should be the reasonable response to our conflicts between hypocrisy and authenticity? I answer: we should blunt rather than sharpen their conflicts by recognizing how dubious are both the blanket condemnation of hypocrisy and the blanket approval of authenticity. Consider the condemnation of hypocrisy first and the approval of authenticity next.

Perhaps the main reason for the condemnation of hypocrisy is that the deliberate misrepresentation of the hypocrite's personal attitude is self-interested. If it were not intended as a means to promoting self-interest but, say, to protecting national security, or misleading a dictator, or protecting the hypocrite's family, or deceiving persecutors, then it might even be praiseworthy. It becomes central, therefore, to the reasonable condemnation of hypocrisy to explain how to identify self-interested motives and how to distinguish them from motives that are not self-interested. The problem is that in most cases this is not easy to do.

No doubt, that there are some clear cases of purely self-interested misrepresentations, but even then their disapproval is often questionable. Was it really wrong for homosexuals even a few decades ago to lie about their sexual preferences in order to avoid prosecution, or for medieval heretics to pretend to be orthodox in order to escape the Inquisition? What would have clearly deserved condemnation is if homosexuals did not merely lie about themselves but actively persecuted other homosexuals in order to divert suspicion from themselves, or if heretics betrayed other heretics in order to curry favor with religious authorities. The point is that what matters is not that hypocrisy involves self-interested misrepresentation of our personal attitude, but whether or not the misrepresentation is reasonable protection against unreasonable threats.

If this is recognized, then the legitimacy of the blanket condemnation of hypocrisy becomes untenable. It depends on the context and times what self-protective misrepresentation of our personal attitude is reasonable and what persecution of what conduct is unreasonable? Are reformed criminals unreasonable if they misrepresent their record in order to get a job? Are politicians unreasonable if they misrepresent their youthful indiscretion to protect themselves from publicity hounding journalists?

Furthermore, in many cases, the hypocritical self-interested misrepresentation of our personal attitude is not only self-interested. The self-interest of hypocrites is often inseparable from the interest of their families; the reelection hypocritical politicians self-interestedly seek may also be in the best interest of those who voted for them; and the self-interested pursuit of wealth by hypocritical physicians posing as dedicated healers may also serve the interest of their patients. The accurate identification of a discreditable motive is not a sufficient reason for condemning the action prompted by the motive. There often are also other and creditable motives for the same action. Identifying a cause for anything is not a sufficient reasons for claiming to have identified the cause of it. Whether or not hypocrisy serves interests in addition to those of the hypocrite cannot be decided a priori. The reasonable evaluation of hypocrisy must be context-dependent and particular. And that makes the blanket condemnation of hypocrisy untenable.

Similar unclarity and context-dependence invalidates the blanket approval of authenticity. Authenticity requires words and actions that express our personal attitude. But the beliefs, emotions, and desires that form our personal attitude often conflict and change. The relative importance we attribute to them shifts as we age, learn from experience, grow in understanding, and respond better to our successes and failures, and to our satisfactions or dissatisfactions with our relationships with others and with the modes of evaluation of our society. Our personal attitude is not always a hard core that endures through peripheral changes. For many people, it is in a state of flux. That need not be a sign of inconstancy, but of reasonable responsiveness to the changing conditions of life and to learning from experience. For most of us, parts of our personal attitude persist for a while through these changes, other parts grow or diminish in importance, and which parts persist and which change is itself changing through time.

These changes can become so frequent and all-embracing as to make it implausible to speak of a personal attitude at all. It is impossible to say in general terms when the frequency of changes leaves us without one. It is sophistical to say that the quiddity a personal attitude may be radical changes throughout a life. It makes sense to speak of a personal attitude only if there is some continuity in its parts, even if the continuing parts themselves change. Nor is it possible to say in general terms when changes indicate weakness of character, or erring on the side of responsiveness, or when the refusal to change indicates pigheadedness, rigidity, or a stubborn refusal to face facts.

The blanket approval of authenticity is unreasonable because it takes no notice of the difficulty of judging whether changes to our personal attitude are too many or too few. Whether or not authenticity is reasonable varies with individuals, circumstances, and contexts, just as does the reasonability of hypocrisy. We need not deny that there are clear cases in which hypocrisy is bad and authenticity is good. It is rather to stress that there are many cases in which it is difficult to evaluate whether either is good or bad. This kind of evaluation is difficult not just for us when we observe and try to evaluate what others do or fail to do. It is difficult also when we try to evaluate whether it would be reasonable for us to act hypocritically or authentically in many of the circumstances we routinely encounter in life. It is often hard to know whether to speak up or keep quiet; stand on principle or compromise;

condemn or tolerate; challenge or leave it alone. That is why the choice between a hypocritical and authentic response is often difficult. How then should we respond when we personally have to make one of these difficult choices?

Against Formulas

After a lifetime of struggle, of great successes and even greater failures, Oedipus has reached Colonus, where he could finally lay down his burden and die in peace. He reflects on "the final things in life (656) [and concludes that] acceptance — that is the great lesson suffering teaches (6) [and resolves that] no more fighting with necessity" (210).[12]

What Oedipus had learned about the final things in life applies to all conflicts we unavoidably face as we try to live as we think we should. And it applies, ipso facto, to the conflict between hypocrisy and authenticity. What we have to accept is that there is no general formula for resolving their conflicts. As we have seen, both hypocrisy and authenticity are sometimes good and sometimes bad. Hypocrisy misrepresents the truth about our personal attitude and authenticity represents it truthfully. There are simple cases in which hypocrisy is clearly bad and authenticity is clearly good. But many cases are far from simple. Often there are strong reasons for and against both hypocrisy and authenticity. If we choose one, we choose against the other. In such cases, the choice between them is difficult.

Making such difficult choices reasonably is a serious problem. And we must often make them in unfavorable conditions created by our forever changing context, by our imperfect knowledge of both ourselves and of those affected by our choice, and by the possibly mistaken beliefs, emotions, and desires that form our personal attitude. We must choose by relying on the prevailing modes of evaluation, even though we are critical of them and they are as much in a state of flux as is our personal attitude. What we have to accept is that we often have to make difficult choices in a state of uncertainty and in complex and imperfectly understood conditions.

How, then, should we proceed? We should not look for simple guides to complex matters. Making a reasonable choice depends on weighing the contrary reasons for the conflicting alternatives, in the light of how we think we should live, how we suppose our choice will affect others, and how we estimate the relevant possibilities of the context in which we have to make the choice. There will be a choice that is more reasonable in these circumstances than any other, but it will be particular, context-dependent, and not generalizable to other choices in other contexts. Much can go wrong: we can err by resolving the conflict in favor of a corrupt policy of hypocrisy or a vicious or self-deceiving policy of authenticity. If we are reasonable, we will be aware of these pitfalls and try to avoid them. We can only try to do as well as we can in unpropitious circumstances that we have not chosen. It may be felt that this answer is feeble and that we need something more robust. This is an understandable sentiment, but it cannot be met. The best we can do is to do the best we can do.

10   The Miasma of Boredom

Understanding Boredom

Boredom may be a short-lived experience we all occasionally have, or
a lasting condition. The latter is a serious problem because it leads to
a general loss of a sense of our values, retreat into ourselves, estrangement from other people, and a pervasive sense of distaste, irritability,
and the futility of all activities. Enjoyments in life are replaced with
scorn, activity with lethargy, the innocent eye with the knowing un-
masking of the corruption that is thought always to lie not far below
the surface of deceptive appearances. The world is not seen and appre-
ciated, but dispiritedly seen through and deplored. Modes of evaluation
are regarded as veils that obscure the bitter truth about the pointlessness of life.

Engagement is a response to boredom. But if boredom is a lasting
condition, not just a passing one, it leads those who are possessed by
it to be bored also with all engagements. All of them are seen as strata-
gems of self-deception that hide the absurdity of human aspirations.
The engagements that might relieve boredom are thus vitiated by the
same of futility that they were intended to relieve. A severe case
of boredom infects its own cure and dooms all attempts to overcome
its deadening malaise.

Boredom is one among many similar more or less overlapping psychological states, such as acedia, alienation, anomie, apathy, doldrums,
ennui, languor, spleen, and tedium. The German word for it is *Lange-
weile*, the French is *ennui*. These terms are imprecise, used in various
senses, and ordinarily leave unclear how they might be defined and distinguished from one another. Several of them have been transformed
from ordinary expressions in one language or another into technical

terms within some theoretical approach. Acedia is one of the deadly sins according to Catholic theology.[1] Alienation is a product of class conflict in Marxist ideology. Anomie has acquired a specialized meaning in Durkheimian sociology.[2] Psychologists explain it as the effect of repetitious activities.[3] And an entire literary genre is devoted to ennui.[4] One characteristic shared by these approaches is that they ignore or denigrate the others. The same is true of the few philosophers—Pascal, Kierkegaard, Schopenhauer, Russell, and Heidegger—who have considered it, although, with the exception of Heidegger, only in unsystematic casual asides, not as a central subject.[5]

I cite three evocative descriptions of boredom separated by many centuries and very different contexts. The first is from *Ecclesiastes*, 1.1–18; 3.16; 4.2–3:

> What does man gain by all the toil at which he toils under the sun? [and answers]: A generation goes, and a generation comes, but the earth remains forever. . . . All things are full of weariness; a man cannot utter it. . . . What has been is what will be, and what has been done is what will be done; and there is nothing new under the sun. . . . All is vanity and a striving after wind. What is crooked cannot be made straight, and what is lacking cannot be numbered. . . . In much wisdom is much vexation, and he who increases knowledge increases sorrow. . . . The fate of the sons of men and the fate of beasts is the same; as one dies, so dies the other. . . . The dead who are already dead [are] more fortunate than the living who are still alive; but better than both is he who has not yet been.

The second is Hamlet's lament in Act II, Scene II, 313–22:

> I have of late—but wherefore I know not—lost all my mirth, forgone all customs of exercises; and indeed it goes so heavily with my disposition that this goodly frame, the earth, seems to me a sterile promontory; this most excellent canopy, the air, look you, this brave o'erhanging firmament, this majestical roof fretted with golden fire, why, it appears no other thing to me, but a foul and pestilent congregation of vapors.

The third comes from Karel Capek's play, *The Makropulos Secret*:

> Boredom . . . everything is so pointless, so empty, so meaningless. . . . One finds out that one cannot believe in anything. Anything. And from that

comes this cold emptiness. . . . You realize that art is useless. It is all in vain. . . . People are never better. Nothing can ever be changed. Nothing, nothing, nothing really matters. If at this moment there were to be . . . the end of the world, or whatever, still nothing would matter. Even I do not matter. [Capek's protagonist says that other people] disgust me. . . . You believe in everything: in love, in yourselves, in honor, in progress, in humanity . . . in pleasure . . . faithfulness . . . power . . . you fools. [As for her] everything tires me. It tires one to be good, it tires one to be bad. . . . In us all life has stopped. . . . And it goes on, goes on, goes on. Ah, this terrible loneliness.[6]

These are fine descriptions of boredom, but the authors do not explain what makes them states of boredom, how they might be distinguished from other similar states, what gets us into those states, what makes them so obviously bad, and why it is so difficult to get out of them. The descriptions are evocative, but not explanatory.

Explanation

I begin with two distinctions. One is between situational and pervasive boredom. Situational boredom is caused by some repetitive activity that is often an unavoidable part of one's life. Chaplin's *Modern Times* is a serio-comic description of the unrelieved drudgery of endlessly repeated tasks his antihero must perform on a production line. But it may be the similarly deadening hard labor of farm hands, slaves, or forced laborers in some Gulag. Of course they are bored. We would all be in those situations. Situational boredom is an understandable reaction to conditions of life that may be temporary and trivial or lasting and genuinely wretched. The obvious remedy of it is to change the conditions, which, unfortunately, those who are bored may not be able to do.

Pervasive boredom involves disengagement from the modes of evaluation on which we depend to provide the possibilities that enable us to live as we think we should. If the possibilities exclude many of the ways in which we want to live, then we have reasons for disengaging ourselves from the prevailing modes of evaluation. But we also have reasons for adhering to them because we derive from them the economic, legal, medical, moral, political, religious, and other evaluations on which we rely for distinguishing between good and bad, and better and worse, possibilities of life in our context. If these contrary reasons persist because we rightly or wrongly think that some of the modes of evaluation on which we rely are defective, then we face a serious conflict that leads to a debilitating uncertainty about how we should live, how to evaluate the available possibilities, and how to make evaluative distinctions. An irritated, resentful retreat into ourselves caused by the apparent futility of all engagements is an understandable reaction. And that is, in part, what boredom involves.

It estranges us from life as we know it. The conditions to which it is a response have no obvious remedy, because they permeate and follow from our dissatisfactions with the modes of evaluation that are the sources of the evaluations we could make. The result is that our evaluations become unreliable and we do not know how we should live and act. We withdraw from our involvement in the whole sorry mess. Pervasive boredom is caused by this kind of estrangement, and that is what I will be discussing.

The second distinction is between episodic and attitudinal boredom. It is close to impossible to avoid episodic boredom. We all have to do some boring things: wait in various offices, stand in line, take long trips, listen to boring speeches, put up with thrice-heard stories of aged relatives, do familiar household chores, and so on. We may get impatient, but these are not life-changing experiences and rarely leave a lasting mark on us. Episodic boredom is a reasonable reaction in contexts that are genuinely boring and would be found so by most of us. Its tedium may be relieved by the realization that putting up with it is a means to something we care about, if indeed we do care about something. Episodic boredom is context-dependent, and caused by genuinely boring conditions in which we may find ourselves. But if we cannot relieve it because we do not care about anything worthwhile to which the repetitious activities may be means, then episodic boredom may turn into a lasting personal attitude to life.

Attitudinal boredom is a pervasive response to life as whole. It is not instrumental to anything worth caring about, but a reaction to the futility of caring about anything. It is a personal attitude that others may not share. The life some of us find boring, others may find interesting. The source of attitudinal boredom is how we feel about our life, not how it actually is. Of course, life may actually be as bad as how we feel about it, but what matters is our estranged, debilitating, personal attitude, not whether it is reasonable. Attitudinal boredom is not about the world, but about ourselves who have the attitude. It is primarily emotional and reactive, and at most only secondarily cognitive and truth-directed.

Experiences of situational and episodic boredom are not particularly bothersome. They are understandable parts of life that need not be laden with ominous significance. In fact, although boredom is usually bad, it is not invariably so. We may yearn for a boring life in the midst of rapid changes in legal, moral, or political evaluations, in times of turmoil caused by foreign or civil war, in the midst of insecurities created by radical changes in sexual practices, communication, terrorist threats, medical practices, and so forth. And we may feel the same yearning as we near the completion of exhausting creative work or moving to a new location; as we are getting accustomed to a new job with new responsibilities and new pressures; as we face prolonged marital strife or the life-threatening illness of someone we love. Moreover, even when boredom is bad, we may welcome it as an alternative to a life of severe pain, humiliation, persecution, and literal or metaphorical enslavement from which we are, with luck and effort, recovering. Boredom may acquire ominous significance if the conditions that cause it are pervasive and lasting, and the episodes are so frequent as to permeate of life. Then they may turn first into disenchantment with and later estrangement from life as a whole. That is the experience of pervasive and attitudinal boredom that I am endeavoring to describe, understand, and evaluate in greater depth than it has been done in the works that I have already cited.

Some explanations of boredom are seriously incomplete. Psychologists tend to ignore pervasive and attitudinal boredom, concentrate on conditional and episodic one, and take no notice of the historically changing social conditions in which it occurs. Sociologists focus on the social conditions, but ignore its historical and psychological aspects, and leave unexplained the glaringly obvious facts that we may respond differently to the same social conditions and are similarly bored in very different social conditions. Catholic theologians condemn pervasive and attitudinal boredom as a deadly sin, because it is contrary to the love of God, which is supposedly the foundation of all virtues, but they do not ask why it is more frequent in some social and psychological conditions than in others, nor why those who do not share their religious views may nevertheless take boredom very seriously indeed. The fine literary evocations of pervasive and attitudinal boredom leave untouched the question of what causes it, and why it assails some of us but not others. And, surprisingly, philosophers are no clearer and more systematic in their occasional discussions of boredom than the preceding ones. Each of these approaches gets something right and ignores much that should not be ignored by an adequate understanding and evaluation of pervasive and attitudinal boredom.

Characteristics

Clear and central cases of boredom have five characteristics. Each may be present to a greater or lesser extent and, when present, stronger or weaker. If they are very strong, they skirt mental illness, typically clinical depression or what has been called melancholia.[7] If they are quite weak, pervasive and attitudinal boredom becomes indistinguishable from situational and episodic ones. The specification of the characteristics, then allows for degrees of boredom, as well as for borderline cases about which it may well be impossible to say whether they qualify as boredom. The characteristics that follow make it possible to identify clear cases of pervasive and attitudinal boredom and to explain what makes some cases unclear. From now I will mean by boredom clear cases of the pervasive and attitudinal forms of it.

The first characteristic is oscillation between *apathy* and *restlessness*. Apathy involves physical and psychological lethargy, enervating lack of motivation, and lassitude. If we are apathetic, we cannot but be aware of how different our condition is from our usual state of active involvement in life and engagement at least in its routine activities. We know that there is something wrong, but we do not know why we have lost whatever motivation we used to have. We become restless in order to get out of our apathetic state and embark on feverish activities in the hope that we will be able to find some relief in them. We go shopping, even though there is nothing we need; watch television programs that do not interest us; become addicted to pornography, although its repetitious predictability becomes tedious after an orgasm provides a momentary satisfaction; take drugs or get drunk. After a while, however, we find no relief in such diversions, and apathy once more sets in. We may vaguely sense, or, if we are honest, realize that we seek diversions because there is nothing, except perhaps the satisfaction of our basic needs, that we really care about. Apathy and restlessness are symptoms of the loss of meaning in our life.

This *loss of meaning* is the second characteristic of boredom. If we are in its grip, we lack lasting interests. Nothing we might do seems more important than alternatives to it. All the available possibilities of life seem equally pointless. As the Ecclesiast says, "all things are full of weariness"; or as Hamlet puts it, life "appears no other thing to me, but a foul and pestilent congregation of vapours," or as Capek's protagonist explains, "everything tires me. It tires one to be good, it tires one to be bad. . . . all life has stopped . . . and it goes on and on." Boredom involves this pervasive sense of meaninglessness.

The third characteristic is *disaffection*. It is the lack of good feelings about life and our own life. We feel desolated and an irritable contempt for all those who cravenly disguise from themselves the awful truth we have faced about the futility of everything. Other people's activities seem stupid, shallow, or motivated by self-deception that they contrive to hide from themselves by phony optimism.

The fourth characteristic is a natural consequence of the preceding ones: *disengagement* from the world and other people. It involves withdrawal, a retreat into our self, but since there is nothing worth withdrawing to, no inner citadel to defend, the disengagement is also from our self. Solace is nowhere to be found. All that previously mattered or might matter in the future has turned into ashes by the devastating loss of anything that might make life worth living. As Mill in his *Autobiography* describes his own experience:

> It occurred to me to put the question directly to myself: 'Suppose all your objects in life were realized . . . would this be a great joy and happiness to you?' And an irrepressible self-consciousness directly answered, 'No!' At this my heart sank within me: the whole foundation on which my life was constructed fell down. . . . I seemed to have nothing left to live for.[8]

The fifth characteristic goes beyond disengagement, which may be no more than a deep private sadness, a grieving for the loss of meaning. In severe cases, disengagement turns into *estrangement* that is full of scorn for all those who do not face the fact that there is nothing to live for. Estrangement makes boredom misanthropic.

Boredom, then involves oscillation between apathy and restlessness, loss of meaning, disaffection, disengagement, and estrangement.[9] Each of these characteristics may be present to a greater or lesser extent. And when their presence is lesser, then pervasive and attitudinal boredom becomes situational and episodic.

The Predicament

Boredom has been present from Biblical times to our own. It must have been familiar to some medieval Christians, otherwise theologians would not have condemned it as a deadly sin. It was certainly no stranger to Chaucer, Shakespeare, and Robert Burton. German and French literature reacting to the Enlightenment is full of descriptions of it. And numerous authors rightly claim that boredom has become a characteristic predicament in contemporary Western life. Part of the problem is to explain why boredom has moved from the periphery to the center. The explanation must surely involve understanding how the contemporary Western modes of evaluation differ from other contexts in which boredom was or is not a central problem.

It is not an original thought that the difference is that we are now critical of our modes of evaluation in a way that others have not been critical of theirs. It would be wrong to suppose that the difference is that they were satisfied with their lives and we are dissatisfied with ours. Virtually all of us chafe under the limits imposed on us, cannot find as close a fit as we would like between the available possibilities and how we think we should live, and feel constrained by our physical, social, and individual circumstances. This was as true in pre-Christian, Christian, Enlightenment, and post-Enlightenment periods as it is in our own. Greater or lesser dissatisfaction in various forms has been felt in many different epochs and conditions is a part of the human predicament. And we, as others, are compelled to respond in some way to our dissatisfactions with life as we know it. The difference is in how we respond. Boredom is a central problem for us, in contrast with past ages in which the predicament may have existed but was nowhere near as acute as it now is for us.

What reason do we have thinking that boredom is now widespread? It is a psychological condition, and we are often wrong even about our own and our intimates' psychological conditions. How then could we reasonably generalize about the psychological conditions of strangers? Lacking clairvoyance, how could we tell what their attitudes are toward their lives?

We can tell in the same way in which we can tell that some people are fair, tactless, untrustworthy, courageous, craven, patriotic, or depressed. We observe what they do in a variety of situations, what possibilities they pursue in preference to other possibilities open to them, and what they say, not when they wear their public face, but when they speak from the heart. We look at how they live and act, and infer what personal attitude motivates them. What then do we find when we observe how people in our context live and act?

We find on Google at the time I write this (2014) about the US that "in 2012, an estimated 23.9% of Americans aged twelve or older were current illicit drug users" (www.drugwarfacts.org); that every day the "average time spent watching television (US) was 5.11 hours" (www .statisticbrain.com); that "adults who regularly visit Internet pornography website are 40 million" (https://wse.edu/pornographystat); that "the daily time spent with media, according to U.S. Consumers in 2012 was [in hours/day] TV: 5:05, Internet 3:07, Video Games: 0:48" (http:// emarketer.com); annually "there are approximately 88,000 deaths attributable to excessive alcohol use" (www.cds.gov/alcohol); and that "197 million adults visit a shopping center each month. This represents 94% of the adult population in the U.S. . . . . Average time spent shopping is 1 hour 27 minutes" (https://www.jsdecauxna.com) and this figure is only of shopping in malls, not in stores outside of malls. I take these figures to indicate that we seek distractions in these ways because we are bored and want relief from it.

Now compare the sensibility these statistics indicate with those that prevailed in two other contexts. The first is in 5th Century B.C. Athens as reflected in Pericles' funeral oration.

Taking everything together then, I declare that our city is an education of Greece, and I declare that in my opinion each single one of our citizens, in all the manifold aspects of life, is able to show himself the rightful lord and owner of his own person, and do this, moreover, with exceptional grace and exceptional versatility. And to show that this is no empty boasting for the present occasion, but real tangible fact, you have only to consider the power which our city possesses and which has been won by those very qualities which I have mentioned. . . . Future ages will wonder at us, as the present age wonders at us now. . . . Our adventurous spirit has forced an entry into every sea and into every land. [10]

The other is in the late Middle Ages:

The contrast between suffering and joy, between adversity and happiness, appeared more striking. All experience had to the minds of men the directness and absoluteness of the pleasure and pain of child-life. Every event, every action, was still embodied in expressive and solemn forms, which raised them to the dignity of a ritual. For it was not merely the great facts of birth, marriage and death which, by the sacredness of the sacrament, were raised to the rank of mysteries; incidents of less importance, like a journey, a task, a visit, were equally attended by a thousand formalities. . . . Calamities and indigence were more afflicting than at present; it was more difficult to guard against them, and to find solace. Illness and health presented a more striking contrast; the cold and darkness of winter were real evils. . . . We, at the present day, can hardly understand the keenness with which a fur coat, a good fire on the hearth, a soft bed, a glass of wine, were formerly enjoyed. . . . All things presenting themselves to the mind in violent contrasts and impressive forms, lent a tone of excitement and passion to everyday life. [11]

There is no trace of boredom in Periclean Athens, at least for adult male citizens. They were wholeheartedly involved in their activities and thereby setting an example to the world to emulate and envy. And boredom was a problem mainly for those few in late medieval Europe who have lived a monastic life or occupied exalted social positions.

What accounts for this difference between those times and our own? The short answer is that people living then were not dissatisfied with their modes of evaluation. They accepted them unquestioningly, not because they were invariably satisfied with their lives, but because they blamed their dissatisfactions on themselves, on the contingencies of life, or on the caprice or wickedness of their rulers or enemies. They assumed that their dissatisfactions were the result of obstacles that prevented them from adhering more closely to the modes of evaluation in accordance with which they thought they should live and act. Their dissatisfactions followed from their culpable or unwitting failure to live as they knew they should.

Why Now?

It is different for us. We are often unsure how we should live, because we have doubts about what possibilities of life we should follow. We resent the limits imposed on us. And we see that the economic, legal, medical, moral, political, religious, and other evaluations we derive from our modes of evaluation are many and conflicting. We are embarrassed by the superabundance of incompatible possibilities and their evaluations. Life has become much too complex for us in a way in which it had not been in ancient Athens and Rome or late medieval Europe. Boredom is the prevalent reaction of the many who seek relief from the resulting uncertainties through the distractions that the statistics I have cited indicate.

What accounts for this difference? It is the combination of several trends that have gradually transformed past conditions into the present ones. Much is changing, but there is also continuity. And the gradual changes in the midst of which we now live make us uncertain about many of our evaluations. This becomes obvious if we reflect on the acute contemporary conflicts, for instance, about abortion, capital punishment, euthanasia, the free market, privacy, security, sexual mores, suicide, taxation, and welfare policies. These changes and the resulting conflicts make our choices difficult.

One of these transforming trends is in our attitude toward the customary evaluations in our context. The dominant view in ancient, medieval, and Enlightenment times was that the modes of evaluation aimed to approximate a providential or natural order that permeates the scheme of things. Lives were good to the extent to which they conformed to that order, and bad if they failed. Failures were blamed on misunderstanding the order or on our weakness or wickedness that led us to act contrary to it. Both were avoidable by the right use of reason.

We continue to accept that there is a natural order, but we think that it sets only minimum conditions to which adequate modes of evaluation must conform. Nature dictates that we must satisfy our basic physiological, psychological, and social needs, but acceptable human lives must have a much richer content than that. We think that this richer content is conventional, constructed by us, not found in nature. Our predicament is that these richer evaluations are many and conflicting, and they reflect ever-changing social conditions. We think of our modes of evaluation as a mixture of natural and conventional elements. And our conflicts, uncertainties, and difficult choices are caused by the loss of an agreed upon standard to which we could appeal to resolve our conflicts, overcome our uncertainties, and make difficult choices easier. The problem is not the lack of standards, but that we have many of them, and they are also conventional, conflicting, and leave us with difficult choices that we often do not know how to make.

This transforming trend toward thinking that our evaluations have a large conventional element would not, by itself, have led to a widespread change of personal attitudes. A handful of cultural commentators may be affected by it, but most of us need not be aware of it at all. But this trend is combined with others that are taking place more or less simultaneously, and they do concern most of us. One is the dramatic improvement in the quality of life. We live longer, in better health, fewer of our children die in infancy, work fewer hours, send our children to school rather than put them to work, social mobility has become possible, women are no longer treated as reproductive tools, we can take ever longer vacations and have time for some leisure after work, and during weekends.

Another trend is away from oppressive societies and toward greater liberty. Religious dissent is no longer regarded as an abomination, sexual mores are more tolerant, education enables more of us to learn more about the possibilities of life than the much narrower circumstances in the past allowed, individual initiative is more often encouraged, we can emigrate in hope of a better future, and our knowledge of other societies and other possibilities of life is now much greater than ever before. These trends jointly force on us the question of how to take advantage of the richer possibilities of life. The question is now more pressing than at earlier times because in contemporary Western life the possibilities continually increase and the scope of individual liberty has grown to an unprecedented extent.

The superabundance of possibilities is now virtually unavoidable as a result of television, the internet, and constant contact with others by means of email, cell phones, face books, and twitter through which we exchange our immediate impressions of such vital matters as the weather, where we happen to be at the moment, what our fleeting frustrations and satisfactions are, what we are seeing or buying in the malls we visit in order to expose ourselves to more merchandise, more information, and more possibilities. And permeating all this are the inescapable advertisements selling ever more and newer products that make this information explosion ever greater. We are numbed by the resulting overload. Our choices are many, and so are the modes of evaluation on which we might rely to guide our choices. We are overwhelmed by a surfeit of information.[12]

The result is that we become frustrated, irritated, lose the ability to judge what is good and bad, and more or less important. We cannot or do not want to escape incessant electronic bombardment, and, like an overloaded grid, turn off. We retreat into a sullen apathy alternating with restlessness and pointless activity. We lose the sense that any of this is meaningful, become disaffected, disengaged, and estranged from our society and its modes of evaluation. In a word, we become bored. These trends and their combination did not exist in the past. They have become combined and are accelerated in contemporary Western life, make boredom an understandable reaction, and that is why, unlike in past ages, boredom is now a central and widespread predicament for us.

Possible Responses

The trends I have described are social, not psychological. Psychological considerations become relevant if we try to understand how we individually respond to the social conditions to which these trends have led. Boredom is one of these responses, but, as we have seen, it is one that we have good reasons to want to avoid. There are other possible responses, and it is a matter of individual psychology which of them is, unavoidably or by choice, our own.

These other responses may be like boredom, in that they take the form of withdrawal from our society. The withdrawal, however, is to some psychological state, and there are several of them. The most drastic one leads to quick suicide. If we think that life is not worth living in the current conditions, then we can put an end to it, as numerous romantic figures in French and German novels have done as a result of finding their usually self-induced *Weltschmerz* intolerable. Or the suicide may be slow and gradual, as was Melville's Bartleby who simply curled up and responded to all inducements by saying "I would rather not." I think such responses are rarely found in real life, although teenagers sometimes toy with them.

A less extreme form of withdrawal is retreat into private life. It may be to the solitary life of a hermit. Or perhaps it is in the company of a few likeminded friends who agree to cultivate their own garden, as Candide had done after his misadventures destroyed his Leibnizian optimism that Voltaire ridiculed with relish and superficial understanding. Or it may take the form of resignation, acceptance of boredom, and living on in quiet desperation, the way various Chekhovian characters have done in endless barren afternoons filled with trips to the samovar and inconsequential conversations about trivial subjects. Or it may involve simply, hopelessly waiting for something, who knows what, that might possibly put an end to lethargy and provide something worth living for, as Vladimir and Estragon have waited for Godot.

These responses, however, are parasitic on others who satisfy the basic needs of those who have withdrawn from engagement. If they cannot depend on others, then they must be willing to put up with poverty, much discomfort, disease, and an uncertain supply of necessities. Most people cannot count on others to provide for their basic needs during their withdrawal and few are willing to accept real poverty if there is an alternative to it.

The psychologically much more likely response is engagement, not withdrawal. But engagement may be inauthentic or genuinely valued. Inauthentic engagement is not just a short-lived restless activity, but a prolonged defensive stratagem. Its aim is to step back from the abyss of losing meaning by making a commitment to some activity, not because it is valuable, but because it relieves boredom. Inauthentic engagement often involves joining others in working for some cause that allows them to say to themselves and others that here is something they value. And it is true that they value it, but not because they are convinced of its value, but because it relieves their apathy, loss of meaning, disaffection, disengagement, and estrangement.

The signs of inauthentic engagement are the fervor of the commitment; the sharp distinction between comrades who are good and true and the rest who are stupid, craven, or corrupt; the dogmatic rejection of criticism by questioning the motives of the critics; and the unshakeable conviction that vitally important matters are at stake in defending the cause. There is a vitally important matter at stake, but it is not the avowed one. It is escape from boredom into commitment to something, it does not matter what it is, provided it yields the desired relief. Such commitments are only superficially to whatever the cause happens to be. Their deep source is the need to avoid the debilitating sense of futility that looms as an alternative to the cause.

I am not suggesting, of course, that all commitment to all causes is inauthentic. There are many genuinely valuable and rightly valued causes. Commitment to them may be a reasonable outcome of considered evaluations. Furthermore, a commitment that starts out as an inauthentic effort to overcome boredom may become a genuine one to a rightly valued cause. We may and often do have more than one motive for what we do. Wanting to avoid boredom may be one of them, but it need not be the only one. It is a simple-minded or cynical mistake to suppose that by identifying *a* motive for doing something we have identified *the* motive for doing it. Motives that coexist with wanting to avoid boredom may be intellectual interests, athletic endeavors, love of family, friends, or adventure, a sense of justice, desire for understanding, artistic creativity, historical or scientific research, and so forth. Such motives may lead to genuinely and rightly valued engagements, even if they start out as inauthentic.

Genuinely valued engagements, however, may not be rightly valued. They may consist in the ruthless pursuit of a noxious ideology, or wealth, or power, or the aggrandizement of a country, religion, or class, or revenge, and so forth. Unboring lives replete with genuine interests and authentic commitments may be deplorable. And the deplorable lives of ideologues, fanatics, terrorists, dictators, sadists, drug lords and their henchmen are unlikely to be boring. There is a great variety of engagements that may help to overcome boredom, but some of them are far worse than enduring boredom.

The problem, then is twofold: to distinguish between inauthentic and genuinely valued engagements, and between genuinely valued engagements that are rightly and wrongly valued. Drawing these distinctions reasonably involves difficult choices. The alternatives among which we must choose are numerous and different, and so are the contexts in which the choices must be made. The choices are difficult because there are reasons both for and against the alternatives, these reasons conflict and make us uncertain. But the choices are only difficult, not impossible. What is it, then, that enables us to make difficult choices reasonably? And why do even reasonably made choices remain difficult? I will now endeavor to answer these questions.

Coping with Boredom

Choices are difficult for two main reasons. One is that there are good reasons for valuing an engagement even if it is inauthentic and wrongly valued because it relieves boredom. It is not unreasonable to think that an inauthentic engagement is preferable to a boring life pervaded by the sense that all engagements are meaningless and futile. After all, an inauthentic engagement may become authentic after a while, as Aristotle pointed out about trying to become virtuous. But there are also reasons for making sure that the engagement is genuinely and rightly valued. Wrongly valued engagements may threaten the conditions of civilized life and require the dissimulation of the ruthlessness called for by the pursuit of whatever aim the engagement has. Since few people are entirely indifferent to legal, moral, political, and other limits, they are likely to be alienated also from their own upbringing and education. These reasons against wrongly valued engagements can be overridden in the name ideological goals, or the desire for wealth, power, glory, or revenge, but doing so has considerable costs that reasonable people will have to weigh before they embark on such quests.

Even if it is acknowledged that there are conflicting reasons for and against inauthentic and wrongly valued engagements, it may be denied that the reasons lead to difficult choices. Reasonable choices depend on evaluating the available alternatives and opting for the one that is most likely to enable us to live as we think we should. This is how we all make choices, if we make them reasonably, and it may be thought that there is no reason why we could not do the same when the choice is between boredom and inauthentic or wrongly valued engagement. We have to evaluate how much boredom we can relieve by the episodic distractions of mindless entertainment, shopping, pornography, drugs, or alcohol. How likely it is that an initially inauthentic engagement may become a genuinely valued one. How deep an alienation from society and other people is an acceptable cost of a wrongly valued engagement. How deeply do we care about the legal, moral, political, and other limits we have been brought up to respect.

It may be thought that we can evaluate these and other similar reasons and choose between boredom and engagement that upon reflection may be found inauthentic or wrongly valued. Doing this is no more difficult than many other choices we make about our finances, political allegiances, career, love affairs, housing, and so forth. We evaluate the alternatives, their likely consequences, the priorities among our preferences, and then make as reasonable a choice as we can. It may still turn out to be mistaken, but we have done what we could to avoid that. But this sanguine view is mistaken.

The choice between boredom and engagement is not like these other choices because, unlike them, boredom is pervasive and attitudinal. It affects everything we do, including the reasonable evaluation of the alternatives and of any engagement to which we might commit ourselves. If we are bored, everything is boring. It is this debilitating effect of boredom that makes it difficult to choose between it and engagement. The obstacles to overcoming pervasive and attitudinal boredom are inherent in the very nature of it. What are these obstacles?

They may be the customary evaluations of our society. Following them is often only apparently a matter of choice. Throughout life we are guided by our upbringing and education, even if we reject parts of them. We conform to many of the prevailing evaluations, and most others around us do the same. We choose our engagements from the possibilities provided by our modes of evaluation, and we at once benefit from them and are critical of the ways they constrain us. Genuinely valued alternative engagements may be open to some few people who are fortunate enough to be acquainted with possibilities beyond those available in their context, but for the majority of us living ordinary lives the possibilities of life are confined to the available readymade patterns. We must fit our lives into one of these patterns, or doom ourselves to estrangement from our society. As Tocqueville memorably writes,

> power is absolute, minute, regular, provident, and mild. It would be like the authority of a parent, if, like that authority, its object was to prepare men for manhood; but it seeks on the contrary to keep them in perpetual childhood: it is well-content that the people should rejoice, provided they think of nothing but rejoicing . . . it chooses to be the sole agent and the only arbiter of that happiness; it provides for their security, foresees and supplies their necessities, facilitates their pleasures, manages their principal concerns, dictates their industry, regulates the descent of property, and subdivides their inheritances—what remains, but to spare them all the care of thinking and all the trouble of living.[13]

Most of us living ordinary lives are not even aware of the insidious, deadening effect on us of the customary evaluations of our society. What we are often aware of is that our lives are boring. We seek relief from it, but most of us can find it only among the customary evaluations which are among the causes of the miasma of boredom.

The possibilities of life are now far richer than those at any other time and place in human history. The sources of widespread boredom, however, are not just customary evaluations, but their combination with affluence, a great deal of liberty, and the overload of information whose quantity makes it very hard to distinguish between what is important and trivial. Added to these conditions is ceaseless bombardment with advertisements calculated to create distractions that would relieve our boredom.

If we wake up to the realization that our life is passing, that we have been on a treadmill going from dissatisfaction to satisfaction and back, and that we have been and are being manipulated, then apathy and disaffection may set in. We cannot get outside of the customary evaluations that surround us, the context in which we and everyone we know have been raised, and from which we derive our evaluations. If strength, stubbornness, or a rebellious spirit prompts us to say no to it, then we become alienated from most people we know who continue on the treadmill. It estranges us from our society, and debilitating boredom follows. If this happens, it is extremely difficult for most of us to find some genuinely valued engagement that would relieve it, since the only source from which we could learn about the possibility of such engagements is the society from which we have become estranged.

Perhaps the most serious obstacle to overcoming boredom once it pervades our entire life and our personal attitude to it is that it affects everything we do, including our efforts to overcome it. Those efforts will seem as valueless as all other efforts to those who have been overpowered by boredom. Its terrible consequence is that it leads to the collapse of the evaluations on which we used to depend. The distinctions between inauthentic and genuine engagements, and rightly and wrongly valued ones becomes pointless since all engagements are regarded as inauthentic and wrongly valued. This is not because of any particular defect in our modes of evaluation. All evaluations, ours and those of others, past and present, Western and non-Western, are seen as vain pretenses that there is something in human life that is genuinely valuable. We are driven by our nature to value the satisfaction at least of our basic needs, but that is just a fact about us, not about the value of the satisfactions we are compelled to seek. It would be neither good nor bad even if the whole of humanity ceased to exist, since nothing is good or bad. Everything that has happened or may happen is just an indifferent fact in the scheme of things. To see this is to see through all evaluations to the futility of all engagements, to the meaninglessness of life.

This is the threat that lurks behind boredom. We have a very strong reason for wanting to avoid getting into this state or for getting out of it once we have fallen into it, namely the awfulness of it. But we also have a very strong reason against any engagement that might avoid or alleviate it, namely, the pointlessness of all engagements. These reasons conflict and that is why the choice between boredom and engagement is difficult.

What can we do about it? It seems to me that there are only three options. One is to resign ourselves to boredom and all that goes with it. This leads to despair. Another is to ignore it, get on with life as well as we can, which is what most people do. Some because they are forced by their circumstances to try to eke out a living without asking about the point of it. But that is not true of us who live in civilized societies and have sufficient leisure to think about how we should live. If we think about it honestly and reasonably, we must either face the difficult choice and struggle with making it, or deceive ourselves by one strata-gem or another. And the third option is to avoid boredom by choosing engagements we think are genuinely valuable. Where might we look for such engagements? We can find them in the classic works in our liter-ary tradition that record and preserve the memory of real or fictional lives that exemplify engagements that seem to us and have seemed to many of our predecessors as genuinely valuable. Teaching that tradition has been the aim of liberal education. But it has fallen on hard times. One deplorable consequence of that is the prevalence of boredom and the frantic search for distraction that might alleviate it.

11 The Prevalence of Evil

What Is Evil?[1]

"Evil" is the most severe one-word condemnation in English. It refers to actions, or people, or customs, or institutions, or evaluative frameworks that are much worse than bad, worse even than very bad. Evil is caused by human beings, primarily, but not exclusively, to other human beings. Man's inhumanity to man is not news. Its familiarity, however, does not make it easier to understand what reasons could lead some human beings to do horrible things to others when they know how horrible it would be if it were done to them.

There are, of course, reasons against doing evil, but there are also reasons for it. Evil actions may be part of the pursuit of personal goals, or they may be dictated by a political, religious, racial, or nationalist ideology. Reasons for and against evil actions conflict and force us to make choices between frustrating or pursuing a goal we have or an ideology to which we are committed. These conflicts are between strong reasons we genuinely think we have. The choices between these reasons are difficult because the reasons are our own, and whatever we decide to do will be contrary to some of the strong reasons we have.

We glean from the histories of all human societies that evil actions are and have been continuously prevalent since the beginning of whatever records we have. Sometimes they are caused by moral monsters, who do it for no other reason than they feel like it, or in unrestrained pursuit of some personal project. But individuals acting on their own behalf can cause only limited evil because their time, energy, and opportunities are limited. The worst and most widespread evil actions that have affected a far greater number of people were and are caused by the cooperative endeavors of individuals acting as agents of an ideology. I will concentrate mainly on evil actions motivated by some ideology. I do not, of course, claim that all ideologies are malignant, nor that all evil actions are caused by ideologues.

Here are some examples of evil actions during the last hundred or so years. Between 1914 and 1918, the Turks massacred about a million and a half Armenian men, women, and children. In 1931, Stalin ordered the murder of prosperous largely Ukrainian peasants and their families, called kulaks, and about two million of them were executed, died of starvation, or deported to concentration camps where they died slowly as a result of forced labor in extreme cold and inadequate clothing. During the great terror of 1937–38, two million Russians were interrogated, tortured, and murdered at Stalin's orders. In 1937–38, Japanese troops raped, tortured, humiliated, and murdered about half million Chinese in Nanking. In Nazi Germany, during WWII, about six million Jews, two million prisoners of war, and half million gypsies, mental defectives, and homosexuals were transported in unspeakable conditions to concentration camps where they were murdered. After India's independence in 1947, over a million Muslim and Hindu men, women, and children were murdered in religious massacres. In the 1950–51 campaign against so-called counterrevolutionaries in Mao's China about one million people, including entire families, were murdered, and the Great Leap Forward of 1959–63 caused the slow death of an estimated sixteen to thirty million people from starvation. Pol Pot in Cambodia presided over the murder of about two million people, once again including the aged and infants, men and women. In 1992–95, about two hundred thousand Muslims were murdered in Bosnia by Serb nationalists. In 1994, almost one million people were murdered in Rwanda. To this list of atrocities many more could be added from Afghanistan, Argentina, Chile, the Congo, Iran, Iraq, Sudan, Syria, Uganda, and numerous other places.

These atrocities were not simple murders. They expressed the ill will of the perpetrators who committed them with as much humiliation and pain as was possible, given the large number of the victims. They were not isolated acts of individuals, but organized systematic patterns of the cruel murder of people simply because they belonged to a vilified ethnic group, religion, class, or nation, not for anything they have done.[2]

The examples above illustrate but do not define evil. The definition I propose begins by focusing on evil actions. It identifies four features that are individually necessary and jointly sufficient to make an action evil. First, the actions cause *grievous harm*. In the examples above, the grievous harm is murder, but it has often been aggravated by rape, mutilation, torture, forced labor, humiliation, and so forth. Second, the victims are *innocent*. They suffer grievous harm only because they belong to a group singled out and persecuted by the evildoers. Their victims are not guilty of anything that would warrant the grievous harm inflicted on them. What is done to them, therefore, cannot be reasonably explained as punishment, revenge, or self-defense. Third, the evildoers are normally intelligent and not incapacitated in some way. They cannot fail to know that torture, dismemberment, forced labor under life-threatening conditions, prolonged starvation, and murder are grievous harms. If they nevertheless cause it, then their actions are *deliberate*. Fourth, their actions are motivated by *ill will*. Cruelty, envy, hatred, jealousy, malevolence, and ruthlessness, or some combination of them, are examples of *active* ill will. But ill will can also be *passive*, as in indifference, callousness, or inattention toward the grievous harm done to the victims, or in the cold, unfeeling efficiency with which it is inflicted on them. Active ill will leads to evil actions; passive ill will is uncaring about the obvious consequences of actions. The atrocities were motivated by the combination of some moral, political, or religious ideology and active ill will. The vilification of members of some group encouraged and were meant to justify large-scale evil actions. I discuss passive ill will in greater detail later.

An action is evil, then, if it deliberately causes grievous harm to innocent victims, and it is motivated by active or passive ill will. Actions that have these features may still be more or less evil, because they may differ in the quantity and quality of the grievous harm they cause, and in the degree of deliberation and ill will involved in them. In normal circumstances, evil actions cannot be reasonably excused or justified. But circumstances may not be normal, and then the vexed question of whether they can be excused or justified needs to be faced. For the moment, I note that this is one reason for the complexities of evil. Another reason is that ideological evildoers do not believe that what they are doing is evil. They believe that their victims are enemies of the great good their ideology aims to being about. Nor do ideological evildoers believe that they are motivated by ill will. They believe that their motives are righteous, their will is good, and the grievous harm they deliberately cause is justified. Their beliefs are obviously mistaken, but they do not think so. Part of the complexity of evil is understanding what leads normally intelligent people, as evildoers often are, to hold and act on obviously false beliefs.

Isolated evil actions do not make human beings evil: they may be counterbalanced by many more good actions. It is then hard to know what should be the overall evaluation of the agents, although, of course, not of their actions. Actions may be good, evil, mixed, or neutral, even if their agents are not. But whatever the actions are, they reflect on their agents. Human beings, then, are evil if their evil actions form a lasting pattern and it is not counterbalanced by a like pattern of good actions. Customs, conventions, institutions, traditions, modes of evaluation, and evaluative frameworks are evil if they prompt those who follow them to perform patterns of evil actions. The ethnic, nationalistic, political, religious, or tribal ideologies that prompted the atrocities are evil for this reason.

The Aztecs

I have discussed the Aztecs briefly in chapter 7, but did so from the point of view of the evil Cortes and his followers did to them. I will now discuss them from the point of view of the evil they inflicted on others before Cortes destroyed them and their society. What Cortes did to the Aztecs, of course, cannot retroactively diminish the evil the Aztecs did to others. The account that follows relies on the work of Inga Glendinnen, *Aztecs: An Interpretation*.[3] She is a respected historian and anthropologist.

The Aztec Empire was dominant from the fourteenth to the sixteenth century. Its center was where Mexico City now is. Central to the Aztec evaluative framework were rituals of exceptional cruelty inflicted on tens of thousands of victims the Aztecs have captured in incessant wars with neighboring people. The rituals involved the large-scale sacrifice of captured warriors. In one way or another, the whole population participated in the rituals. Only the priests did the killing, but they did it in plain view of the assembled people who celebrated what was done. The killings took place not just in Huizilpochtli's [one of their god's] pyramid, the main site of their rituals, but also in neighborhood temples and on the streets.

> The people were implicated in the care and the preparation of the victims, their delivery to the place of death, and then in the elaborate processing of their bodies: the dismemberment and distribution of heads and limbs, flesh and blood and flayed skins. On high occasions warriors carrying gourds of human blood and wearing the dripping skins of their captives ran through the streets, to be ceremoniously welcomed into their dwellings; the flesh of their victims seethed in domestic cooking pots. . . . [All this was done by] people notable for a precisely ordered polity, a grave formality of manner, and a developed regard for beauty (2).

After weeks in captivity, the victims

> were paraded through the elaborate routines which were a prelude to their assent to Huizilpochtli's pyramid. There they would be seized, forced back over the killing stone, a priest pressing down each limb to keep the chest tautly arched, while a fifth drove the flint blade of the sacrificial knife into the chest and dragged out the still-pulsing heart. The heart was raised to the Sun and the plundered body let to fall aside. It was then sent suddenly rolling down the pyramid steps, to be collected at the base by old men . . . who would carry it away through the streets for dismemberment and distribution (89). [The priest] tore the heart from the victim and with it fed the [sacred] fire. When the watching populace saw the flames leap up they all (even the babies) had their ears cut, and splattered the fast flowing blood repeatedly in the direction of the fire's glow, intent in their turn on initiating their own individual and household relationship with this most powerful lord (238).

This was not done on rare occasions, but as a regular part of life, as long as the Aztec evaluative framework lasted. One of the reasons for the incessant wars the Aztecs waged was to obtain captives for their ghastly rituals.

What reason did the Aztecs have for their rituals? They believed that their continued existence depended on the mercy of gods whose caprice made life uncertain. Their sense of the uncertainty of life and their fear that it may all come to an end unless the gods are propitiated by the blood of the sacrificed victims and the self-mutilation of the Aztecs—even of their infants—was one of the deepest beliefs on which their evaluative framework rested. It dictated their evaluations that overrode all other considerations.

The uncertainty of life was symbolized by the sacred fire. It was the absolute duty of the priests in charge to keep it burning. While it was burning, human life could go on and threats to it could be kept under control, but as it flickered so did human lives and fortunes. The less it flickered, the more steady human fortunes were. The sacred fire was the link between the Aztecs and their gods. The capricious gods had to be propitiated by valuable sacrifices. And that was why the sacrificial victims were honored warriors the Aztecs captured, not common people, and why even the common people mutilated themselves as a token of their submission. All the blood and the ministrations of their priests kept the sacred fire burning.

The Aztecs could not have failed to know the grievous harm they had deliberately inflicted on tens of thousands of victims, as well as on themselves, throughout the centuries. Their ill will was not active. They did not despise their victims, but valued them as worthy objects of sacrifice. Their ill will was passive, in that they were indifferent to the suffering they have inflicted on their victims. They regarded that as insignificant compared to the great good of placating the gods so that their society and its evaluative framework could continue to flourish.

What made it even more horrible is that it was refined by an aesthetic element that beautified it: elaborate ceremonial clothing, precious implements, grave and dignified manner, and a punctilious observance of the sequence of the rituals. The more beautiful it was, the more it would please the gods. It was "aesthetic, expressive, interrogative, and creative." Interrogative because the priests could tell from how the fire flickered whether the sacrifice was well received by the gods. By enhancing the ritual with the aesthetic element, they hoped to make their offerings more attractive to the gods. They created high art. Huizilpochtli's blood-drenched pyramid was the Aztecs' cathedral dedicated to the glory of the gods.

As the Aztecs saw it, their horrible evil practices underpinned all else they had. If they had not offered the frequent human sacrifices that involved cutting the heart out of tens of thousands of living human beings, then they could not propitiate Huizilpochtli, and they would be subject to the uncertainties of life that would sooner or later destroy their civilization and all they valued in life. They believed that they had to choose between what it took to propitiate the god on whose good will everything depended and forfeiting what made their lives worth living. They naturally chose the former and committed the great evils they regarded as necessary for continued divine favor.

It may occur to readers that a similar account could be given of evil actions in Christian Europe and elsewhere, but I will put that thought aside. The more basic question is whether there can be good reasons for a pattern of evildoing, regardless of whose it is. If we consider this question, we will realize that strong reasons can be and have been given both for and against patterns of evil actions. These reasons may conflict, and if we think about them deeply, we will become conflicted about our evaluation of these reasons. This will force us to make difficult choices between evaluating the relative strength of these reasons. Evaluative frameworks throughout history, as well as in the contemporary world, have often led to such conflicts and forced participants in them to make difficult choices. Do we, then, have strong enough reasons to resolve these conflicts and make the choices for or against evil?

The End of Reasons?

It may be thought that even to raise this question is to concede too much to misguided attempts to defend evil. It should go without saying that evil actions ought not be done. That does not require justification. What does require justification is doing them. This thought has been widely accepted for several reasons, one among which is Wittgenstein's support of it. He thought that there comes a point at which everyone runs out of reasons:

> If I exhausted the justifications I have reached bedrock, and my spade is turned. Then I am inclined to say: 'This is simply what I do.' [At that point,] what has to be accepted, the given, is—so one could say—*forms of life*.[4]

This raises obvious questions: what exactly are forms of life? what is the connection between them and evaluative frameworks? and why must forms of life be accepted, rather than doubted or rejected?

I do not know how Wittgenstein would answer these questions. But there are answers that have been given in a Wittgensteinian spirit. An answer to the first question is that

> the idea of a form of life applies . . . to historical groups of individuals who are bound together into a community by a shared set of complex, language-involving practices. These practices are grounded in biological needs and capacities, but . . . our human form of life is fundamentally *cultural* (rather than biological) in nature. . . . It is this vital connection between language and the complex system of practices and activities binding a community together that Wittgenstein intends to emphasize in the concept of a 'form of life.'[5]

The answer to the second question might be that an evaluative framework is part of the form of life of a society. A form of life must include, in addition to the prevalent modes of evaluations, also non-evaluative demographic, geographical, historical, linguistic, technological, and other conditions which basically influence life in a society. But an evaluative framework is also a part of a form of life, and if the form of life has to be accepted, then, apparently, so must be the evaluative framework that is part of it.

This then brings us to the third question to which I find the Wittgensteinian answer most doubtful. Our form of life has to be accepted because we cannot do otherwise:

> Inside the general structure or web of human attitudes and feelings . . . there is endless room for modification, redirection, criticism, and justification. But questions of justification are internal to the structure or relate to modifications internal to it. The existence of the general framework of attitudes itself is something we are given with the fact of human society. As a whole, it neither calls for, nor permits, an external 'rational' justification.[6]

The Wittgensteinian view is then that we can give reasons for or against evaluations, but the reasons are internal to our evaluative framework. This must be so because our evaluative framework determines what count for us as reasons. We can disagree about the relative merits of various reasons, but that is the end of the matter. Asking for reasons for reasons must come to an end. It is futile to ask for them because if we did, and, impossible as it is, actually found some reason, then the same question would arise about that reason, and the demand for reasons would lead to a never-ending regress. We have to stop somewhere, and the reasonable stopping point is the evaluative framework that is part of our form of life and guides how we live. Others have other evaluative frameworks and from them perhaps other reasons follow, but we have ours, and we derive from it all the reasons we need and only ones we can have for our evaluations.

There are strong reasons against this view. There may come a point at which we run out of reasons, but that point is certainly not the evaluative framework we happen to have. We know that some evaluative frameworks are bad. And since we are often critical of our own we may wonder whether it may not be also bad. This is not unreasonable when we behold the injustice, harm, killings, and worse that have been inflicted and justified by reasons derived from our evaluative framework. And when our evaluative framework is called into question by our children, students, and domestic or foreign critics, we need a better answer than "this is simply what I do."

If the Wittgensteinian view were correct, it would be unreasonable to question our entire evaluative framework. But such radical questions have been and are being asked by poets, rebels, philosophers, prophets, revolutionaries, reformers, and skeptics. Their questions cannot be disarmed by saying that they are only about some parts of the evaluative framework while they rely on other parts of it. Thoughtful critics often question all parts of it. And they could question even those parts that they themselves have accepted. Critics can be also self-critical. Countless critics have disowned their own evaluative framework and abandoned it for another they regarded as better. Surely, it is far too cavalier to condemn as unreasonable all those who emigrate, convert, lose faith, or become disenchanted because they have demanded and failed to get reasons for the evaluative framework they have come to distrust. Yet, consistency requires Wittgensteinians to do just that.

Perhaps the truth is that the demand for reasons for our entire evaluative framework cannot be met because there are no such reasons. In that case, we rely on a fairy tale we have been told, convinced ourselves of, and adhere to because we have nothing better. If true, this would be a devastating indictment of how we live, but it would not be a reason against asking for reasons for so much of what we believe and do. This is especially so if we bear in mind the widespread criticisms of how we live now, as well as the wars, crimes, and political and social turmoil that permeate contemporary Western societies.

The Need for Reasons

Defenders of the Wittgensteinian view are right to stress that our form of life with its evaluative framework is given to us, but they are wrong to claim that we have to accept it. We should accept it only if the reasons for it are better than the reasons against it. The Aztecs have accepted their evaluative framework. If they had not, it could not have endured for centuries. Nor can it be doubted that they had reasons for accepting it. They made sense of their lives, drew the necessary evaluative distinctions, and ordered their lives in terms of the evaluations they derived from their evaluative framework. Moreover, their authorities, whom they trusted, vouchsafed for it, and its rituals appeared to them to succeed in propitiating the gods, since their lives had been going on as far as their memories could stretch back in time. But there were also reasons against accepting it.

The first reaction of someone steeped in our evaluative framework is to say about the Aztecs that regardless of what they believed and did, their beliefs were false and their actions were evil. Even if we set aside the vexing question of the existence of God or gods, it is not true that human lives and the entire world depend on the ghastly ritual murder of tens of thousands of people, on eating their flesh, and on wallowing in their blood. We know that these beliefs are false because human lives and the world have been going on both before the Aztecs and after their rituals have been consigned to the graveyard of defunct horrors.

We would say that any reasonable evaluative framework must meet certain minimum conditions, among which have to be the condemnation of Aztec rituals. The Aztec evaluative framework systematically cultivated large-scale patterns of cannibalism, self-mutilation, and human sacrifice. They deliberately caused grievous harm to innocent victims, therefore they were evil. The prohibition of evil actions is among the minimum conditions that all reasonable evaluative frameworks must met. Furthermore, the social cost of the rituals was enormous. It required training and maintaining a class of warriors who went to war to supply the victims for the ritual and a priestly class whose members sanctified the proceedings. And above them all were the few hundred aristocrats who lived in great luxury that far exceeded what was enjoyed by contemporary European rulers, priests, and warriors. The cost of all this had to be borne by the multitude of common people (estimated at 25 million), who served the elite, produced the food, mined the gold and silver, made the weapons, built the monuments, and lived short lives close to the subsistence level.

These reasons for or against the Aztec evaluative framework conflict, but they follow from two different points of view. The reasons for it are reasons the Aztecs had. The reasons against it are reasons we have. The Aztecs were not in the position to know the reasons we have because they relied only on their evaluative framework. They believed, even if mistakenly, that the survival of their society depended on their rituals, and that justified the evil they inflicted on their innocent victims. From their point of view, that was reason enough. We cannot reasonably condemn the Aztecs for not having the reasons we have, since their evaluative framework prevented them from having it. But we can reasonably say, knowing that their beliefs were false, that there are better evaluative frameworks than the Aztec's, and that the Aztec evaluative framework is unreasonable. We have good reasons for condemning the actions that followed from it, even if we do not have good reasons for condemning the Aztec agents who performed those actions.

This is not a conclusion that follows only from our contemporary form of life and evaluative framework. It does that, but it also does more. It follows from the human point of view. All reasonable evaluative frameworks should condemn rituals that involve the torture and massacre of innocent people, of waging war in order to obtain victims, and keeping large numbers of people in servitude in order to sustain these rituals. Evaluative frameworks that lead to valuing such practices violate minimum conditions that any reasonable evaluative framework must meet. Since this conclusion appeals to reasons that are not just internal but also external to our form of life and evaluative framework, the Wittgensteinian view is mistaken.

Matters, however, are more complex than this conclusion suggests. It might be said in defense of the Aztecs that they did not know that they were mistaken about having to propitiate their god. They had reason to believe and no reason to doubt the effectiveness of their rituals. They did not know what happened in the world before their society and its evaluative framework came in to existence, and they certainly could not know what happened after it was destroyed. They could also agree that a reasonable evaluative framework must protect the minimum conditions under which human life can go on. And then tell their critics that they were doing just that by their rituals. They could acknowledge the enormous cost in human lives and resources of providing that protection, and say about it that they had reason to believe that the alternative to it would have been disastrous. They could reasonably deny that what they did was evil. They might agree that they deliberately inflicted grievous harm on innocent victims, but they were motivated by good rather than ill will. They acted in good faith, did as well as they could, in, what they had reason to believe, were the prevailing conditions.

Two considerations may be added to this. First, those who committed the ideological atrocities with which this chapter began could say just what the Aztecs might have said. But the ideological evildoers would make it even stronger by denying that their victims were innocent. They would say that their victims were guilty of being enemies of the great good that their ideology aimed to bring about. Second, if our hypothetical successors look back on us from a distance, say, of five centuries, they may well be as horrified by what we do in wars, in the exploitation of natural resources, and in letting technology rule our lives, as we are by the rituals of the Aztecs and their ideological atrocities.

Might it be then that the Wittgensteinian view is, after all, reasonable? I deny it on the basis of two reasons: the availability and importance of alternative evaluative frameworks, and the significance of good will that is also part of our motivation.

The Importance of Alternatives

Part of the reasons why I have discussed the Aztecs is to compare our evaluative framework with theirs. They must have had conflicts between various possibilities and made choices between them. Their conflicts and choices, however, were not as difficult as our own now are. There are two reasons for this difference. One is that they knew of no alternatives to their own modes of evaluation and evaluative framework, so they could not have examined them in the light of others. We, however, know about alternatives to ours and we can compare ours with them. The other is that the Aztec evaluative framework was hierarchical, and ours is not. In a hierarchical evaluative framework, all conflicts can be resolved in favor of what is regarded as the overriding value. For the Aztecs, it was the propitiation of their capricious gods on whose mercy they believed they depended. We have many modes of evaluation, each has many values, and none is always overriding. And that leaves us without an obvious way of choosing between our conflicting evaluations.

Consider first the importance of the availability to us of alternative evaluative frameworks. We know a great deal about the evaluative frameworks of ancient Athens, Rome, early and medieval Christianity, Confucian China, Hindu and Buddhist India, Parsi Persia, Muslim Middle East, Japanese Shinto, Socialist Soviet Union, Nazi Germany, and of the many others in early America, Africa and the South Sea Islands that generations of anthropologists have tirelessly studied. None of these, or indeed any other, was known to the Aztecs.

My point is not that it is a realistic option for most of us to cope with our conflicts, make choices, abandon what we have and opt for one of these alternative evaluative frameworks. Some few people have done that, of course, but the vast majority of us is tied by language, family, morality, politics, religion, work, comfort, education, and habit to our familiar evaluative framework. The importance for us of the availability of alternatives is that we can compare our own with them. This makes it possible for us to criticize, justify, revise, and improve our own evaluative framework. The availability of alternatives liberates us from the condition of those who are locked into their own evaluative framework without the possibility of comparing their own evaluations with those available elsewhere. We have often misused the knowledge we have acquired of other evaluative frameworks for titillation about their sexual practices, getting a frisson out of horror stories, condescending to their simple-mindedness, or using them in support of a naive relativism that refuses to make adverse evaluative judgments. Nevertheless, having the knowledge gives us important possibilities that those without the knowledge lack.

The deep mistake of the Wittgensteinian view is that it assumes that we are bound to consider other evaluative frameworks from the point of view of our own. We can and often do that, of course. But we are not doomed to be as parochial as that. We can imaginatively enter into the literature, religion, philosophy, customs, and practices of evaluative frameworks that are not our own. We can, as it were, vicariously walk in their shoes for a while, and try see the world as it appears from their point of view, not ours. This is the possibility whose importance defenders of the Wittgensteinian view miss. Its importance is not just the description and interpretation of such alternatives—anthropologists do that very well—but that when we return home from this imaginative journey, we can see our own possibilities with fresh eyes and our conflicts and choices with greater detachment than we could muster before.

The knowledge of alternative possibilities on which all this depends yields great benefits, but it also carries with it great burdens. For with the comparisons it provides come conflicts between what we can have, given the possibilities of our evaluative framework, and what we might have if we adopt those of evaluative frameworks into which we have imaginatively entered. The resulting conflicts are not between staying here and moving there, but between remaining committed to the possibilities we have and reforming, enlarging, or replacing them by others, knowledge of which we have brought home with us. Reflective people in all but the most primitive evaluative frameworks had to struggle with the question of whether their criticisms of what they have are serious enough to call for deep changes that may endanger their entire evaluative framework. Nothing less is at stake for such people, as it now is for us, than the sense they or we have of life and of the evaluative distinctions that need to made between the good, bad, and in-between possibilities of life. The burdens that come with the growth of knowledge are conflicts about how to cope with the conflicting evaluations that follow from our nonhierarchical evaluative framework. Among the consequences of such conflicts are the difficult choice we have to make.

In hierarchical evaluative frameworks, there are conflicts but there is a clear way of resolving them. At the peak of the hierarchy there is an overriding value, Conflicts between evaluations can be resolved by deciding which of them is more important for the pursuit or the protection of the overriding value. There may be disagreements about that, but there is no disagreement about how such disagreements should be resolved. There is general agreement about the overriding value and the method for settling disagreements. The rest are matters of detail. In our evaluative framework, there are many candidates proposed as an overriding value and many methods favored for resolving conflicts among evaluations, but there is no general agreement to accept any of them. The reason for this is that our evaluative framework is not hierarchical, it has numerous modes of evaluation, and none is always overriding.

There have been and continue to be persistent tendencies in our evaluative framework to claim that conflicts among evaluations that follow from different modes of evaluation should always be resolved in favor of the overriding mode. Such claims have been made, at one time or another, for each of our modes of evaluation. But none of these claims has been or should have been accepted by all reasonable people.

The central problem with all such claims is that those who advance them cannot give a reasonable account of the force of the "should" in their claim that the favored mode of evaluation should be overriding. If their claim is that the reason why it should be overriding follows from the supposedly overriding mode of evaluation, then they arbitrarily assume what needs to be justified. They will convince only those who already accept that their favored mode of evaluation is overriding, and then they do not need to be convinced. But if the "should" is not derived from any of the modes of evaluation, then what is the reason for it? Any such reason must ultimately appeal to some evaluation, and the same question will arise about that evaluation, whatever it is.

We should recognize, of course, that economic, legal, moral, political, religious, and other modes of evaluation are indispensable parts of our evaluative framework. But from that it does not follow that any of them should always override the others. If the conflicts concern vital matters, then reason requires resolving them in one way or another. But it is a mistake to suppose that reason always requires resolving them in the same way. Sometimes one kind of evaluation should override a conflicting one, sometimes the reverse should happen. We need to decide the relative importance of the reasons for conflicting evaluations in the context in which their conflicts occur. Contexts, of course, change, and the relevance and importance of the reasons for different modes of evaluation change with them.

In the light of these consideration, I conclude that the Wittgensteinian view is mistaken. Knowledge of alternative evaluative frameworks enables us to appeal to considerations external to our own and compare our possibilities with those of other evaluative frameworks. Reasons, therefore, do not come to an end with what we do because we could do differently.

This, however, leaves us with reasons for and against nonhierarchical evaluative frameworks. The reason against them is that they saddle us with conflicts and difficult choices between incompatible evaluations, which are familiar features of our evaluative framework. But they are wrenching, not just familiar, because most of us, who are not fanatics, are committed to several different modes of evaluation and that makes the conflicts not only public and social but also private and personal.

The availability of evaluations that follow from other frameworks and the frequency of conflicting evaluations that follow from our own make it a serious problem of how we should cope with the resulting conflicts. The Aztecs and ideologues had no such conflicts and did not have to make difficult choices. But we do. These reasons against our evaluative framework, however, are counterbalanced by reasons for it.

We have an alternative to hierarchical evaluative frameworks from which evil actions follow. We do not have to vilify people who disagree with our evaluations. We can recognize that there will be reasonable disagreements about which mode of evaluation should reasonably override others in particular contexts. That, however, still leaves us with the problem that commitment to a particular mode of evaluation in a particular context may be so strong as to be thought to justify the infliction of evil on those who oppose it. I now turn to that problem.

Good Will

We have our modes of evaluation and evaluative frameworks, and we do what we can, given the facts and our evaluations of them. But there is a set of facts whose evaluation is of exceptional importance: those involved in deliberately causing grievous harm to other human beings who do not deserve it. For the moment I leave aside the question of whether causing grievous harm is motivated by ill will. It is enough for my present purposes that these facts are and have been parts of human lives since time immemorial. The vast majority of humanity has a visceral reaction to coming face to face with the spilled blood and guts, the visible signs of excruciating pain, and the cries for mercy of the victims, especially if they are helpless children or feeble and aged. We feel pity, outrage, and even if we cannot do anything about it, we feel that something ought to be, or have been, done.

We may call what prompts this emotional reaction benevolence, compassion, fellow-feeling, pity, solidarity, sympathy, or, as I will do, good will. I do not know whether it is innate or acquired. It is not universally shared because some may be altogether without it and, others may culpably or otherwise lose it because their experiences harden them. It may be overwhelmed by ill will, such as cruelty, envy, hatred, jealousy, malevolence, and ruthlessness; or by reason; or by other urgent and pressing concerns. Good will motivates action, but the motive may not be acted on because of fear, prudence, helplessness, or because we are at a great spatial or temporal distance from what provokes it. Good will makes us outraged by actions that deliberately cause grievous harm to innocent victims, regardless of whether they are motivated by ill will. What is important for my present purposes is that good will prompts us to challenge defenders of a mode of evaluation who, supposing it to be overriding in a particular context, think that acting on its dictates is justified even if the actions deliberately cause grievous harm to innocent people. But since this may happen in a just war, triage, or the distribution of badly needed but scarce resources, the challenge can be met. Being contrary to good will is a reason against such actions, but certainly not a conclusive one. If the actions are the least bad in wretched circumstances, then good will may actually motivate causing deliberate grievous harm to innocent people.

Good will is a reason we have for condemning an evaluative framework, regardless of whether it is our own, if it involves the deliberate infliction of grievous harm on innocent victims. But we may also have reason for defending such an evaluative framework if it enables us to live as we think we should, evaluate the possibilities of life, cope with adversities, and do not believe that there is a better alternative available. Thus we can have strong reasons both for and against modes of evaluation and evaluative frameworks, and these reasons may conflict. If we are motivated by both good and ill will, as most of us often are, and by the need to rely on the evaluative framework on which we and our society depend for living as we think we should, then our conflicting good and ill will and the conflicting reasons we have for and against our evaluative framework become conflicts within us. We have to choose between them, and the choice is difficult because so much depends on how we make it. Since conflicts between our good and ill will are frequent, as we know from personal experience, and since we often have to make difficult choices between them in particular situations—think of deep moral, political, and religious disputes—the reasonable way of coping with such conflicts and choices had to be faced again and again throughout the past and the present.

This, however, is no more than a bare beginning of grappling with the complexities involved in finding reasonable ways of coping. Both our good and ill will may be misguided. And our belief that there are or are not better alternatives available to our evaluative framework that leads to such conflicts and choices may also be mistaken. How could we tell whether or not good or ill will in a particular situation, at a particular time, directed toward particular societies, people, or actions is misguided? Whether it is really good or ill will that motivates us or others when we or they deliberately cause grievous harm? There are no reasonable unconditional answers to these questions. There are reasonable answers but they are conditional on the context and particular circumstances.

Were the Aztecs reasonable in believing that their survival depended on propitiating their god by tens of thousands of ghastly human sacrifices and the blood-drenched rituals that accompanied them? Obviously not. They had commercial and other dealings with neighboring societies whose evaluative framework did not involve similar hideous rites, and yet they survived without them. And even if we accept for a moment their belief, it does not explain the frequency with which they murdered their victims, nor eating their corpses and cutting their children to mix their blood with their victims'. Why then did they do what they did? Because they were motivated by ill will, by cruelty and ruthlessness. The evil they inflicted on their victims was disproportionately more than their belief called for. At the foundation of their evaluative framework were orgiastic evil practices that cannot be justified.

A similar condemnation is warranted of the ethnic, nationalistic, political, religious, and tribal atrocities I listed earlier in this chapter. What was done could not be explained by the ideology alone that motivated the evildoers. To adapt a catchphrase of the gun lobby, ideologies do not kill people: people kill people. Ideologies enable them to express their ill will by providing them with a justification for it. It is enough if the ideology has a semblance of reason in its favor. The vilification of Armenians by Turks; the Chinese by the Japanese; city dwellers by rural Maoists; gypsies, homosexuals, and Jews by Nazis; the bourgeois by Communists; Hindus by Muslims and vice versa; members of a tribe by members of another tribe; one and all rest on patently false beliefs that involve indefensible generalization. It proceeds from a few individuals, who may have acted the way their persecutors condemn, to countless others who belong to the same group but have not acted in the condemned way. These atrocities were not motivated only by ideologies. Ideologies encouraged and justified the evil actions that ill will motivated evildoers to perform.

It is reasonable to condemn active ill will that has motivated evil actions in the past and the present. But what about passive ill will that takes the form of callousness, indifference, or inattention? It enables but does not motivate evil actions. Are the reasons against it as strong as they are against active ill will? No, they are not because there are also strong reasons for it. This is one of the hard lessons that history teaches those who pay attention to it.

The great civilizations of ancient Greece and Rome were based on slavery. Christendom was enabled to flourish by the feudal system that century after century doomed millions of serfs to short lives and unceasing toil that made it possible for religious and secular rulers to live piously and fight with Muslims, who were also enabled by their serfs to do the same. The settlement of America was coextensive with the murder of well over half of the native Indian population. A large majority of the natives of South America were massacred by the conquistadores. A semblance of law and order was established in Europe by the Westphalian Peace, but only after 30 years of war, disease, and starvation that killed a substantial percentage men, women, and children because they were Catholics or Protestants. England derived immense wealth from the slave trade and West Indian slave labor. The industrial revolution was enabled by the labor of children and adults during long hours, in dangerous conditions, and for barely subsistence wages dooming them short, disease-ridden, and miserable lives. The French Revolution of 1789 and the defeat of the armies of Napoleon and Hitler cost countless innocent lives. And so on.

Now consider the predicament of reflective people who lived in these circumstances. They were as committed to protecting their evaluative frameworks as we are to protecting ours. They knew that it enabled them to live civilized lives, although at the cost of causing deliberate often grievous harm to innocent people. And they let it happen because they thought that it was justified, that the protection of civilized life was more important than the lives of the victims. And that gave them a strong reason for passively condoning the ill will directed against those who seriously threatened the conditions on which the evaluative framework of life depended. Of course they also had strong reasons against it. Indifference, callousness, and inattention to the grievous injury done to innocent people in their name and for their benefit is wrong.

These reasons for and against passive ill will forced them to choose. For those who are sufficiently reflective, honest, and decent, such conflicts will not be remote and social but personal, and they will find the choices they have to make difficult. The hard lesson history teaches us is that having to face such conflicts and make such choices are not rare episodes in life, but frequent and recurrent problems of life. In Bernard Williams's eloquently words:

> We are in an ethical condition that lies . . . beyond Christianity. . . . We have an ambivalent sense of what human beings have achieved, and have hopes for how they might live (in particular, in the form of a still power-ful ideal that they should live without lies). We know that the world was not made for us, or we for the world, that our history tells no purpo-sive story, and that there is no position outside the world or outside his-tory from which we might hope to authenticate our activities. We have to acknowledge the hideous costs of many human achievements that we value, including this reflective sense itself, and recognise that there is no redemptive Hegelian history or Leibnizian cost-benefit analysis to show that it will come out well enough in the end.[7]

What, then, should we do? We should face the fact that the world is not hospitable to our endeavors. We are vulnerable to forces we cannot control. But much of what makes us vulnerable is caused by us. The great evils of human life—war, slavery, atrocities, torture, tyrannies, mass murders—are caused by human beings to other human beings. Sometimes they are moral monsters motivated by ill will. But far more often they are human beings who believe that they are acting for the good of humanity in pursuing reasonable ideals that override contrary considerations. Those who resist it must be educated, and those who remain recalcitrant must be forced to act as they would if they were reasonable enough to join the cause serving the great good of humanity. And then follow the great evils that were throughout history deliber-ately inflicted on those who were condemned as enemies. This should not be obfuscated by stressing that there are also good things in life.

Those who face these facts naturally ask why human beings cause evil knowing what consequences it has. The answer is that all of us are motivated by both good and ill will and whether one or the other is dominant partly depends on the evaluative framework of our society. Most evaluative frameworks proceed as if good will were dominant and ill will motivated its participants only when social arrangements were bad. But social arrangements are bad because those who make and maintain them are motivated by active or passive ill will. Bad social arrangements cannot be the causes of the frequency of ill will because

without active or passive ill will there could not be bad social arrangements.

We all have to struggle with personal conflicts between good and ill
will and make choices between them that are difficult because however
we make them we have to go against part of ourselves. These conflicts
and choices may involve personal decisions or social arrangements, but
they always take particular forms in particular contexts. Our personal
response should be to do what we can to understand the details of our
ambivalent motivation, strengthen our good, and weaken our ill will.
Of course this is easy to say and hard to do, but that cannot be helped.
The social response should be to favor social arrangements that encourage the expression of good will and discourage the expression of ill will.
This is a platitude, if it remains a generality. It becomes realistic if it
leads to the critical examination of particular social arrangements and
to the readiness to revise or abandon them in the light of the changing
conditions in particular contexts. There is, I think, some hope in this
respect by the emergence of nonhierarchical evaluative frameworks.
But finding a reasonable way of coping with our ambivalent motives remains as difficult as it has always been.

12   The Danger of Innocence

The Conflict

Innocence is a natural, spontaneous, simple, genuine state of mind. Its expression in words and actions is without artifice or pretense, and unconcerned with making an impression. Reflection involves standing back from everyday life, trying to understand and evaluate our relations with others, the evaluative framework of our society, the circumstances in which we live, the work we do, and how our life is going. It is a state of mind in which we thoughtfully examine our ordinary activities.

Innocence and reflection are both fallible, prone to self-deception, to mistakes about our motives, and both may have good, bad, or mixed consequences. But however lasting, episodic, or characteristic our innocence and reflection are, they conflict. The more reflective we are, the less innocent we can be. And the purer is our innocence, the less reflective we will be. I will return at the end of this chapter to the possibility of resolving their conflicts, but I begin with noting that most of us do not simultaneously sustain them.

We may or may not be aware of the conflict between innocence and reflection. If unaware, then, perhaps without knowing or meaning it, we have already opted for innocence over reflection. But that may be a mistake because too much innocence may make us incapable of coping with the problems caused by human predicaments. If, however, we are aware of their conflict, then, once again, we have chosen, because the awareness involves at least some reflection.

The choice between innocence and reflection is between two personal attitudes to how we should live. One involves simple, unquestioning trust both in ourselves and in the ways of the world. The other is complex, questioning, and places us at some distance from the flow of life. How we think we should live partly depends on what we choose, and since the choice we make may be mistaken, much depends on whether we cultivate innocence or reflection as our personal attitude to life. The choice is difficult because there are strong reasons for and against both attitudes. If we decide that the balance of reasons favors one choice over the other, the weaker reasons will not disappear. We and our circumstances may change, and the balance may tilt in the other way, the conflict will have to be faced again, and the choice has to be made once more. And if we make it in one area of life, say about work, in one way, we may make it in the opposite way in another area, for instance about friendship. We can be reflective in some ways and innocent in others.

The Ideal of Innocence[1]

Once upon a time, there was a Garden, called Eden. Adam and Eve lived innocently in it, until they did what they were forbidden to do, and, at the behest of the Serpent, ate the apple from the Tree of Good and Evil. They became aware of good and evil possibilities of which they had been hitherto ignorant. Their innocence was shattered, and they had to recognize and again and again choose between good and evil. These choices put paid to their innocent existence, and their problems ensued.

The ancient myth of innocence remains alive in our imagination. We want life to be as innocent and good as it supposedly was in the Garden. That imagined possibility, as well as the necessities of life, compel us to struggle. Having eaten the apple, we know what our primordial ancestors did not know before their disobedience, namely, that we cannot trust our innocent responses because we are forever doomed to choose between good and evil possibilities.

At the risk of trespassing on hallowed grounds, I amend the ancient myth. Why did Eve listen to the Serpent, Adam to Eve, and why did they eat the apple? They did so, I suggest, because they were bored. They had all they wanted, they had each other, and the living was easy. The Sun was always shining, a balanced diet grew on trees, mosquitoes bit only the Serpent, there was no humidity or indigestion, and they were not inconvenienced by hardship or illness. But day in and day out they had nothing to do apart from eating, making love, and, I assume, sleeping, although Genesis is silent about it. So they yearned for some excitement, for opportunities to put their talents to use, having some interesting projects, and they got what they wanted. The consequences that followed are still with us, although the Serpent has become protean and our unboring lives involve conflicts and difficult choices.

The second amendment is to enlarge the scope of the knowledge eating the apple gave Adam and Eve. They came to know, I am supposing, not only good and evil possibilities, but also merely bad ones. The bad includes not just evil but also cowardice, tactlessness, vulgarity, stupidity, imprudence, self-destructiveness, irrationality, self-deception, and many other all too familiar ways in which we can go wrong in life. The reason for the enlargement is that it is hard to make a mistake about many evil possibilities, such as making baked babies part of our diet, but it is not at all hard to mistake cowardice for prudence, tactlessness for forthrightness, vulgarity for simple tastes, stupidity for inattention, and so forth. Knowing what is bad requires much more reflection than knowing what is evil. Losing innocence, as Adam and Eve did, involves becoming aware of these more complex and more problematic possibilities of life.

My third amendment is to consider the implications of the richness of the possibilities Adam and Eve had. Even if all their possibilities had been good, they still would have had to evaluate their relative desirability, ask themselves which they desired more, find a happy medium between too many and too few satisfactions, compare physical and mental pleasures, postpone some satisfactions in order enjoy others more fully, weigh the consequences of their choices, avoid jadedness, and decide how much or how little variety they wanted in their lives. And since there were two of them, they would have had to coordinate the satisfaction of their own desires with those of their mate's, an experience familiar to everyone who lives with someone else. The more aware they became of the richness of their possibilities, the more reflective, and consequently the less innocent, they had to become. The conditions of life for beings like us make pure unalloyed innocence impossible, even in circumstances as idyllic as they were in the Garden of Eden.

The myth of the Garden of Eden, however, is more plausibly understood, neither as a description of a state of affairs that has existed in the distant past, nor of one that may exist in the future, but as an ideal that we may try to approximate. The ideal is to know the good and be guided by it. In that ideal frame of mind it would be unthinkable for us even to consider what is bad as a possibility that has to be rejected. Choosing the bad would not be an option for us if we truly live according to this ideal. We would, then, live and act simply, naturally, and spontaneously — in a word, innocently. We would trust ourselves, others, and the world. Whatever attractions bad possibilities may have for others, they would have none for us if we were inspired by the good. In this ideal condition, we would face no conflicts, need make no choices, because we would know how we should live and live that way. To do otherwise would be unthinkable, if we were innocent.

Thinking of the Garden of Eden as an ideal, however, is no more tenable than thinking of it as a description of a past or future state of affairs. It is psychologically impossible for normal human beings to live without conflicts and difficult choices. We have to control our fear, desire, anger, envy, jealousy, and hostility. We have to identify and learn from our past mistakes and decide which practical courses of action we should follow in the future. We have to balance present and future satisfactions. We have to live with others and make prudent judgments about their motives, trustworthiness, how they feel about us, and how they might respond if our actions affect them one way or another. We have to face problems in the form of injustice, illness, accidents, failure, social changes, competition, ignorance, prejudice, and so forth.

The same is true of others with whom we come into contact. And that makes our interactions with them even more open to misunderstandings than do our fallibility, self-deception, wishful thinking, and unreasonable hopes and fears that handicap our understanding of ourselves. Acquiring such understanding is difficult and always a matter of degree because ultimately we have nothing else to rely on than our possibly false beliefs, unruly emotions, and ill-understood desires. But even if we have managed to acquire a great deal of understanding, we could have done so only because we have learned from our past mistakes in coping with our conflicts and making difficult choices.

The myth of innocence is dangerous because it leads to pursuing an impossible ideal while ignoring the problems of life. The myth makes a virtue of superficiality about human motivation, including our own. Reflecting on the illusion he shared with his Bloomsbury friends, Keynes memorably writes:[2]

We repudiated all versions of the doctrine of original sin, of there being insane and irrational springs of wickedness in most men. We were not aware that civilisation was a thin and precarious crust erected by the personality and the will of a very few, and only maintained by rules and conventions skillfully put across and guilefully preserved. We had no respect for traditional wisdom or the restraint of custom. We lacked reverence . . . for everything and everyone. It did not occur to us to respect the extraordinary accomplishments of our predecessors in the ordering of life . . . or the elaborate framework which they have devised to protect this order. . . . As a cause and consequence of our general state of mind we completely misunderstood human nature, including our own. The rationality which we attributed to it led to superficiality, not only of judgment, but also of feeling. . . . I can see us as water-spiders, gracefully skimming, as light and reasonable as air, the surface of the stream without any contact with the eddies and currents underneath.

The illusion Keynes condemns is that of cultivating an Epicurean garden in the company of like-minded friends, repudiating the prevailing evaluative framework, and living by rules they have made for themselves. It is now and it was then an illusion because they innocently and uncritically assumed that what they happened to value is valuable, what seemed good or bad to them really was good or bad, and that their own motives were unsullied by malice, selfishness, and contempt for those who thought differently from them about how they should live. And it was an illusion also because living as they did was made possible only in a society in which the prevailing legal, moral, and political conventions enabled some privileged individuals to live as they pleased, while scorning those who made it possible for them to live that way. They were inexcusably innocent about human nature, including their own, and about the fragility of the system that sustained them. They could and should have known better. And those of us who succumb to the same illusory ideal of innocence should also know better.

Not all innocence is inexcusable. There are many who are unreflective because their lives are hard, face debilitating adversities, live in poverty, or are terrorized by authorities who dictate how they should live. Yet others are born into the evaluative framework of a society in which innocence counts as a virtue and reflection is condemned as a vice that leads to disobedience.

Deianera

I now turn to Sophocles' "The Women of Trachis," a classic treatment of the tragic consequences of the non-culpable innocence of a woman, Deianera, who could not have known better.³ She was the wife of Heracles, the greatest hero of ancient Greek mythology. He had accomplished many feats, conquered formidable opponents, and as the play opens he is on the way home after his latest triumph. Along the way he enslaved young Iole with whom he was besotted and whom he intended to keep at home as a concubine. Deianera remained loving and faithful while her husband was away adding laurels to his already unsurpassed glory, and she was burning with desire for her husband.

When she learned about Iole, she resolved to rekindle Heracles' desire for her and sent her husband a potion, which she believed will overpower him with desire for her, rather than for Iole. She was given the potion by Nessus, a half-human monster, who assaulted her sexually and whom Heracles killed for that. As the monstrous Nessus lay dying, she gave Deianera the potion, telling her that it was by way of expiating for his obscene attack. And Deianera, in her innocence, believed him. But the potion was in fact a poison that caused excruciating death to those who were exposed to it. And that is what Deianera innocently gave Heracles, who died an awful death because of it. Deianera tried to win back her husband's love, but destroyed him instead. Acting out of love, she caused the horrible death of the man she loved most in life. That was the tragedy—the tragedy of innocence.

Sophocles shows the innocence of Deianera in many ways. She was trusting because throughout her young life she was protected, first by her father the King and then by her heroic husband. She trusted Nessus the monster, the Messenger who told her lies, and her husband who betrayed her. They all told her what to do and, she says, "I only did what I was told to do" (684) by the men who protected her. She expressed her feelings, even the bad ones about herself and her husband, plainly, ingenuously, without pretense or dissimulation. Speaking of Heracles, she says "I only know he's gone and left me a sharp pain for him" (40–41); she is "terrified to think that I may have to live deprived of the one man who is finest of all" (176–77); "Oh, I am miserable, miserable" (376); as "are my feelings . . . so too shall I act" (479); "I cry out for all I suffer" (534); "I am afraid that he may be called my husband but be the younger woman's man" (549–50); and "I am not a woman who tries to be . . . bad and bold" (582–83). There is no distance between how she feels and how she speaks or acts. This innocence leaves her helpless when she encounters evil: "I see something unspeakable, incomprehensible to human reason" (693–94); "I do not know what to think" (704); "my only wish is to be truly good" (721), and she innocently destroys the greatest hero whom her world has seen, the one she loved, and who had prevailed over all other adversaries.

When she realizes what she had done, she persists in her innocence and thinks that what she did was evil, even though she knew it was unintentional. No less innocently, she concludes that "I could not bear to live and hear myself called evil when my only wish is to be truly good" (720–21), and kills herself. In her innocence, she does not realize that she cannot be blamed for the unintended consequences of her action, nor that being called evil does not make one evil. Her innocence prevents her from recognizing and coping with the problems of her life.

In this as in all the extant plays, Sophocles shows our vulnerability to the human predicaments. Oedipus supposed that reflection can protect him, but it was his reflection that led to his disaster. Deianera, the mirror image of Oedipus, was utterly without reflection. Innocence, however, did not make her invulnerable, it destroyed her beloved and herself. We are vulnerable, Sophocles shows, whatever we do and however we live. If for "the Gods" we read "human predicaments," as perhaps Sophocles had intended, then we can conclude with the last lines of the play:

No one can foresee what is to come,
What is here now is pitiful for us . . .
but of all men it is hardest for him
who is the victim of this disaster. . . .
You have seen a terrible death
and agonies, many and strange, and there is
nothing here which is not Zeus (1269–78).

The innocent are destroyed and are destructive because they are helpless in the face of their predicaments. They think that good will is enough and that if they mean well, then all will be well. But that is a dangerous illusion. We, in our day, age, and circumstances, rely on the ideal of reflection to dispel our innocence and cope with human predicaments.

The Ideal of Reflection

Reflection, of course, can take as many forms as beliefs, emotions, and desires. The reflection that conflicts with innocence, however, has a particular form, and that is the one I now want to discuss.[4] In the interest of brevity I will refer to it simply as reflection. The general focus of reflection is how we do and should live, but that is much too general because our life has many different inward and outward aspects and we may be concerned with it and its aspects from many different points of view, which may be aesthetic, ecological, economic, historical, legal, medical, moral, political, religious, psychological, scientific, and so forth. The focus of this chapter is on evaluative, not descriptive, points of view, and, more specifically, on the evaluation of how closely we actually live comes to how we think we should live. Our reflection on the gap between the life we have and the one we should have is prone to mistakes. The temptations are many of evaluating ourselves more favorably than we should. So we have to be critical of our evaluations.

The point of reflection, then, is first to step back from how we live, understand it, evaluate it, and then question, criticize, or justify it. But this involves a realistic view of the possibilities we have, the psychological and social limits to which we are subject, and the evaluative framework of the society in which we live. And the evaluative framework by which we are, for better or worse, unavoidably influenced may also be partly or entirely mistaken. All of this makes reflection hard and prone to mistakes. Why, then, should we reflect? Because without it we could not respond reasonably to the problems we encounter when we try to live as we think we should.

The problem with innocence is that it excludes reflection, and the less we reflect, the less able we are to cope with the conflicts and choices that stand in the way of living as we think we should. But there is a problem also with reflection: it is very difficult to do it well. We need help with it, and, it is thought, that reasonable evaluative frameworks and their modes of evaluation can provide that help by means of an ideal theory of reflection. Just as the ideal of innocence is a state of mind in which it is unthinkable that we would follow possibilities contrary to how we should live, so the ideal of reflection is to be wholeheartedly committed to an ideal theory which, if accepted and realized, would make following such possibilities unthinkable.

I have argued throughout the book that the search for an ideal theory involves chasing a dangerous illusion. I do so one last time because the search for it interferes with a reasonable way of coping with the conflict between innocence and reflection. The present form of the ideal is that rightly conducted reflection will make it unthinkable to be committed to possibilities that are contrary to living as we should.

For the innocent some possibilities are unthinkable because they have not thought of them. That leaves open the question of what would happen if they did so. The reason why some possibilities are unthinkable for the innocent may be their cognitive or imaginative failings, not their goodness or virtues. Another reason why reflection may lead to regarding some possibilities as unthinkable is that they have been thought of and unequivocally rejected because commitment to an ideal theory rules them out. In John McDowell's apt words, a person's judgment who is committed to live and act according to an ideal theory is not

> a result of balancing reasons for and against. The view of a situation he arrives at . . . is one in which some aspect of the situation is seen as constituting a reason for acting in some way; this reason is apprehended, not as outweighing or overriding any reason for acting in other ways . . . but as silencing them.[5]

The state of mind arrived at by commitment to an ideal theory is that some possibilities become unthinkable because they are silenced by commitment to an ideal theory.

If we are reflective, we may become so committed because we believe that reasonable modes of evaluation and our personal attitude that jointly guide how we think we should live rule out some possibilities. That is why, if we are ideally reflective, we reach the point at which possibilities contrary to how we should live are silenced and become for us unthinkable. We have reflected in the past, committed ourselves to living that way, and now no longer have to reflect, just as we do not have to reflect when we use our native language. The unthinkable is silenced, not because we are unreflective, as the innocent are, but because reflection has done its work, and it is now behind us.

If we are ideally reflective, we naturally regard some possibilities as unthinkable because reflection has made that our second nature. If we are purely innocent, we follow whatever possibilities our first nature prompts us to follow. We may be among the exceptional few who have a saintly first nature, spontaneously live as we rightly think we should, and life goes well for us and for those who are affected by our actions. Or we may be like most of humanity and start out with good and bad dispositions, mixed motives, and ambivalent personal attitudes. That is why for most of us innocence is dangerous and reflection necessary.

Reflection, Innocence, and Ideal Theories

We have seen that complexities and conflicts make the ideal of innocence an unattainable and ill-advised illusion. I think that the same is true of the illusion that an ideal theory can be formulated. There are several reasons for this. One is that although numerous ideal theories have been proposed throughout the world during past millennia, not one of them has been generally accepted. This has not been because ideal theorists have not been sufficiently reasonable and reflective. Some of the best minds in the world have dedicated themselves to formulating an ideal theory as the key to living as we all should. But no less reasonable and reflective critics have always found faults with the proposed one, and then proceeded to formulate their own ideal theory, which then met the same fate.

The basic reason for this unbroken record of failure is that the attempts rest on the mistaken assumption that there is one, and only one, overriding ideal that everyone, always, in all circumstances should be guided by. The assumption is often only tacitly held, but sometimes it is explicitly expressed, usually by philosophers. In Kant's words,[6]

> an absolutely good will, whose principle must be the categorical imperative, will . . . contain only the *form of willing*, and that as autonomy. In other words, the fitness of the maxim of every good will to make itself a universal law is itself the sole law which the will of every rational being spontaneously imposes on itself.

According to Mill,

> the general principle to which all rules of practice ought to conform, and the test by which they should be tried, is that of conduciveness to the

happiness of mankind, or rather, of all sentient beings: in other words
. . . the promotion of happiness is the ultimate principle.[7] That is . . . the
foundation of morality . . . the standard of morality . . . and the criterion
of morality.[8]

Contrary to this assumption, we know from history and personal experience that there is a wide plurality of ideals that have been and are
followed by different people, at different times, in different contexts,
derived from different ideal theories as guides to how they should live.

Part of my reason for having discussed anthropological, historical,
and literary possibilities throughout the book has been to stress this
plurality of ideals. It follows from their plurality, contrary to the mistaken assumption on which ideal theories rest, that there are many
ideals that may reasonably guide how we should live. The search for the
ideal theory is not misguided because the ideal it favors is unreasonable, but because there are many reasonable ideals that may guide how
we should live, depending on our personal attitude and the evaluative
framework of the society in which we live. This is not because any ideal
is as reasonable as any other, but because, as I have tried to show again
and again in preceding chapters, there are different ideals in different
contexts and they may or may not be reasonable.

Another reason why there can be no ideal theory that reason requires
everyone, always, everywhere to accept as a guide to how all human
beings should live is that not only is there a plurality of ideals but also
a plurality of modes of evaluation. The moral mode of evaluation must
certainly be part of any reasonable guide to how we should live, but it
is not the only reasonable guide. Economic, legal, medical, political,
and religious modes of evaluations are no less important than moral
ones. The problem is that from each of these modes of evaluation several conflicting evaluations follow, and the evaluations that follow from
one mode often conflict with the evaluations that follow from other
modes. It cannot be reasonably supposed, as ideal theorists routinely
do, that reason requires that such conflicts be always settled in favor of
the evaluations of one mode.

Why should moral evaluations always override scientific ones? Could
not scientific research show that some factual assumptions on which
moral evaluations rest are mistaken? Could not moral evaluations be
dogmatic, dictated by merely local conventions? Could not they be the
expression of prejudices or of the self-serving interests of illegitimate

authorities? Such questions often and reasonably arise about conflicting evaluations that follow from all modes of evaluation, not just from the moral one. And when they do arise, it cannot be reasonably supposed that the evaluations that follow from one mode should always, in all contexts, and in all cases override all conflicting evaluations. But that is just what ideal theorists routinely suppose.

Most contemporary ideal theorists in our society claim that the overriding mode of evaluation should be moral. But in numerous other contexts, the overriding mode has been economic, political, or religious. Surely, if we face epidemics and natural disasters, medical evaluations may reasonably override economic, legal, moral, political, and religious evaluations. And is it not obvious that the possibility of worrying about the conflicting evaluations that follow from various modes of evaluation presupposes the availability of at least sufficient economic resources to meet the basic needs for nutrition, shelter, and hygiene. It is unreasonable to suppose, as ideal theorists do, that one mode of evaluations should always, in all contexts, in all circumstances override all other conflicting modes of evaluation. If this were recognized, the search for ideal theories would have to be abandoned. But it is not recognized, the search goes on, ideal theories are contested by other ideal theories, which, in turn, are criticized by yet others. The general impression created by all this ferment is that of very earnest people banging their stubborn heads against very hard walls, when, actually, the door is open and they could leave their self-imposed confinement.

There is yet a further reason why the search is fruitless for an ideal theory that would provide the overriding evaluation to which we could appeal to resolve conflicts between and within modes of evaluation. The reason is that if the overriding evaluation, impossible as it is, were miraculously found, it could not be reliably applied. According to ideal theorists, we need an overriding evaluation because otherwise we could not resolve conflicts among evaluations and make the difficult choices we have to make. They rightly suppose that our choices may be based on a personal attitude that involves mistaken beliefs, overwrought emotions, or misguided desires. And even if we form our beliefs, emotions, and desires that guide how we think we should live by relying on the evaluative framework of our society, that too may be flawed. That is why we need, ideal theorists wrongly suppose, an objective, context-independent, universally applicable, overriding evaluation on which we could rely for evaluating both our beliefs, emotions, and desires and our evaluative framework.

Having such an overriding evaluation, however, would not be enough. We would have to apply it to resolve the conflicts we face and make the difficult choices between the conflicting good and bad, better and worse possibilities we think we have. And we would have to apply it to what we understand as the context in which the conflicts arise and the choices have to be made. Such understanding and application, of course, may be mistaken. In order to avoid the mistakes, we could not reasonably rely on the supposedly overriding evaluation we are trying to apply unless we have ascertained its reliability. How else, then, could we ascertain the reliability of the supposedly overriding evaluation than by our beliefs, emotions, and desires that guide how we think we should live? And if, as ideal theorists insist, they too may be mistaken, then, even if we have and want to follow an objective, context-independent, universal, and overriding evaluation, its application in particular contexts would be as prone to mistakes as is the personal attitude on which we rely in applying it.

Ultimately we can do no better than rely on our fallible reflections in order to cope with our conflicts and make difficult choices. Ideal theories are supposed to replace our fallible reflections with an overriding evaluation that reason requires everyone to accept. But they cannot do that. There are many conflicting evaluations that follow from many conflicting modes of evaluation. And we have to rely on our fallible reflections to apply in particular contexts whatever evaluations there may be. Reason does require us to try to cope with our conflicts and make difficult choices, but we cannot do that by relying on any ideal theory. We are left with a choice between two personal attitudes: innocence that cannot cope with human predicaments, and reflection that is an unavoidably fallible guide to coping with our conflicts and making the choices we have to make.

I conclude that we have strong but conflicting reasons both for and against trying to approximate the ideal of innocence or of reflection. The reason for aiming at innocence is that it would free us from the conflicts and choices with which we, who have not come even close to the ideal, have to struggle. We would, then, live simply, feel safe and untroubled, because we knew how we should live and live that way. We would have returned to the Garden of Eden.

The reason against trying to approximate the ideal of innocence is that not even the best intentions are sufficient for coping with human predicaments and the problems to which they lead. The context in which we live forces us to face conflicts and make choices between good and bad, better and worse economic, legal, medical, moral, political, religious, and scientific evaluations. And our own beliefs, emotions, and desires that guide how we think we should live also conflict and force us to make choices that are difficult because whatever we choose we must go against some of our own evaluations in order to follow some others.

These problems are for beings like us unavoidable. The ideal of innocence is the illusion that we can free ourselves from conflicts and choices. But we cannot because they are inherent in the efforts we might make to free us from the very conflicts and choices of which we are trying to free ourselves. We cannot raise ourselves by our bootstraps, not even if we try very hard.

The reason for aiming at the ideal of reflection is that we need some reasonable approach to coping with conflicts and making choices. Reflection is supposed to be that approach. It would be a very strong, perhaps conclusive, reason for reflection if we could rely on it for that purpose. And it certainly is a possible approach. It involves understanding and evaluating the conflicting alternatives between which we have to choose. But is it a reliable approach? Ideal theorists say that it would be reliable if it were guided by the right ideal theory. As we have seen, however, millennia of search has not led to a generally accepted ideal theory. All ideal theories that have been hitherto proposed arbitrarily privilege some mode of evaluation at the detriment of other no less reasonable modes. And all ideal theories have to be applied to particular conflicts and choices, but the efforts to apply them are also handicapped by conflicts and choices. Reflection on how we should live involves our fallible and conflicting beliefs, emotions, and desires. We have to choose between them, and those choices also involve fallible and conflicting beliefs, emotions, and desires. The strong reason against reflection based on any ideal theory is that it cannot free us from conflicts and choices.

The ideal of reflection rests on the mistaken assumption that an ideal theory would allow us to transcend our condition. But that is, I repeat, as much an illusion as is relying on the ideal of innocence. It cannot be done. The ideals of innocence and reflection are both superficial for the same reason: they fail to recognize how deep and subversive are the human predicaments that cause our conflicts and the difficult choices we have to make.

Toward Deeper Understanding[9]

What, then can we do? My answer is in several steps. The first is to consider what I think is a mistaken claim by Bernard Williams. He writes that once we embark of reflection, "there is no route back, no way in which we can consciously take ourselves back from it."[10] In one way, Williams is obviously right: once we have reflected and came to understand that human predicaments are unavoidable, we cannot just return to our previous innocence about them. We will, then, have understood that we face the conflicts and have to make the difficult choices I have discussed in the preceding chapters. Williams is right to think that innocence is like youth, once lost, it stays lost. But reflection is not like that. It is a lasting achievement that may be sufficiently deep to allow us to face the problems, rather than innocently ignore them, or console ourselves with the dream of an ideal theory. Once we have achieved that, we no longer have to do it again. It has become part of us and forms the background of how we live and act.

The route back from reflection is to have reached a point beyond which we can live and act as if we were innocent. But it is a different kind of innocence, based on a deeper understanding of the problems we have to face, not an unreflective innocence based on ignorance about them. The innocence that deeper understanding may allow us to reach is an enduring and calm acceptance of the conflicts with which we have to cope, the difficult choices we have to make, and the unavoidability of human predicaments. This is compatible with a simple, spontaneous, genuine, natural way of living and acting that is free of pretense and self-deception. It is, however, an expression of a second nature that we have cultivated through deepening understanding, rather than of our first nature with which we have innocently started out in life, and which many of us have not entirely lost.

The second step toward my answer is to consider the content of such deeper understanding. What does it exclude and include? It excludes the expectation that if we try hard enough, we can make ourselves immune to human predicaments. We, then, realize that the complexities, conflicts, and choices we encounter are not episodic emergencies visited upon us by bad luck, but ineluctable conditions. They are conditions with which we have to cope as reasonably as we can. Conflicts and difficult choices are among the consequences these conditions.

Some conflicts are inherent in the often conflicting modes of evaluation of the evaluative framework of our society. There is very little any of us can do to change them. Perhaps we can leave our society, but we leave it for another, and it will also have conflicting modes of evaluation that require us to make difficult choices. We have very little control over these conflicts. They force difficult choices on us between unwanted and threatening alternatives.

Nor can we free ourselves from the choices I have discussed between conflicts and self-knowledge, choices and decisions, fate and autonomy, fear and prudence, contingency and justice, our present and future self, social and personal evaluations, hypocrisy and authenticity, boredom and engagement, evil and reasons, and innocence and reflection. We have seen how unavoidable and difficult are the choices most of us have to make between them. We have strong reasons for and against both alternatives, and whichever we choose, we must give up something we regard as important for living as we think we should.

Deeper understanding excludes the expectation that if we try hard enough, we can free ourselves from such problems. This expectation is the tacit assumption that motivates ideal theories. But if we reach a deep enough understanding, we will know that the assumption is mistaken because problems, conflicts, and choices are part of our condition. Perhaps we cannot give up the dream of transcending our condition and living free of problems, but it nevertheless remains only a dream, although a persistent one.

Deeper understanding includes a realistic attitude that enables us to see life steadily and as a whole. It is, of course, not to see the entirety of life — no one can do that — but to see what is important in it for living as we should. And it is not to do nothing else except contemplate it — no one can or indeed should try to do that either — but to see it steadily, without self-deception, obfuscation, or fantasizing it away. This is admittedly very hard to do. Mentioning only some of the great and dead, Sophocles, Euripides, and Shakespeare in their tragedies, Thucydides and Burckhardt in their histories, Montaigne and Hume in their essays, Nietzsche in scattered aphoristic remarks, Conrad in some novels, and, closer to our time, perhaps E. R. Dodds, Wallace Stevens, Wislawa Szymborska, Isaiah Berlin, Stuart Hampshire, and Bernard Williams did it in some of their works.

I am not suggesting that seeking deeper understanding requires sharing the content of these fine writers' various and very different attitudes and responses to human predicaments. Their responses certainly leave room for reasonable dissent, and they certainly do not exhaust possible responses. But they have seen the futility of dreaming about ideal theories. They have seen in Peter Winch's fine words, that

> a man's sense of the importance of something to him shows itself in all sorts of ways: not merely in precautions to safeguard that thing. He may . . . contemplate it, to gain some sense of his life in relation to it. He may wish thereby, in a certain sense, to *free* himself from dependence on it. I do not mean by making sure that it does not let him down, because the point is that, *whatever* he does, he may still be let down. The important thing is that he should understand *that* and come to terms with it . . . a man may equally well be transfixed and terrified by the contemplation of such a possibility. He must see that he can still go on even if he is let down by what is vitally important to him; and he must so order his life that he still *can* go on in such circumstances.[11]

To have reached this is to have reached part of an attitude that must be part of the deeper understanding toward which I am gesturing. But it is only a part of it. If it included nothing more, it would be a bleak view of our life. It is certainly true that if we give up the expectation that we can free ourselves from human predicaments, then we will not be shocked if we are assailed by them. But if the best we can do is to be prepared to go on even if lose what is vitally important to us, then deeper understanding is a paltry thing indeed. Why should we go on if we realize how little control we have over what we most value, how much at risk is what we live for, and how easily we can lose what makes our life worth living?

This brings us to the third step toward deeper understanding. It involves acknowledging that the best efforts we can make to cope with human predicaments may fail. But it also involves the realization that this is not a reason against making them. On the contrary, it is a reason for making the best efforts we can, because if we do not, we increase the chances of the very failure that we want to avoid. This is no more than plain common sense. But it takes depth, not just common sense, to respond appropriately to the acknowledgment of our vulnerability.

One seductive response is to turn toward despair, cynicism, quick gratification, seeking consolation in mysticism, oriental cults, misanthropy, religious or ideological fanaticism, or in numbing ourselves with work or with physical exertion. These are all unreasonable overreactions to the realization that we are vulnerable to human predicaments. If we no longer believe that life is bound to go well for us if we try really hard, we need not conclude that everything is hopelessly going to hell. To recognize that we are vulnerable, does not mean that calamity awaits us just around the corner. Contingencies may benefit, not just harm, us; there is also good will and a sense of justice in human life, not just evil; and the evaluative framework that is a bulwark between civilized life and barbarism, although porous, may be strong enough to withstand barbaric assaults, especially if we face them resolutely. We are at risk, but we are not doomed. To have reached this depth of understanding is to have gone far, but it is possible to go still farther.

The evolutionary process that our natural conditions have made possible allows us to interpose an evaluative framework between the human and the non-human parts of the world. With reason and good judgment we can use the limited control we have to protect that framework and increase such control as we have over ourselves and the conditions in which we live. We can thus humanize a minute segment of the vast world by relying on our evaluative framework. Of course, our efforts at control and at increasing the control we have are limited by conditions beyond our control. But normally, which is most of the time, our limits do not deprive us from all of our possibilities.

A deeper understanding combines the acknowledgment of our limits and encourages the pursuit of our possibilities as the only means we have of facing human predicaments. This acknowledgment and encouragement are the third step toward deeper understanding. But it follows from it also that it excludes misunderstanding our condition by benighting ourselves with the illusion that our condition is better than it is, or by making things worse and succumb to the disillusion that it is worse than it is. A deep enough understanding lies between these stultifying extremes: between the unsubstantial dreams of illusions and the corrosive nihilism of disillusion. And this deeper understanding gives us the modest hope that we can reasonably have. What then is this hope?

I have been referring to our condition, but that is only a convenient abstraction we can use to refer collectively to our particular and individual conditions. A general description of these conditions is that we are all trying to live as we think we should, given our experiences, preferences, upbringing, ambient conditions, and the evaluative framework of our society. We try, more or less reasonably, with greater or lesser success, to live accordingly.

The modest hope allowed by the deeper understanding I have been describing is that there is a route back from reflection to the kind of innocence that a deeper understanding allows. It excludes the vain hope nurtured by ideal theorists that if we are reasonable enough, we can escape from human predicaments. And it combines the acknowledgments of our vulnerability to them with the realistic recognition that we have not only problems but also possibilities and some control that enables us to try to live as we think we should. But it gives us only modest hope because our control is limited, both our personal attitude and the evaluative framework on which we rely are fallible. Nevertheless, we still need to cope with our conflicts and make difficult choices.

It will be said, especially by ideal theorists, that this hope is pretty thin gruel for those who yearn for more substantial nutrition. My response is that ideal theorists are like the man with the blue guitar to whom it was

> Said, "You have a blue guitar,
> You do not play things as they are."
> The man replied, "Things as they are
> Are changed upon the blue guitar."

The man with the blue guitar wanted more than anything to be heard, but he was not listened to by his meager audience because they did not believe he could change things by his blue guitar. He climbed on a table to be heard by more people but they still paid no attention to him. He put a chair on the table, stood on it, and people began to take notice, but only to laugh at him. Then he put a long ladder on the table and balanced the chair on top of it, and a few people actually stopped laughing and paid interest. He was encouraged. He balanced an even longer second ladder on the first, balanced the chair on the second latter, and climbed on the chair with his blue guitar. Crowds gathered and watched his incredible balancing act. They were awed by his skill. Then, being very careful not to lose his balance, he played for them on his blue guitar. But he was too high up and nobody could hear him. He played and played, balanced and balanced, but he was too involved in what he was doing to notice that only he could hear it. It was all very sad — as sad as ideal theorists are. Finally, he climbed down and came to the deeper understanding that

> To say more than human things with human voice,
> That cannot be; to say human things with more
> Than human voice, that also, cannot be:
> To speak humanly from the height or from the depth
> Of human things, that is acutest speech.[12]

Notes

Chapter One

1   My way of understanding evaluative frameworks is not new, although it has often been referred to by various different names. According to an anthropologist,

> one of the broadest and surest generalizations that anthropology can make about human beings is that no society is healthy or creative or strong unless that society has a set of common values that can give meaning and purpose to group life, that can be symbolically expressed, that fit with situation of the time as well as being linked to the historical past, and that do not outrage man's reason and at the same time appeal to their emotions (Clyde Kluckhohn, "Culture and Behavior," in *Collected Essays of Clyde Kluckhohn*, ed. R. Kluckhohn [New York: Free Press, 1962], 297–98).

A classicist writes that

> there remains embedded in the very substance of all our thought about the world and about ourselves an inalienable and ineradicable framework of conception, which is not our own making, but given to us ready-made by society—a whole apparatus of concepts and categories, within which . . . all our individual thinking . . . is compelled to move. This common inherited scheme of conception, which is all around us and comes to us as naturally and unobjectionably as our native air, is none the less imposed upon us and limits our intellectual movements in countless ways (F. M. Cornford, *From Religion to Philosophy* [New York: Harper & Row, 1912/1957], 44–45).

A philosopher sees it as

> our sharing routes of interest and feeling, modes of response senses of humor and of significance and of fulfillment, of what is outra-

geous, of what is similar to what else, what a rebuke, what forgive-
ness, of when an utterance is an assertion, when an appeal, when
an explanation — all the whirl of organism Wittgenstein calls "form
of life." Human speech and activity, sanity and community, rest
upon nothing more, but nothing less, than this (Stanley Cavell, "The
Availability of Wittgenstein's Later Philosophy," in *Must We Mean
What We Say?* [Cambridge: Cambridge University Press, 1976], 52).

2   I am not sure who first named it ideal theory, but it is so named in John
Rawls's *A Theory of Justice* (Cambridge, MA: Harvard University Press,
1971).

3   The phrase is Bernard Williams'. See *Philosophy as a Humanistic Discipline*,
ed. A. W. Moore (Princeton, NJ: Princeton University Press, 2006).

4   This tradition includes Pyrrhonian skeptics, Epicureans, Stoics, Montaigne, Pascal, many of Hume's essays, Nietzsche, aspects of the later work
of Wittgenstein, Pierre Hadot, Peter Winch, Iris Murdoch, Stuart Hampshire, Bernard Williams, Annette Baier, and such presently active thinkers as, among others, Stanley Cavell, Timothy Chappell, John Cottingham,
Richard Eldridge, Raimond Gaita, Daniel Hutto, Jonathan Lear, Stephen
Mulhall, Alexander Nehamas, and Anthony O'Hear. They disagree, of
course, about many things, and I with them. But we agree that one central task of philosophy is to seek reasonable answers to the question of how
we, fallible human beings, should understand and cope with the particular
forms in which we have to face problems of life.

Chapter Two

1   Plato, *Republic*, trans. Robin Waterfield (Oxford: Oxford University Press,
ca. 380 BC/1993), 443d–e.

2   Stuart Hampshire, *Thought and Action* (London: Chatto & Windus, 1960),
177.

3   See Charles L. Griswold, *Self-Knowledge in Plato's Phaedrus* (New Haven,
CT: Yale University Press, 1986).

4   See, e.g., Erich Heller, *The Artist's Journey into the Interior* (London: Secker
& Warburg, 1965); W. H. Buford, *The German Tradition of Self-Cultivation*
(Cambridge: Cambridge University Press, 1975); and Robert E. Norton,
The Beautiful Soul (Ithaca, NY: Cornell University Press, 1995).

5   The theory was proposed by Leon Festinger, *A Theory of Cognitive Disso-
nance* (Stanford, CA: Stanford University Press, 1957). A recent refined
and revised restatement of it is Joel Cooper, *Cognitive Dissonance* (Los
Angeles: Sage, 2007). For surveys of the literature and bibliographies, see
Mary L. Loach, "Cognitive Dissonance," *Encyclopedia of Human Behavior*
(San Diego: Academic Press, 1994); and Elliot Aronson, "Cognitive Dis-

sonance," *Encyclopedia of Psychology* (New York: Oxford University Press, 2000).

6 See, e.g., Richard Wollheim, *The Mind and Its Depths* (Cambridge, MA: Harvard University Press, 1993); and Jonathan Lear, *Open Minded* (Cambridge, MA: Harvard University Press, 1998).

7 I rely on E. E. Evans-Pritchard's 1948 Frazer Lecture, published as "The Divine Kingship of the Shilluk of the Nilotic Sudan," in *Social Anthropology and Other Essays* (New York: Free Press, 1948/1962). References are to the pages of this book.

8 Edward Gibbon, *The Decline and Fall of the Roman Empire*, chap. 2. There are many editions and it would be pedantic to cite any one.

9 Stuart Hampshire, *Innocence and Experience* (London: Allen Lane, 1989), 101.

Chapter Three

1 For a survey and bibliography, see C. A. J. Coady, "The Problem of Dirty Hands," *Stanford Encyclopedia of Philosophy*, http//:plato.stanford.edu /entries/dirty-hands/.

2 Michel de Montaigne, "Of the Vanity of Words," in *The Complete Works of Montaigne*, trans. Donald M. Frame (Stanford, CA: Stanford University Press, 1588/1943), 220.

3 J. B. Schneewind, *The Invention of Autonomy* (Cambridge: Cambridge University Press, 1998), 4.

4 Louis Dumont, *Homo Hierarchicus: The Caste System and Its Implications*, trans. Mark Sainsbury, et. al. (Chicago: University of Chicago Press, 1966/1970); and *Essays on Individualism: Modern Ideology in Anthropological Perspective* (Chicago: University of Chicago Press, 1986).

5 Clifford Geertz, *Negara: The Theatre State in Nineteenth-Century Bali* (Princeton, NJ: Princeton University Press, 1980), and in parts of *Local Knowledge* (New York: Basic Books, 1983). Reference in the text are to the pages of the second work.

6 Schneewind, Invention of Autonomy, 4.

7 What I say about defeasible commitments is similar to what Ross says about prima facie duties. See W. D. Ross, *The Right and the Good* (Oxford: Clarendon, 1930).

8 Arthur O. Lovejoy, *The Great Chain of Being* (New York: Harper & Row, 1960), 312.

Chapter Four

1   Arthur Schopenhauer, *The World as Will and Representation*, trans. E. F. Payne (New York: Dover, 1844,1969), 1:252–53.

2   The only recent defense of fatalism I know of is Richard Taylor's "Fatalism," in *Philosophical Review* 71 (1962): 56–66; and "Fate" in his *Metaphysics* (Englewood Cliffs, NJ: Prentice-Hall, 1963). It provoked numerous attempts to refute it. See Hugh Rice, "Fatalism," *Stanford Encyclopedia of Philosophy*, http://plato.stanford.edu/archives//entries/fatalism/, as well as Steven M. Cahn and Maureen Eckert, eds. *Fate, Time, and Language* (New York: Columbia University Press, 2011). Fatalism, of course, has been long recognized as a metaphysical conundrum in Aristotle's *Categories* and *De Interpretatione*, but, as far as I know, it is not now a live issue.

3   I rely on the immensely learned "Fate," in *Encyclopedia of Religion and Ethics*, ed. James Hastings (New York: Scribner's, 1912), vol. 5. Also, Vincenzo Cioffari, "Fortune, Fate, and Chance," in *Dictionary of the History of Ideas*, ed. Philip P. Wiener (New York: Scribner's, 1973), vol. 2. And for West African religions, on Meyer Fortes, *Oedipus and Job in West African Religion* (Cambridge: Cambridge University Press, 1959); and *Religion, Morality, and the Person: Essays on Tallensi Religion*, ed. Jack Goody (Cambridge: Cambridge University Press, 1987).

4   For the history of autonomy, see J. B. Schneewind, *The Invention of Autonomy* (New York: Cambridge University Press, 1998). For a survey and bibliography following the cited passage, see John Christman, http://plato.stanford.edu/archives/spr2011/entries/autonomy-moral/.

5   Isaiah Berlin, "Two Concepts of Liberty," in *Four Essays on Liberty* (Oxford: Oxford University Press, 1958/1969), 131.

6   Bernard Williams, "The Women of Trachis," in *The Sense of the Past*, ed. Myles Burnyeat (Princeton, NJ: Princeton University Press, 1996/2006), 54.

7   Sophocles, *Oedipus at Colonus*, in *The Three Theban Plays*, trans. Robert Fagles (New York: Viking, 1982). References are to the lines of this translation, unless otherwise noted.

8   Isaiah Berlin, "European Unity and Its Vicissitudes," in *The Crooked Timber of Humanity*, ed. Henry Hardy (London: John Murray, 1959/1990).

9   Plato, *Republic*, trans. Robin Waterfield (Oxford: Oxford University Press, ca. 380 BC/1993). References are to the lines of this translation and edition.

10 Paul Shorey, *Republic* in *Plato: Collected Dialogues*, eds. Edith Hamilton and Huntington Cairns (Princeton, NJ: Princeton University Press, 1961).

11 Hiromichi Yahara, *The Battle for Okinawa*, trans. Roger Pineau and Masatichi Uehara (New York: Wiley, 1995).

12 Aristotle, *Nicomachean Ethics*, trans. W. D. Ross, rev. J. O. Urmson, in *The

Complete Works of Aristotle, ed. Jonathan Barnes (Princeton, NJ: Princeton University Press, 1984). References are to the lines of this translation.

13　The remarks that follow rely on Ivan Morris's *The Nobility of Failure: Tragic Heroes in the History of Japan* (New York: Farrar, Straus and Giroux, 1975); and Yukio Mishima, *The Way of the Samurai*, trans. Kathryn Sparling (New York: Basic Books, 1977).

Chapter Five

1　This is not the place for a review of the relevant works. Interested readers will find an excellent survey and a much fuller bibliography than I can give in Ronald de Sousa's, http://plato.stanford.edu/archives/spr2013/entries /emotion/.

2　For the Aristotelian view, see David Konstan, *The Emotions of the Ancient Greeks* (Toronto: University of Toronto Press, 2006); Alexander Nehamas, "Pity and Fear in the *Rhetoric* and the *Poetics*," and Martha C. Nussbaum, "Tragedy and Self-Sufficiency: Plato and Aristotle on Fear and Pity," both in *Essays on Aristotle's Poetics*, ed. Amelie Rorty (Princeton, NJ: Princeton University Press, 1992).

3　Aristotle, *Nicomachean Ethics*, trans. W. D. Ross, rev. J. O. Urmson, in *The Complete Works of Aristotle*, ed. Jonathan Barnes (Princeton, NJ: Princeton University Press, 1984), 1109a23–29.

4　Blaise Pascal, *Pensees*, trans. W. F. Trotter (New York: Random House, 1670/1941), 205–6.

5　Bertrand Russell, "A Free Man's Worship," in *Mysticism and Logic* (Harmondsworth, UK: Penguin, 1902/1953), 51.

6　This possibility of course has been much discussed. See, e.g., Albert Camus, *The Myth of Sisyphus* (New York: Random House, 1942/1955); Thomas Nagel, "The Absurd," in *Mortal Questions* (Cambridge: Cambridge University Press, 1979), and chap. 11 in *The View from Nowhere* (New York: Oxford University Press, 1986); and Richard Taylor, chap. 18 in *Good and Evil* (New York: Macmillan, 1970).

7　Bernard Williams, *Ethics and the Limits of Philosophy* (London: Collins, 1985), 118.

8　G. F. W. Hegel, *Reason in History*, trans. R. S. Hartman (New York: Liberal Arts, 1953), 6–7.

9　Mary Douglas, *Purity and Danger* (London: Routledge, 1966).

10　E. E. Evans-Pritchard, *Witchcraft, Oracles and Magic among the Azande* (Oxford: Oxford University Press, 1936). For interesting discussions of it, see Michael Polanyi, *Personal Knowledge* (Chicago: University of Chicago Press, 1958), 287–94; Peter Winch, "Understanding a Primitive Society," in *Ethics and Action* (London: Routledge, 1964/1972); and Robin Horton,

"Professor Winch on Safari," in *Patterns of Thought in Africa and the West* (Cambridge: Cambridge University Press, 1976/1993), 138–60.

11 David Hume, *A Treatise of Human Nature*, 2nd ed., ed. P. H. Nidditch (Oxford: Clarendon, 1739/1978), 268.

12 Horton, "African Traditional Thought and Western Science," in *Patterns*, op. cit. 197–258, at p. 246.

13 Michel de Montaigne, *Essays* in *The Complete Works of Montaigne*, trans. Donald M. Frame (Stanford: Stanford University Press, 1588/1979). References are to the pages of this edition.

14 René Descartes, "Discourse on the Method . . . ," in *The Philosophical Writings of Descartes*, trans. John Cottingham, et. al. (Cambridge: Cambridge University Press, 1637/1985), 1:122.

15 Hume, *Treatise*, 268–69.

16 Karl R. Popper, "Towards a Rational Theory of Tradition," in *Conjectures and Refutations* (New York: Harper, 1968), 131.

17 Thomas Reid, *Essays on the Active Powers of the Human Mind* (Cambridge, MA: MIT Press, 1814/1969), 349.

18 W. V. O. Quine, "Two Dogmas of Empiricism," in *From a Logical Point of View* (Cambridge, MA: Harvard University Press, 1953), 42–43.

19 Bernard Williams, *Truth and Truthfulness* (Princeton, NJ: Princeton University Press, 2002), 268.

20 Friedrich Nietzsche, *Human All Too Human*, trans. R. J. Hollingdale (Cambridge: Cambridge University Press, 1878/1996), 1:517.

Chapter Six

1 What I say about justice is in a long tradition according to which the primary concern of justice is with desert. The tradition is that "life for life, eye for eye, tooth for tooth, hand for hand, foot for foot, burn for burn, wound for wound, stripe for stripe." *Exodus* 21:24. "I the LORD search the mind and try the heart, to give to every man according to his ways, according to the fruit of his doings." *Jeremiah* 17:10. "Awards should be according to merit; for all men agree that what is just in distribution must be according to merit in some sense." Aristotle, *Nicomachean Ethics*, 1131b24–26. "Justice is a constant and unceasing determination to render everyone his due." Justinian, *Institutes*, I.iii.1. "Justice is a constant and abiding will that renders every person his desert." Thomas Aquinas, *Summa Theologiae*, 2a2ae.58.1. "As every man doth, so it shall be done to him, and retaliation seems to be the great law which is dictated to us by nature. . . . The violator of the laws of justice ought to be made to feel himself that evil which he has done to another." Adam Smith, *The Theory of Moral Sentiments* (Indianapolis: Liberty Classics, 1853/1969), 160. "It is universally considered

just that each person should obtain that (whether good or evil) which he *deserves*; and unjust that should obtain a good, or be made to undergo an evil, which he does not deserve. This is, perhaps, the clearest and most emphatic form in which the idea of justice is conceived by the general mind." John Stuart Mill, *Utilitarianism*, chap. 5 (1861/2006) in *The Collected Works of John Stuart Mill*, vol. 10 (Toronto: University of Toronto Press), 242.

2   Theognis, *Elegies* (New York: Arno, ca. 6th cent. BC/1979). Reference is to the lines. The translation is by E. R. Dodds. See his *The Greeks and the Irrational* (Berkeley: University of California Press, 1971), 30.

3   I have found most thoughtful Dodds, *The Greeks and the Irrational*, op. cit.; Hugh Lloyd-Jones, *The Justice of Zeus* (Berkeley: University of California Press, 1971); and Meyer Fortes' *Oedipus and Job in West African Religion* (Cambridge: Cambridge University Press, 1959).

4   Aristotle, *Nicomachean Ethics*, trans. W. D. Ross, rev. J. O. Urmson, in *The Complete Works of Aristotle*, ed. Jonathan Barnes (Princeton, NJ: Princeton University Press, 1984), 1177b31–1178a.

5   For an interesting exploration of this, see Genevieve Lloyd, *Providence Lost* (Cambridge, MA: Harvard University Press, 2008), chap. 1.

6   See Owen McCleod, http://plato.stanford.edu/archives/win2008/entries /desert.

7   I draw on a fine and largely forgotten work by Vivian Charles Walsh, *Scarcity and Evil* (Englewood Cliffs, NJ: Prentice-Hall, 1961).

8   Isaiah Berlin, "European Unity and Its Vicissitudes," in *Crooked Timber of Humanity*, ed. Henry Hardy (London: Murray, 1990), 185, 187, 192.

9   Michel de Montaigne, "Of Presumption," in *The Complete Works of Montaigne*, trans. Donald M. Frame (Stanford, CA: Stanford University Press, 1588/1943), 488.

10   John Rawls, *A Theory of Justice* (Cambridge, MA: Harvard University Press, 1971), 3.

Chapter Seven

1   T. S. Eliot, "The Metaphysical Poets," in *Selected Essays* (New York: Harcourt, 1921/1960).

2   John Keats, Letter to George and Georgina Keats, December 21, 1819. In Hyder Edward Rollins, ed. *The Letters of John Keats, 1814–1821* (Cambridge, MA: Harvard University Press, 1958).

3   Eliot, "Metaphysical Poets," 247–48.

4   R. W. B. Lewis, *The American Adam: Innocence, Tragedy, and Tradition in the Nineteenth Century* (Chicago: University of Chicago Press, 1955), 1–2.

5   Isaiah Berlin, "The Hedgehog and the Fox," in *The Proper Study of Mankind*, eds. Henry Hardy and Roger Hausher (New York: Farrar, Straus and Giroux, 1951/1998), 436–37.

6   Charles Taylor, "Introduction," in *Human Agency and Language* (New York: Cambridge University Press, 1985), 1.

7   Ibid., 18.

8   Charles Taylor, *Sources of the Self* (Cambridge, MA: Harvard University Press, 1985), 4. References in the text are to this work.

9   Walter Pater, "Conclusion," in *Studies in the History of the Renaissance*, 2nd ed. (Oxford: Oxford University Press, 1873).

10 My primary source for Cortes's life, achievement, and motivation is J. H. Elliott's *Spain and Its World: 1500–1700* (New Haven, CT: Yale University Press, 1989). References in the text are to this work. I also relied on F. A. Kirkpatrick's *The Spanish Conquistadores* (New York: World Publishing, 1934/1969) and B. Levy's *Conquistador* (New York: Random House, 2008), which tells a very good story indeed of Cortes's quest.

11 The letters are collected in Simone Weil, *Waiting on God*, trans. Emma Craufurd (London: Routledge, 1950–51); and *Letter to a Priest*, trans. A.F. Wills (London: Routledge, 1953). I refer to the first volume as "*Letters*" and to the second as "*Last Letter*."

12 E. W. F. Tomlin, *Simone Weil* (New Haven, CT: Yale University Press, 1954), 5–6.

13 Ibid., 5.

14 Jean-Jacques Rousseau, *Emile*, trans. Barbara Foxley (London: Dent, 1762/1986).

15 John Keats, Letter to George and Thomas Keats, December 21, 1817, in Walter Jackson Bate, *John Keats* (Cambridge, MA: Harvard University Press, 1963), 249.

16 Ibid.

17 Isaiah Berlin, "John Stuart Mill and the Ends of Life," in *Four Essays on Liberty* (Oxford: Clarendon, 1969), 188.

Chapter Eight

1   John Stuart Mill, *On Liberty* (Indianapolis: Bobbs-Merrill, 1859/1956), 69.

2   John Stuart Mill, *Utilitarianism* (Indianapolis: Hackett, 1861/1979).

3   See Raymond Guess, *Public Goods, Private Goods* (Princeton, NJ: Princeton University Press, 2001) on this point.

4   Thomas Hobbes, *Leviathan*, ed. Richard Tuck (Cambridge: Cambridge University Press, 1651/1991), chap. 15.

5   F. H. Bradley, *Ethical Studies* (Oxford: Clarendon, 1876/1927).

6   A sociological example is Emile Durkheim's "Cours de science sociale,"
     Revue internationale de l'enseigment, trans Steven Lukes, XV(1888): 23–48,
     at p. 47.

> Our society must regain the consciousness of its organic unity; the
> individual must feel the presence and influence of that social mass
> which envelops and penetrates him, and this feeling must continu-
> ally govern his behaviour . . . [sociology] will enable the individual
> to understand what society is, how it completes him and what a
> small thing he is when reduced to his own powers. It will tell him
> that he is not an empire enclosed within another empire, but the
> organ of an organism, and it will show him what is valuable in con-
> scientiously performing one's role as an organ. . . . These ideas
> should spread throughout the deepest levels of the population.

And an anthropological example is Clifford Geertz's "The Impact of
the Concept of Culture on the Concept of Man," in *The Interpretation of
Cultures* (New York: Basic Books, 1973), 52: "Becoming human is becoming
individual, and we become individual under the guidance of cultural patterns, historically created systems of meaning in terms of which we give
form, order, point, and direction to our lives."

7   Mill, *On Liberty*, 71.
8   Friedrich A. Hayek, *The Road to Serfdom* (London: Routledge, 1944).
9   Hobbes, *Leviathan*, chap. 13.
10   W. D. Falk, "Morality, Self, and Others," in *Ought, Reasons, and Morality*
     (Ithaca, NY: Cornell University Press, 1963/1986), 198–231.
11   Stuart Hampshire, *Justice Is Conflict* (Princeton, NJ: Princeton University
     Press, 2000), 33–34.
12   Isaiah Berlin, "From Hope and Fear Set Free," in *Concepts and Categories*,
     ed. Henry Hardy (London: Hogarth, 1978), 198.
13   This is the subject of my *How Should We Live?* (Chicago: University of Chi-
     cago Press, 2014).
14   Niccolò Machiavelli, *The Prince*, trans. David Wootton (Indianapolis:
     Hackett, ca. 1514/1994), chap. 15, p. 48.
15   References are to the pages of Michel de Montaigne, in *The Complete
     Works*, trans. Donald M. Frame (Stanford, CA: Stanford University Press,
     1588/1948).
16   Hobbes, *Leviathan*, chap. 15.
17   Isaiah Berlin, "Two Concepts of Liberty," in *Four Essays on Liberty* (Oxford:
     Oxford University Press, 1958/1969), 135.
18   David Hume, *A Treatise of Human Nature* (Oxford: Clarendon, 1739/1960–
     71), 241.
19   Jean-Jacques Rousseau, *Discourses on the Origin and Foundation of Inequality
     Among Man*, trans. Donald A. Cress (Indianapolis: Hackett, 1988/1754), 89.

20 Immanuel Kant, *Religion within the Bounds of Reason Alone*, trans. Theodore M. Greene and Hoyt H. Hudson (New York: Harper & Row, 1960/1794), 39, 31.

21 John Stuart Mill, *Utilitarianism* (Indianapolis: Hackett, 1861/1979), 31–32.

22 John Rawls, *A Theory of Justice* (Cambridge, MA: Harvard University Press, 1971), 245.

23 Sigmund Freud, *Civilization and Its Discontents*, trans. James Strachey (New York: Norton, 1930/1961), 82.

Chapter Nine

1 I know of no better discussion of hypocrisy than Judith Shklar's "Let us not be hypocritical" in *Ordinary Vices* (Cambridge, MA: Harvard University Press, 1984). My discussion is indebted to it. Much has been written about hypocrisy in politics. See, for instance, Ruth W. Grant, *Hypocrisy and Integrity* (Chicago: University of Chicago Press, 1997); and David Runciman, *Political Hypocrisy* (Princeton, NJ: Princeton University Press, 2008), but politics is not my topic.

2 Edmund Burke, *Reflections of the Revolution in France* (Harmondsworth, UK: Penguin, 1790/1968), 171.

3 David Hume, *An Enquiry concerning the Principles of Morals*, ed. Tom L. Beauchamp (Oxford: Oxford University Press, 1751/1998), 150.

4 Edward N. Luttwak, review of Archie Brown, *The Myth of Strong Leader* in *TLS*, (May 23, 2014), 9.

5 For a sustained defense of the ideal of authenticity, see Charles Taylor's *The Ethics of Authenticity* (Cambridge, MA: Harvard University Press, 1992). Unless otherwise noted, references in the text are to the pages of this work.

6 Jean-Jacques Rousseau, "The Creed of a Savoyard Priest," in *Emile*, trans. Barbara Foxley (London: Dent: 1762/1974), 249.

7 See Joel F. Harrington, *The Faithful Executioner* (New York: Farrar, Straus and Giroux, 2013). References in the text are to the pages of this work.

8 Martin Luther, cited in Joel F. Harrington, *The Faithful Executioner* (New York: Farrar, Straus and Giroux, 2013), 32–33. This is Harrington's translation of "Ob Kriegsleute in seligem Stande konnen" 1526; D. Martin Luthers Werke: Kritische Gesamtausgabe (Weimer: Herman Bohlau, 1883), 19:624–26.

9 Charles Taylor, *Sources of the Self* (Cambridge, MA: Harvard University Press, 1989).

10 Molière, *The Misanthrope*, trans Richard Wilbur (New York: Harcourt Brace, 1666/1965), act 1, scene 1.

11 Ibid.

12   Sophocles, *Oedipus at Colonus*, in *The Three Theban Plays*, trans. Robert
      Fagles (New York: Viking, ca. 441 BC/1982). References are to the lines.

Chapter Ten

1   See Siegfried Wenzel, *The Sin of Sloth: Acedia* (Chapel Hill: University of
      North Carolina Press, 1960).

2   See Steven Lukes, *Emile Durkheim* (New York: Harper & Row, 1972);
      Robert K. Merton, *Social Theory and Social Structure*, rev. ed. (New York:
      Free Press, 1957); and Wolf Lepenies, *Melancholy and Society*, trans. Jeremy
      Gaines and Doris Jones (Cambridge, MA: Harvard University Press, 1992).

3   See John D. Eastwood, et. al., "The Unengaged Mind," *Perspectives on
      Psychological Science* 7 (2012): 448–49; and Mihaly Csikszentmihalyi,
      Beyond Boredom and Anxiety (San Francisco: Jossey-Bass, 1975).

4   Perhaps the greatest of such works are Proust's *Remembrance* and Thomas
      Mann's *Magic Mountain*. But see also, among others, Flaubert's *Bouvard and
      Pecuchet*, a novel as boring, no doubt intentionally, as the state it is about;
      and Fernando Pessoa's *The Book of Disquiet*, whose quiet desperation drives
      its readers to share the attitude. An outstanding historical account of the
      genre is Richard Kuhn, *The Demon of Noontide* (Princeton, NJ: Princeton
      University Press, 1976). An oddly selective postmodernist survey is Eliza-
      beth S. Goldstein, *Experience without Qualities* (Stanford, CA: Stanford Uni-
      versity Press, 2005). And an even more selective feminist survey of refer-
      ences to boredom in English literature from the eighteenth century on is
      Patricia Meyer Spacks, *Boredom* (Chicago: University of Chicago Press,
      1995).

5   Heidegger's discussion is in Martin Heidegger, *The Fundamental Concepts
      of Metaphysics*, trans. William McNeill and Nicholas Walker (Bloomington:
      Indiana University Press, 1983/1995), pt. 1. Other philosophical works on
      boredom are surveyed by Sean Desmond Healy, *Boredom, Self, and Culture*
      (Cranbury, NJ: Associated University Presses, 1984); and Lars Svenden,
      A Philosophy of Boredom, trans. John Irons (London: Reaktion, 1999/2005).

6   Karel Capek, "The Makropulos Secret," trans. Yveta Sinek and Robert T.
      Jones, in *Toward the Radical Center* (Highland Falls, NJ: Catbird, 1990),
      110–77.

7   See Stanley W. Jackson, "Acedia the Sin and Its Relationship to Sorrow and
      Melancholia," in *Bulletin of the History of Medicine* 55 (1981): 172–85.

8   John Stuart Mill, *Autobiography* (Indianapolis: Bobbs-Merrill, 1873/1957),
      86–87.

9   Bertrand Russell, *The Conquest of Happiness* (London: Routledge,
      1930/1993), 44: "Boredom as a factor in human behavior has received, in
      my opinion, for less attention than it deserves. It has been, I believe, one

of the great motive powers throughout the historical epoch, and is so at the present day more than ever." Martin Heidegger, "What Is Metaphysics?," in *Existence and Being*, ed. W. Brock (Chicago: Regnery, 1949), 364, 366: "This profound boredom, drifting hither and thither in the abysses of existence like a mute fog, drowns all things [an odd fog that drowns!], all men and oneself along them. . . . All things, and we with them, sink into a kind of indifference. . . . There is nothing to hold onto." Healy, *Boredom, Self, and Culture*, op. cit. 15: "There would at first glance seem to be no good reason for supposing that boredom . . . should have steadily and continuously increased in modern times. . . . And yet the records of man's thought and experience indicate otherwise . . . boredom has a history and has gradually emerged from near obscurity to center stage." Karl E. Scheibe, *The Drama of Everyday Life* (Cambridge, MA: Harvard University Press, 2000), 19: "Boredom . . . is the paramount motivational issue of our times." O. E. Klapp, *Overload and Boredom* (Westport, CT: Greenwood, 1986), 11–12: "A strange cloud hangs over modern life. At first it was not noticed; now it is thicker than ever. It embarrasses claims that the quality of life is getting better. . . . It is thickest in cities where there are the most varieties, pleasure, and opportunities. Like smog, it spreads to all sorts of places it is not supposed to be. . . . The most common name for this cloud is boredom." Kuhn, *Demon of Noontide*, op. cit. 331: "In the twentieth century ennui is not one theme among others; it is the dominant theme, and, like a persistent obsession, it intrudes upon the work of most contemporary writers." Jacques Barzun, *From Down to Decadence* (New York: Harper Collins, 2000), 788, 801:

> Whether sports events or soap opera or rock concert, entertainment in its main 20C forms was seated and passive. The amount supplied was unexampled. . . . It became people's chief object in life, because for the millions work had lost its power to satisfy the spirit. Yielding no finished object, taking place only abstractly on paper and in words over a wire, it starved the feeling of accomplishment. It was drudgery without reward, boredom unrelieved. . . . After a time, estimated a little over a century, the western mind was set upon by a blight: it was boredom.

10 Thucydides, *The Peloponnesian War*, trans. Rex Warner (Harmondsworth, UK: Penguin, ca. 5th cent. BC/1954), bk. 2, chap. 4.

11 Johan Huizinga, *The Waning of the Middle Ages* (New York: Doubleday, 1949/1954), 9–10.

12 O.E. Klapp, *Overload and Boredom*, op. cit.

13 Alexis de Tocqueville, *Democracy in America*, trans. Henry Reeve (New York: Schocken, 1835–40/1961), 2:318.

Chapter Eleven

1   The discussion draws on my *Facing Evil* (Princeton, NJ: Princeton University Press, 1990) and *The Roots of Evil* (Ithaca, NY: Cornell University Press, 2005).

2   For further examples, see, e.g., Robert Conquest, *The Great Terror* (New York: Oxford University Press, 1990); Stephanie Courtois, et. al., *The Black Book of Communism* (Cambridge, MA: Harvard University Press, 1999); Martin Gilbert, *The Holocaust* (New York: Henry Holt, 1985); Jonathan Glover, *Humanity: A Moral History of the Twentieth Century* (New Haven, CT: Yale University Press, 1999); Paul Hollander, ed., *From the Gulag to the Killing Fields* (Wilmington, DE: ISI Books, 2006), and my own *The Roots of Evil* (Ithaca, NY: Cornell University Press, 2005).

3   Inga Glendinnen, *Aztecs: An Interpretation* (New York: Cambridge University Press, 1991). References in the text are to pages of this book.

4   Ludwig Wittgenstein, *Philosophical Investigations*, trans. G. E. M. Anscombe (Oxford: Blackwell, 1986), p. 217 and p. 226.

5   Marie McGinn, *Wittgenstein* (London: Routledge, 1997), 51.

6   Peter.F. Strawson, "Freedom and Resentment," in *Freedom and Resentment* (London: Methuen, 1962/1974), 23.

7   Bernard Williams, *Shame and Necessity* (Berkeley: University of California Press, 1993), 166.

Chapter Twelve

1   My thinking about innocence is indebted to Herbert Morris's "Lost Innocence," in *On Guilt and Innocence* (Berkeley: University of California Press, 1976); and Stuart Hampshire's *Innocence and Experience* (London: Allen Lane, 1989).

2   John Maynard Keynes, *Two Memoirs* (New York: Augustus M. Kelley, 1949), 99–103.

3   Sophocles, "The Women of Trachis," trans. Michael Jameson, in *Sophocles II*, eds. David Grene and Richmond Lattimore (Chicago: University of Chicago Press, 1957). References in the text are to the lines of this play.

4   For a discussion of contemporary approaches and bibliography, see Valerie Tiberius, *The Reflective Life* (New York: Oxford University Press, 2008); and Joel J. Kupperman, *Ethics and the Qualities of Life* (New York: Oxford University Press, 2007).

5   John McDowell, "Virtue and Reason," in *Mind, Value, & Reality* (Cambridge, MA: Harvard University Press, 1998), 55–56.

6   Immanuel Kant, *Groundwork of the Metaphysics of Morals*, trans. H. J. Paton (New York: Harper, 1785/1964), 112.

7   John Stuart Mill, *A System of Logic* (London: Longmans, 1872), bk. 6, chap. 12, secs. 6–7.

8   John Stuart Mill, *Utilitarianism* (Indianapolis: Hackett, 1979), 16, 17, 31.

9   In the remarks that follow I draw on parts of chap. 10 of my *The Human Condition* (Oxford: Oxford University Press, 2010).

10   Bernard Williams, *Ethics and the Limits of Philosophy* (London: Collins, 1985), 163–64.

11   Peter Winch, "Understanding a Primitive Society," in *Ethics and Action* (London: Routledge, 1964/1972), 38–39.

12   Both stanzas quoted are from Wallace Stevens. The first from "The Man with a Blue Guitar." The second from "Chocorua to Its Neighbors," both in *The Collected Poems* (New York: Random House, 1982).

Bibliography

Aquinas, Thomas. *Summa Theologiae* (numerous editions).

Aristotle, *Nicomachean Ethics*. Translated by W. D. Ross, and revised by J. O. Urmson. In *The Complete Works of Aristotle*, edited by Jonathan Barnes. Princeton, NJ: Princeton University Press, 1984.

Aronson, Elliot. "Cognitive Dissonance." *Encyclopedia of Psychology*. New York: Oxford University Press, 2000.

Barzun, Jacques. *From Down to Decadence*. New York: Harper, 2000.

Bate, Walter Jackson. *John Keats*. Cambridge, MA: Harvard University Press, 1963.

Berlin, Isaiah. *Concepts and Categories*. Edited by Henry Hardy. London: Hogarth, 1978.

———. *The Crooked Timber of Humanity*. Edited by Henry Hardy. London: John Murray, 1959/1990.

———. *Four Essays on Liberty*. Oxford: Oxford University Press, 1958/1969.

———. *The Proper Study of Mankind*. Edited by Henry Hardy and Roger Hausher. New York: Farrar, Straus and Giroux, 1998.

Bradley, F. H. *Ethical Studies*. Oxford: Clarendon, 1876/1927.

Buford, W. H. *The German Tradition of Self-Cultivation*. Cambridge: Cambridge University Press, 1975.

Burke, Edmund. *Reflections of the Revolution in France*. Harmondsworth, UK: Penguin, 1790/1968.

Cahn, Steven M., and Maureen Eckert, eds. *Fate, Time, and Language*. New York: Columbia University Press, 2011.

Camus, Albert. *The Myth of Sisyphus*. New York: Random House, 1942/1955.

Capek, Karel. "The Makropulos Secret." Translated by Yveta Sinek and Roert T. Jones. In *Toward the Radical Center*. Highland Falls, NJ: Catbird, 1990.

Cavell, Stanley. *Must We Mean What We Say?* Cambridge: Cambridge University Press, 1976.

Chong, Kim Chong. "The Practice of Jen." *Philosophy East and West* 49 (1999): 298–316.

Christman, John. "Autonomy." http://plato.stanford.edu/archives/spr2011 /entries/autonomymoral/.

Cioffari, Vincenzo. "Fortune, Fate, and Chance." In *Dictionary of the History of Ideas*, edited by Philip P. Wiener. New York: Scribner's, 1973.

Coady, C. A. J. "The Problem of Dirty Hands." http//:plato.stanford.edu/entries /dirty-hands/.

Conquest, Robert. *The Great Terror*. New York: Oxford University Press, 1990.

Cooper, Joel. *Cognitive Dissonance*. Los Angeles: Sage Publications, 2007.

Cornford, F. M. *From Religion to Philosophy*. New York: Harper & Row, 1912/ 1957.

Courtois, Stephanie, et. al. *The Black Book of Communism*. Cambridge, MA: Harvard University Press, 1999.

Csikszentmihalyi, Mihaly. *Beyond Boredom and Anxiety*. San Francisco: Jossey-Bass, 1975.

Descartes, René. *The Philosophical Writings of Descartes*. Translated by John Cottingham, et. al. Cambridge: Cambridge University Press, 1637/1985.

Dodds, E. R. *The Greeks and the Irrational*. Berkeley: University of California Press, 1971.

Douglas, Mary. *Purity and Danger*. London: Routledge, 1966.

Dumont, Louis. *Essays on Individualism: Modern Ideology in Anthropological Perspective*. Chicago: University of Chicago Press, 1986.

———. *Homo Hierarchicus: The Caste System and Its Implication*. Translated by Mark Sainsbury, et. al. Chicago: University of Chicago Press, 1966/1970.

Durkheim, Emile. "Cours de science sociale." *Revue internationale de l'enseignement*. Translated by Steven Lukes, XV (1888): 23–48, at p.47.

Eastwood, John D. et. al. "The Unengaged Mind." *Perspectives on Psychological Science* 7 (2012): 448–49.

Eliot, T. S. *Selected Essays*. New York: Harcourt, Brace, 1921/1960.

Elliott, J. H. *Spain and Its World: 1500–1700*. New Haven, CT: Yale University Press, 1989.

Evans-Pritchard, E. E. *Social Anthropology and Other Essays*. New York: Free Press, 1948/1962.

———. *Witchcraft, Oracles and Magic among the Azande*. Oxford: Oxford University Press, 1936.

Falk, W. D. *Ought, Reasons, and Morality*. Ithaca, NY: Cornell University Press, 1986.

Festinger, Leon. *A Theory of Cognitive Dissonance*. Stanford, CA: Stanford University Press, 1957.

Freud, Sigmund. *Civilization and Its Discontents*. Translated by. James Strachey. New York: Norton, 1930/1961.

Fortes, Meyer. *Oedipus and Job in West African Religion*. Cambridge: Cambridge University Press, 1959.

————. *Religion, Morality, and the Person: Essays on Tallensi Religion*. Edited by Jack Goody. Cambridge: Cambridge University Press, 1987.

Geertz, Clifford. *The Interpretation of Cultures*. New York: Basic Books, 1973.

————. *Local Knowledge*. New York: Basic Books, 1983.

————. *Negara: The Theatre State in Nineteenth-Century Bali*. Princeton, NJ: Princeton University Press, 1980.

Geuss, Raymond. *Public Goods, Private Goods*. Princeton, NJ: Princeton University Press, 2001.

Gibbon, Edward. *The Decline and Fall of the Roman Empire*. (Numerous editions)

Gilbert, Martin. *The Holocaust*. New York: Henry Holt, 1985.

Glendinnen, Inga. *Aztecs: An Interpretation*. New York: Cambridge University Press, 1991.

Glover, Jonathan. *Humanity: A Moral History of the Twentieth Century*. New Haven, CT: Yale University Press, 1999.

Goldstein, Elizabeth S. *Experience without Qualities*. Stanford, CA: Stanford University Press, 2005.

Grant, Ruth W. *Hypocrisy and Integrity*. Chicago: University of Chicago Press, 1997.

Griswold, Charles L. *Self-Knowledge in Plato's Phaedrus*. New Haven, CT: Yale University Press, 1986.

Hampshire, Stuart. *Innocence and Experience*. London: Allen Lane, 1989.

————. *Justice Is Conflict*. Princeton, NJ: Princeton University Press, 2000.

————. *Thought and Action*. London: Chatto & Windus, 1960.

Harrington, Joel F. *The Faithful Executioner*. New York: Farrar, Straus and Giroux, 2013.

Hastings, James, ed. *Encyclopedia of Religion and Ethics*. New York: Scribner's, 1912.

Hayek, Friedrich A. *The Road to Serfdom*. London: Routledge and Kegan Paul, 1944.

Healy, Sean Desmond. *Boredom, Self, and Culture*. Cranbury, NJ: Associated University Presses, 1984.

Hegel, G. F. W. *Reason in History*. Translated by R. S. Hartman. New York: Liberal Arts, 1953.

Heidegger, Martin. *Existence and Being*. Edited by W. Brock. Chicago: Regnery, 1949.

————. *The Fundamental Concepts of Metaphysics*. Translated by William McNeill and Nicholas Walker. Bloomington: Indiana University Press, 1983/1995.

Heller, Erich. *The Artist's Journey into the Interior*. London: Secker & Warburg, 1965.

Hobbes, Thomas. *Leviathan*. Edited by Richard Tuck. Cambridge: Cambridge University Press, 1651/1991.

Hollander, Paul ed. *From the Gulag to the Killing Fields*. Wilmington, DE: ISI Books, 2006.

Horton, Robin. *Patterns of Thought in Africa and the West*. Cambridge: Cambridge University Press, 1993.

Huizinga, Johan. *The Waning of the Middle Ages*. New York: Doubleday, 1949/1954.

Hume, David. *An Enquiry concerning the Principles of Morals*. Edited by Tom L. Beauchamp. Oxford: Oxford University Press, 1751/1998.

———. *A Treatise of Human Nature*. 2nd ed. Edited by P. H. Nidditch. Oxford: Clarendon, 1739/1978.

Jackson, Stanley W. "Acedia the Sin and Its Relationship to Sorrow and Melancholia." *Bulletin of the History of Medicine* 55 (1981): 172–85.

Justinian, *Institutes*, I.iii.1. (Numerous editions)

Kant, Immanuel. *Groundwork of the Metaphysics of Morals*. Translated by. H. J. Paton. New York: Harper, 1785/1964.

———. *Religion within the Bounds of Reason Alone*. Translated by Theodore M. Greene and Hoyt H. Hudson. New York: Harper & Row, 1794/1960.

Kekes, John. *Facing Evil*. Princeton, NJ: Princeton University Press, 1996.

———. *How Should We Live?* Chicago: University of Chicago Press, 2014.

———. *The Human Condition*. Oxford: Oxford University Press, 2010.

———. *The Roots of Evil*. Ithaca, NY: Cornell University Press, 2005.

Keynes, John Maynard. *Two Memoirs*. New York: Augustus M. Kelley, 1949.

Kirkpatrick, F. A. *The Spanish Conquistadores*. New York: World Publishing, 1934/1969.

Klapp, O. E. *Overload and Boredom*. Westport, CT: Greenwood, 1986.

Kluckhohn, Clyde. *Collected Essays of Clyde Kluckhohn*. Edited by R. Kluckhohn. New York: Free Press, 1962.

Konstan, David, *The Emotions of the Ancient Greeks*. Toronto: University of Toronto Press, 2006.

Kuhn, Richard. *The Demon of Noontide*. Princeton, NJ: Princeton University Press, 1976.

Kupperman, Joel J. *Ethics and the Qualities of Life*. New York: Oxford University Press, 2007.

Lear, Jonathan. *Open Minded*. Cambridge, MA: Harvard University Press, 1998.

Lepenies, Wolf. *Melancholy and Society*. Translated by Jeremy Gaines and Doris Jones. Cambridge, MA: Harvard University Press, 1992.

Levy, B. *Conquistador*. New York: Random House, 2008.

Lewis, R. W. B. *The American Adam: Innocence, Tragedy, and Tradition in the Nineteenth Century*. Chicago: University of Chicago Press, 1955.

Loach, Mary L. "Cognitive Dissonance." *Encyclopedia of Human Behavior*. San Diego: Academic Press, 1994.

Lloyd, Genevieve. *Providence Lost*. Cambridge, MA: Harvard University Press, 2008.

Lloyd-Jones, Hugh. *The Justice of Zeus*. Berkeley: University of California Press, 1971.

Lovejoy, Arthur O. *The Great Chain of Being*. New York: Harper & Row, 1960.

Lukes, Steven. *Emile Durkheim*. New York: Harper & Row, 1972.

Luther, Martin. *Werke: Kritische Gesamtausgabe*. Weimer: Herman Bohlau, 1883.

Luttwak, Edward N. Review of Archie Brown, *The Myth of Strong Leader* in *TLS*, May 23, 2014.

Machiavelli, Niccolò. *The Prince*. Translated by David Wootton. Indianapolis: Hackett, ca. 1514/1994.

McCleod, Owen. "Desert." http://plato.stanford.edu/archives/win2008/entries /desert.

McDowell, John. *Mind, Value, and Reality*. Cambridge, MA: Harvard University Press, 1998.

McGinn, Marie. *Wittgenstein*. London: Routledge, 1997.

Merton, Robert K. *On Liberty*. Indianapolis: Bobbs-Merrill, 1859/1956.

―――. *Social Theory and Social Structure*. Rev. ed. New York: Free Press, 1957.

Mill, John Stuart. *The Collected Works of John Stuart Mill*. Toronto: University of Toronto Press, 2006.

Mishima, Yukio. *The Way of the Samurai*. Translated by Kathryn Sparling. New York: Basic Books, 1977.

Molière, Jean Baptiste Poquelin, de. *The Misanthrope*. Translated by Richard Wilbur. New York: Harcourt Brace, 1666/1965.

Montaigne, Michel de. *The Complete Works of Montaigne*. Translated by Donald M. Frame, Stanford, CA: Stanford University Press, 1588/1943.

Morris, Herbert. *On Guilt and Innocence*. Berkeley: University of California Press, 1976.

Morris, Ivan. *The Nobility of Failure: Tragic Heroes in the History of Japan*. New York: Farrar, Straus and Giroux, 1975.

Nagel, Thomas. *Mortal Questions*. Cambridge: Cambridge University Press, 1979.

―――. *The View from Nowhere*. New York: Oxford University Press, 1986.

Nehamas, Alexander. "Pity and Fear in the *Rhetoric* and the *Poetics*." In *Essays in Aristotle's Poetics*, edited by Amelie Rorty. Princeton, NJ: Princeton University Press, 1992.

Nietzsche, Friedrich. *Human All Too Human*. Translated by R. J. Hollingdale. Cambridge: Cambridge University Press, 1878/1996.

Norton, Robert E. *The Beautiful Soul*. Ithaca, NY: Cornell University Press, 1995.

Nussbaum, Martha C. "Tragedy and Self-Sufficiency: Plato and Aristotle on Fear and Pity." In *Essays on Aristotle's Poetics*, edited by Amelie Rorty. Princeton, NJ: Princeton University Press, 1992.

Pascal, Blaise. *Pensees*. Translated by. W. F. Trotter. New York: Random House, 1670/1941.

Pater, Walter. *Studies in the History of the Renaissance*. 2nd ed. Oxford: Oxford University Press, 1873.

Plato. *Republic*. Translated by Robin Waterfield. Oxford: Oxford University Press, ca. 380 BC/1993.

———. Republic in *Plato: Collected Dialogues*. Edited by Edith Hamilton and Huntington Cairns. Princeton, NJ: Princeton University Press, 1961.

Polanyi, Michael. *Personal Knowledge*. Chicago: University of Chicago Press, 1958.

Popper, Karl R. *Conjectures and Refutations*. New York: Harper, 1968.

Quine, W. V. O. *From a Logical Point of View*. Cambridge, MA: Harvard University Press, 1953.

Rawls, John. *A Theory of Justice*. Cambridge, MA: Harvard University Press, 1971.

Reid, Thomas. *Essays on the Active Powers of the Human Mind*. Cambridge, MA: MIT Press, 1814/1969.

Rice, Hugh. "Fatalism." http://plato.stanford.edu/archives//entries/fatalism/.

Rollins, Hyder Edward, ed. *The Letters of John Keats, 1814–1821*. Cambridge, MA: Harvard University Press, 1958.

Rorty, Amelie, ed. *Essays on Aristotle's Poetics*. Princeton, NJ: Princeton University Press, 1992.

Ross, W. D. *The Right and the Good*. Oxford: Clarendon, 1930.

Rousseau, Jean-Jacques. *Discourses on the Origin and Foundation of Inequality among Man*. Translated by Donald A. Cress. Indianapolis: Hackett, 1754/1988.

———. *Emile*. Translated by Barbara Foxley. London: Dent, 1762/1986.

Runciman, David. *Political Hypocrisy*. Princeton, NJ: Princeton University Press, 2008.

Russell, Bertrand. *The Conquest of Happiness*. London: Routledge, 1930/1993.

———. *Mysticism and Logic*. Harmondsworth, UK: Penguin, 1902/1953.

Scheibe, Karl E. *The Drama of Everyday Life*. Cambridge, MA: Harvard University Press, 2000.

Schneewind, J. B. *The Invention of Autonomy*. Cambridge: Cambridge University Press, 1998.

Schopenhauer, Arthur. *The World as Will and Representation*. Translated by E. F. Payne. New York: Dover, 1844/1969.

Shakespeare, William. *Macbeth*. (Numerous editions)

Shklar, Judith. *Ordinary Vices*. Cambridge, MA: Harvard University Press, 1984.

Smith, Adam. *The Theory of Moral Sentiments*. Indianapolis: Liberty Classics, 1853/1969.

Sophocles. *Oedipus at Colonus*. In *The Three Theban Plays*, translated by Robert Fagles. New York: Viking, 1982.

————. "The Women of Trachis." Translated by Michael Jameson. *Sopho-cles II*, edited by David Grene and Richmond Lattimore. Chicago: University of Chicago Press, 1957.

Sousa, Ronald de. "Emotion." http://plato.stanford.edu/archives/spr2013/entries/emotion/.

Spacks, Patricia. *Boredom*. Chicago: University of Chicago Press, 1995.

Stevens, Wallace. *The Collected Poems*. New York: Random House, 1982.

Strawson, Peter F. *Freedom and Resentment*. London: Methuen, 1962/1974.

Svenden, Lars. *A Philosophy of Boredom*. Translated by John Irons. London: Reaktion, 1999/2005.

Taylor, Charles. *Human Agency and Language*. New York: Cambridge University Press, 1985.

————. *Sources of the Self*. Cambridge, MA: Harvard University Press, 1985.

————. *The Ethics of Authenticity*. Cambridge, MA: Harvard University Press, 1992.

Taylor, Richard. "Fatalism." *Philosophical Review* 71 (1962): 56–66.

————. *Good and Evil*. New York: Macmillan, 1970.

————. *Metaphysics*. Englewood Cliffs, NJ: Prentice-Hall, 1963.

Theognis, *Elegies*. New York: Arno, ca. 6th cent. BC/1979.

Thucydides. *The Peloponnesian War*. Translated by Rex Warner. Harmondsworth, UK: Penguin, ca. 5th cent. BC/1954.

Tiberius, Valerie. *The Reflective Life*. New York: Oxford University Press, 2008.

Tocqueville, Alexis de. *Democracy in America*. Translated by Henry Reeve. New York: Schocken, 1835–40/1961.

Tomlin, E. W. F. *Simone Weil*. New Haven, CT: Yale University Press, 1954.

Walsh, Vivian Charles. *Scarcity and Evil*. Englewood Cliffs, NJ: Prentice-Hall, 1961.

Weil, Simone. *Letter to a Priest*. Translated by A. F. Wills. London: Routledge, 1953.

————. *Waiting on God*. Translated by Emma Craufurd. London: Routledge, 1950–51.

Wenzel, Siegfried. *The Sin of Sloth: Acedia*. Chapel Hill: University of North Carolina Press, 1960.

Williams, Bernard. *Ethics and the Limits of Philosophy*. London: Collins, 1985.

————. "Philosophy as a Humanistic Discipline." In *Philosophy as a Humanistic Discipline*, edited by A. W. Moore. Princeton, NJ: Princeton University Press, 2000/2006.

————. *Shame and Necessity*. Berkeley: University of California Press, 1993.

————. *Truth and Truthfulness*. Princeton, NJ: Princeton University Press, 2002.

————. "The Women of Trachis." In *The Sense of the Past*, edited by Myles Burnyeat. Princeton, NJ: Princeton University Press, 1996/2006.

Winch, Peter. *Ethics and Action*. London: Routledge, 1972.

Wittgenstein, Ludwig. *Philosophical Investigations*. Translated by G. E. M. Anscombe. Oxford: Blackwell, 1986.

Wollheim, Richard. *The Mind and Its Depths*. Cambridge, MA: Harvard University Press, 1993.

Yahara, Hiromichi. *The Battle for Okinawa*. Translated by Roger Pineau and Masatichi Uehara. New York: Wiley, 1995.

Index